Contents

Crime policy
in Europe

Good practices
and promising examples

Council of Europe Publishing

Cover design: Graphic Design Workshop, Council of Europe
Photo: Ellen Wuibaux, © Council of Europe
Layout: Desktop Publishing Unit, Council of Europe

Edited by Council of Europe Publishing
http://book.coe.int
F-67075 Strasbourg Cedex

ISBN-10: 92-871-5486-4
ISBN-13: 978-92-871-5486-6
© Council of Europe, December 2004
Reprinted February 2006
Printed at the Council of Europe

Contributors

Pierre V. Tournier is a Director of Research at the National Centre for Scientific Research (CNRS). He teaches at the Centre of Twentieth-Century Social History, University of Paris I Pantheon-Sorbonne. He is President of the French Association of Criminology (AFC) and a member of the Criminological Scientific Council of the Council of Europe. He was also responsible for initiating the compilation of the Council of Europe's Annual Penal Statistics (SPACE).

Denis Ribeaud is preparing a doctoral thesis on drug-crime links at the University of Lausanne. He has been involved in various research projects on heroin trials and the disruptive behaviour of primary schoolchildren.

Martin Killias is a professor at the School of Criminal Sciences, University of Lausanne. He is one of the co-founders of the international crime victimisation surveys, Chairman of the group of experts associated with the European sourcebook of crime and criminal justice statistics and co-founder, as well as first President, of the European Society of Criminology.

Marcelo F. Aebi is Professor of Criminology and Deputy Director of the Andalusian Institute of Criminology, University of Seville. He is a member of the group of experts associated with the European sourcebook of crime and criminal justice statistics and is currently responsible for the Council of Europe's Annual Penal Statistics (SPACE), as well as Executive Secretary of the European Society of Criminology.

Birgitt Haller is a researcher at the Institute of Conflict Research, Vienna, and a lecturer at the Institute of Political Science, University of Vienna. She has conducted two evaluations of Austria's Protection against Domestic Violence Act.

Christa Pelikan is a researcher at the Institute of Sociology of Law and Criminology, Vienna. She was involved in the drafting of the Council of Europe's recommendation on mediation in penal matters and was a member of the Criminological Scientific Council of the Council of Europe. She is currently a member of the Board of the European Forum for Victim-Offender Mediation and Restorative Justice.

Petra Smutny is a judge at the Regional Civil Court of Vienna and Commissioner for Equal Treatment in the Austrian Federal Ministry of Justice. She has advised the Austrian Federal Ministry of Justice on the Code of Criminal Procedure, mediation in criminal and family law, crime prevention, domestic violence and human rights.

Ivo Aertsen is Professor of Criminology at the Catholic University of Leuven. He has carried out several research projects on victimology, mediation and restorative justice, and has worked as a practitioner in the prison system and in victim support. He is Chair of the European Forum for Victim-Offender Mediation and Restorative Justice and leads COST Action A21 on Restorative Justice Developments in Europe

Vincent Delbos is a judge in France. He has worked in the fields of crime prevention, juvenile delinquency and alternatives to imprisonment.

Helena Válková teaches criminal law and criminology at the Faculty of Philosophy, Charles University, Prague, and the Faculty of Law, University of West Bohemia, Pilsen, where she is Head of the Department of Criminal Law. She has been a member of the Criminological Scientific Council of the Council of Europe.

Jana Hulmáková teaches criminal law and criminology at the Faculty of Law, University of West Bohemia, Pilsen.

Hanns von Hofer is Professor of Criminology at the University of Stockholm. He has been a member of the Criminological Scientific Council of the Council of Europe and a member of the Editorial Board of the *European Journal of Criminology.*

Frieder Dünkel teaches criminology, penology, juvenile justice, criminal procedure and criminal law at the University of Greifswald (Germany). He has conducted a wide range of empirical studies on juvenile criminology, penology, prisons and community sanctions, alcohol and drunken driving, and human rights. He is the co-editor of *Neue Kriminalpolitik* and member of the Editorial Board of the *European Journal of Criminology.* He has been Chair of the Criminological Scientific Council of the Council of Europe.

Tapio Lappi-Seppälä is Director of the National Research Institute of Legal Policy of Finland. He has been a member of the criminal code committee, prison system reform committee and the juvenile criminal justice system reform committee in Finland, as well as a member of the Select Committee of Experts on Sentencing of the Council of Europe. He has been recently elected as a member of the Criminological Scientific Council of the Council of Europe.

Annie Kensey is a sociologist-demographer specialising in, amongst other things, recidivism and the evolution of the prison population in France. She is a researcher at the Office for Studies of the French Prison Service and a member of the Scientific Council of the National Institute for Demographic Studies (INED).

Francesco De Leo is a public prosecutor at the National Anti-Mafia Bureau of Italy. He has participated in the EU's Phare-Horizontal project. He is a central contact point of the European Judicial Network.

Mariavaleria Del Tufo is Professor of Criminal Law at the Faculty of Law, University of Naples II. She has served as an ad hoc judge for Italy at the European Court of Human Rights. She is a member of the Criminological Scientific Council of the Council of Europe and has reviewed several draft laws of Council of Europe member states. She has participated in the EU's Phare-Horizontal project and has been a member of the EU Expert Committee on Victims of Crime. She was also a member of the Italian Delegation at the UN Diplomatic Conference on the Establishment of an International Criminal Court.

Gualtiero Michelini is a judge at the Court of Rome. He has advised the Italian Ministry of Justice on international co-operation and has participated in the work of the Council of Europe and the EU (including the Phare-Horizontal project).

Francesco Patrone is a judge at the Court of Rome . He has been a prosecutor and has worked at the Prisons' Department of the Italian Ministry of Justice. He has also participated in the EU's Phare-Horizontal project.

Preface

Frieder Dünkel and Hanns von Hofer

At the end of the year 2000 the Council of Europe edited a book entitled *Crime and criminal justice in Europe*. This comparative reader had been proposed by members of the Criminological Scientific Council of the Council of Europe (PC-CSC) with the then President, Alenka Selih from Slovenia. The contributions – written by members of the PC-CSC and other scholars in criminal policy and criminological research – covered a wide range of topics: from crime trends and crime prevention to different forms of sentencing and prisons in Europe. The positive reception of this reader encouraged preparation of this present publication on criminal policy in the member states of the Council of Europe. This time it was felt that the focus should be on examples of promising practice in specific countries, which could be encouraging to other countries whilst being aware that the transfer of such practices has always to take into consideration the cultural and legal background of national systems.

Recent research in criminology has greatly emphasised "what works" in the field of crime policy and it is fully acknowledged that the approach used in this volume does not meet the strict criteria of famous meta-analyses like the University of Maryland report conducted by Lawrence Sherman and his research institute[1] or of other studies like the one presented by the British Home Office[2] or the mostly unpublished meta-analyses of Lipton et al.[3] The present exercise falls under the category of "promising examples" that need further evaluative research. However, the examples presented in this volume deserve attention in so far as they demonstrate that under certain circumstances crime

---

1. See Sherman, L. et al., *Preventing crime. What works, what doesn't, what's promising*, University of Maryland, 1997. See also Office of Justice Programs, US Department of Justice, and National Institute of Justice, *Research in brief*, July 1998; the extended version is available at www.preventingcrime.org
2. See Goldblatt and Lewis (eds.), *Reducing offending: an assessment of research evidence on ways of dealing with offending behaviour*, UK Home Office, 1998; in particular Vennard and Hedderman, "Effective interventions with offenders", pp. 101-119.
3. See Lipton, "The effectiveness of correctional treatment revisited thirty years later: preliminary meta-analytic findings from the CDATE study", paper presented at the 12th World Congress of Criminology, Seoul, 24 to 29 August 1998 (available through douglipton@earthlink.net); Pearson and Lipton, "The effectiveness of educational and vocational programs: CDATE meta-analyses", paper presented at the annual meeting of the American Society of Criminology, Toronto, 17 to 20 November 1999.

policy can have a positive impact and projects can be successfully implemented with respect to criminal law reform. Again, the term "successfully" needs further clarification as Pierre Tournier points out in his chapter.

The examples of "good practice" have been grouped together in the present volume under the headings of crime prevention (see chapters 1-3), mediation and other community sanctions (chapters 4-10), the prison system (chapters 11-12) and criminal procedure (chapter 13). Most of the authors are members of the PC-CSC. Others have been asked by the PC-CSC to contribute as they are important researchers in their countries.

As already indicated, in the first chapter Pierre Tournier reminds us that we should be aware of possible pitfalls when declaring that something "works". The statement that something works has to be related to something else: for example, is a new penal sanction more promising than another and how can we measure it? We have to consider problems of net-widening and the possibility that the new sanction replaces other minor sanctions and not – as intended – imprisonment. However, he also provides some interesting examples, such as the experiences in France with early (conditional) release, which is described in more detail by Annie Kensey in chapter 12. The difficulties in judging a practice as successful lead to two conclusions: that there has to be a clear definition of what "success" means (taking also into consideration the barely measurable further consequences of such practices; for example, for third persons and their quality of life) and, secondly, the need to employ high methodological research standards.

In chapter 2, Denis Ribeaud, Martin Killias and Marcelo Aebi describe the long-term effects of a heroin prescription programme for serious addict offenders in Switzerland. After a four-year follow-up period the treated persons showed significant lower prevalence and incidence rates concerning drug abuse, and also violent and other crimes, particularly property crimes. The effects seem to be independent of natural "maturing out", although those who dropped out of the programme also showed some (less impressive) decline in their prevalence rates. The consequences of the Swiss drug policy are evident: a health care or "harm reduction" approach looks much more promising than the traditional repressive penal law approach. This is true not only for the drug-addicted offenders, but also for their (possible) future victims when taking into consideration, for example, violent or property offences committed in order to get drugs or money, etc., for buying drugs.

Austrian legislation for protection against domestic violence came into force in 1997. Austria was one of the "forerunners" in this field; for example, Germany followed with a similar law only at the end of 2001. The Protection against Domestic Violence Act created new interventions against perpetrators of domestic violence, combining instruments of civil law, police law and penal law. The aim of the new law was to assert the victim's right to protection, security and support. Therefore much emphasis is given to the so-called "intervention

centres" providing free counselling and support. The so-called "go-order" forbids the (mostly male) offender to stay in the same household as the victim. This eviction or barring order issued by the police lasts for ten days and can be prolonged by the district court. Such orders have been used increasingly since 1997. About half of the cases resulted in a dispute settlement, and another 43% in longer eviction/barring orders. In chapter 3, Birgitt Haller, Christa Pelikan and Petra Smutny report that, according to research, victims and the police seem to be satisfied. Maybe this shift in perspective is important as domestic violence is no longer seen as a private conflict, but as a ground for receiving protection from state agencies.

The second part of the volume focuses on mediation and other community sanctions.

In chapter 4, Christa Pelikan reports on a comparative research initiative to evaluate the impact of the Council of Europe's Committee of Ministers Recommendation No. R (99) 19 on mediation in penal matters. The results are very encouraging, demonstrating that victim-offender mediation has spread rapidly throughout Europe. In some countries the influence has not been so strong as mediation "was on its way" already with a widespread network of mediation schemes, such as those in Germany, whereas in many other countries new legislation has been passed in order to extend existing model projects nationwide or to transfer juvenile justice experiences into the field of general penal law. On other occasions, the impact is mainly restricted to NGOs and academics and therefore the recommendation may have only an indirect influence on national penal policy. The report is not an evaluation of mediation schemes, but of the influence of the Council of Europe's work in member states. It is furthermore a good example of how important an evaluation of a recommendation is, and of why this exercise should become "routine" in the Council of Europe's work.

Mediation is increasingly used in Europe and in some countries not only on an experimental basis, but nationwide. Belgium is one of the "forerunner" countries in developing mediation. The idea of restorative justice has spread from the well-known Leuven Department of Criminology (Lode Walgrave, Tony Peters et al.) and gained importance in the criminal justice system. However, it is often stated that cases dealt with by mediation schemes only concern minor crimes and petty, first-time offenders. Often the focus is on juvenile offenders and diversion procedures. The crucial question for a more widespread implementation is whether mediation also works with more serious offences and offenders. The Belgian results (with references to similar experiences in England and the Netherlands), presented by Ivo Aertsen in chapter 5, are encouraging and demonstrate that even in prisons some cases, when selected carefully, can result in a positive solution for the victim as well as the offender. However, this is a demanding task and needs much time, energy and professional skill as it sometimes comes close to a therapeutic intervention. The majority of serious cases (inside and outside prisons) apparently work through indirect mediation, that is, the victim does not necessarily have to meet the offender face to face. As a consequence of the experiments in prisons, the programme on "restorative justice in prisons" has been implemented in every Belgian prison since the end of 2000.

In chapter 6, Vincent Delbos describes experiences with a specific mode of community service order in France that has existed since the end of 1999 (the traditional form of community service order was introduced in 1984 in France). The experiment now includes (in addition to working hours) eighteen hours of social training where the juvenile offenders in a group are confronted with members of victim assistance or probation services and other representatives of the civil society. The aim is to establish a civic dialogue and to increase the young person's responsibility and integration into society. These training sessions have also been offered recently to prison inmates. The French experiment of civic dialogue has not yet been evaluated in the strict sense, but the approach of integrating "normal" civil society in offender treatment programmes deserves much attention and opens perspectives not only for a justice system oriented to the idea of restorative justice but also to restorative neighbourhoods and a restorative civil society in general.

The Czech Republic is one of the central European countries with a penal tradition much influenced by the former Soviet Union. At the end of the 1980s, a strong reform movement started which resulted, on the one hand, in reforms of penal law in 1995 and 1997 (introducing or amending community sanctions, such as community service, or suspended sentences with or without the supervision of the probation service) and, on the other, of the Criminal Procedure Act in 1993 and 1995 (expanding the possibilities of diversion and mediation). A new Probation and Mediation Service was established at the beginning of 2001, covering social work in the pre-trial, trial and post-trial stages, but mainly occupied with the execution of community service and probation orders. In chapter 7, Helena Válková describes the changes in sentencing practice during the 1990s, which show an important increase in community sanctions and a decrease in unconditional prison sentences from 28% of all convictions in 1998 to 15% in 2002. Whilst the absolute numbers of convicted offenders has increased since 1998, the number of persons sentenced to unconditional imprisonment has declined. The follow-up period is too short to draw final conclusions, but the idea of reducing imprisonment seems to work.

A major problem in many countries is not only long-term prison sentences, but also short-term sentences, which cause a lot of bureaucratic work and cannot really be seen as rehabilitative because of their short-term nature. One really disturbing case is the issue of fine defaulters. In most countries those who are not able or willing to pay their fine finally get detained (see the example of Germany described in chapter 9). There is, however, the interesting exception of Sweden. Hanns von Hofer's report in chapter 8 demonstrates that alternative provisions – for example, instalment schemes – need not necessarily have a negative influence on honest payment of fines imposed on offenders. It seems to be of importance that responsibility for collecting fines has been transferred to the tax administration and therefore the payment of fines has acquired a clear fiscal and civil overtone, pushing the idea of penal retribution into the background. Sweden has practically abolished detention for fine defaulters, although fines are the most prominent sentences and used very extensively. Only in the case where an offender takes active steps to evade collection systematically is detention possible, but this rule has only been used in a very few cases. Hanns von Hofer establishes a link to the historical reform movement in Sweden, which enabled such a reform before retribution made its return to other penal law areas. Fortunately, there has been no demand to reverse this alternative approach to fine defaulters' detention in Sweden up to now.

The legal background in Germany is different. In chapter 9, Frieder Dünkel describes the German system relying very much on the ultimate resort of detention for fine defaulters. Due to the general economic problems in the country and a sentencing practice which in more than 80% of cases imposes fines, the number of fine defaulters in the 1990s has dramatically increased. The problems have been even more serious in the "new" federal states (*neue Bundesländer*) of the former GDR. In the north-east German federal state of Mecklenburg-Western Pomerania in 1996 no less than 22% of the daily prison capacity was occupied by fine defaulters. This was the starting point for a project that increased the possibilities of replacing this kind of short-term detention by community service. As fine defaulters often show very serious behavioural, alcohol and other problems, special pedagogical assistance had to be provided. More than 1 600 institutions where offenders can perform community service have been established, 62 of them with special pedagogical assistance.

The evaluation of the project demonstrates a reduction of the number of fine defaulters in prison by half. More than 80% of those transferred to community service before entering the prison, and even 55% of the very problematic inmate population, completed community service successfully. The most promising element in ensuring that offenders took part in community service was a proactive case management system where social workers systematically visited the offenders at home and tried to motivate them through personal contacts. The project was a success not only in terms of diverting offenders from prison, but also in terms of cost-benefit analysis: the costs for the staff and social pedagogical assistance were far less than the costs of imprisonment. The Ministry of Justice of Mecklenburg-Western Pomerania has therefore implemented the project on a permanent basis. At the end of 2003 the Federal Ministry of Justice proposed the extension of community service through a draft bill at the federal level, referring to the positive example of Mecklenburg-Western Pomerania.

An outstanding "natural experiment" has been the post-war reduction of the prison population in Finland. The prisoners' rate went down from about 190 per 100 000 inhabitants in 1950 to less than 60 per 100 000 at the end of the 1990s. This has been a result of long-lasting law reforms and changes in sentencing policies. The movement towards a more lenient system of sanctions and a more lenient sentencing practice (particularly for property offences and drunken driving) cumulatively contributed to this "reductionist" approach. Community service and conditional prison sentences replaced unconditional prison sentences to a considerable degree. In chapter 10, Tapio Lappi-Seppälä points out the background factors which made such a change possible. The political will and consensus among Finnish experts and in society, the reasonable attitudes of the media towards issues of criminal policy, the readiness of the judiciary and a rather peaceful and safe crime situation in Finland favourably contributed to the changes described above. The rise of the prison population between 1999 and 2002, up to about 70 per 100 000 inhabitants, may be explained by an increase in foreign prisoners (mainly drug dealers, etc.) as well as by an expansion of the fine-defaulter and remand-prisoner population. It cannot yet be decided if the somewhat reverse development in the last three years is the beginning of a "politicisation" of crime policy with a trend towards more severe punishment. Finland is probably just being faced with global problems such as drug trafficking and the mobility of offenders, which counteract the "reductionist" approach. However, it seems that official criminal policy will react and try to fight against unfounded repression.

In the third part of this volume two chapters are dedicated to the prison system, although both of them also deal with "alternatives". One deals with partly replacing the prison sentence by conditional release (France) and the other deals with the relaxation of the closed prison regime by prison furloughs, day leave and opening the prison system in general (Germany).

In chapter 11, Frieder Dünkel refers to prison reform in West Germany in the 1970s, which was taken up in 1990 in the East German federal states after the re-unification of Germany. The Prison Act of 1977 in Germany provides several forms of leave of absence (day leave, prison furlough, work release) that are used for preparing the offender for release and to maintain social bonds with the outside world. The number of home leaves has been tripled in the last twenty years. In the same period the failure to return from leave has decreased to a mere 1%. Furthermore, tension in prison and aggressive behaviour towards prison staff have also decreased. In the early 1990s the number of violent assaults against members of the prison staff in East Germany was twice as many as in West Germany. With the extension of rehabilitative measures and the opening up of prisons, the ratio has now dropped to the low West German level.

Several studies demonstrate that different forms and periods of prison leave contribute to rehabilitation, especially when they are followed by conditional release (parole). Prison leave in Germany is seen as a fundamental right of prisoners and the Constitutional Court in this context has repeatedly emphasised the constitutional principle of rehabilitation. Although relaxation of the prison regime, which leads to reduced violence, can be judged as a humane and "good" practice, recent trends in prison policy in some conservative federal states are oriented to more severe and less rehabilitative regimes. Thus a comparison of the prison regimes in the different federal states will probably show disparity, which – under the same federal law – is problematic.

In chapter 12, Annie Kensey reports on a research project on the recidivism of French prisoners granted early release in comparison to those who fully served their sentence. Independent of crime categories, age and prior convictions, the early release group showed significant lower recidivism rates than the "control group". Although some methodological reservations may be made, this result is very much in line with international research. The implications for criminal policy are evident and there are strong arguments for regular early release, at best combined with intensive social after-care by the probation service.

The last part of this volume deals with the important issue of victim protection in criminal procedure.

In chapter 13, Francesco De Leo, Mariavaleria del Tufo, Gualtiero Michelini and Francesco Patrone describe the experiences of the Italian reform concerning persons co-operating with the justice system and witnesses in anti-Mafia proceedings. Persons co-operating with the justice system have a key position in the fight against organised crime. They risk their lives if the state does not provide effective protection for such witnesses. The Italian criminal justice system provides a variety of protective measures, as well as a sentencing scheme allowing considerable mitigation of a sentence for persons who been involved in crime themselves. The favourable treatment granted to collaborators is not restricted to more lenient sentencing; it also concerns the prison regime (*inter alia,* privileges in prison life). A very important point is the protection of persons co-operating with the justice agencies at the first level through different forms of surveillance up to their transfer to another municipality, social reintegration or special custody measures. The second level comprises measures leading to an alternative life programme with a new identity.

Furthermore, special programmes exist for witnesses including long-distance proceedings through video-conferences (which enable, for example, interviews with dangerous prisoners without them having to leave a secure prison unit to go to the court). The chapter does not offer an empirical evaluation of the new regulations, but does provide extensive material on the legislation and on certain problems concerning its implementation. There may be other countries that have introduced similar regulations for witness protection, etc., but it is, unfortunately, undoubtedly true that Italy has the most experience in dealing with criminal proceedings against members of organised crime groups.

Although the heterogeneous examples of this volume certainly give no clear picture of what works in criminal policy, at least some examples could be useful for further consideration. The main emphasis is on what works in community sanctions and how to reduce the prison population. The example of Finland shows a possible alternative to "getting tough" and mass incarceration ideologies that prevail in the United States and certain other countries. Europe might also discover a more humane and effective way of sanctioning offenders and crime reduction. Maybe one should look not only for good practices and what works, but also for the pitfalls of criminal policy, because one can learn more about what works if one considers what has been a failure and what did not work. This might form the basis for another criminological exercise of the Council of Europe.

PART I
CRIME PREVENTION

Chapter 1

Aspects of good practice in the criminal justice system

Pierre V. Tournier

In March 2003 the Office of the Solicitor General of Canada invited me to give a paper[1] at the first conference in a series entitled "What works", the theme of which was "What works in conditional release and community reintegration". In the presentation document, Wayne Easter, Solicitor General of Canada, also spoke of "exemplary practices" and "innovative ideas". In May 2004, on the initiative of the American Society of Criminology (ASC), the first conference of societies of criminology will be held in Paris on the theme of "What works in reducing crime". The French Association of Criminology (AFC), which I chair, will be taking part in this important event. I have translated the title of the conference as "*Réduire la délinquance et la criminalité: ce qui marche*". The Council of Europe's Criminological Scientific Council of which I have been a member since June 2001 has undertaken to prepare a document presenting "promising examples". I therefore have three opportunities to look pragmatically at these problems; a clear response to the "Nothing works" emanating from the other side of the Atlantic; three opportunities to examine the conditions for appropriate use of the concept of "good practice".

Let us begin with an example: electronic monitoring orders (EMOs), introduced in France by the act of 19 December 1997. The measure is innovative, at least for France, but does it work? Is it effective? A good practice? A promising practice? It can be seen that the various formulations are not synonymous but, though the last expression is tinged with a degree of caution by projecting us into a future by its very nature uncertain, in the final analysis, they are surely all stylistic devices referring to the same thing, namely criminal sanctions and measures that should be supported and developed, or even sold, in one international authority or another.

The need for definitions

Before replying to the question "Does it work?", the first methodological requirement is surely to state clearly what we are talking about. Criminal

---

1. Tournier, P.V., "La libération conditionnelle en Europe. Modèle discrétionnaire vs modèle de libération d'office", Conference on What Works in Conditional Release and Social Reintegration, Montreal, 2003.

sanctions and measures are frequently polymorphous: an analysis relevant to one may prove erroneous for another. The 1997 act established electronic monitoring orders as a means of enforcing custodial sentences. Article 723-7 of the Code on Criminal Procedure provides that where a person is sentenced to one or more custodial sentences the total length of which does not exceed one year, or where the remainder of a prisoner's term for one or more custodial sentences does not exceed one year, the judge responsible for enforcement of sentences (JAP) may decide that the sentence should be enforced by electronic monitoring. Electronic monitoring orders may also be used as a probationary measure for a period not exceeding one year following conditional release. Thus there are three types of electronic monitoring orders in French law: adjustment of a sentence of less than a year (type 1), adjustment of the remainder of a sentence not exceeding one year (type 2) and its imposition as a probationary measure following conditional release (type 3). I should add that, since the act of 9 September 2002, there has been a fourth type used as a special condition of a judicial supervision order (type 4). In this last, very different, case, the person has not yet been tried. Unlike in the other three situations, he or she has not been placed on the prison register. Without for the time being making it clear what the question "Do electronic monitoring orders work?" means, it can easily be seen that the answer may vary according to type since, while the technical measure is the same, it can be applied in widely differing contexts: to a person who has never been imprisoned or even convicted (type 4), or to a prisoner who has just served fifteen years (types 2 and 3). The first methodological requirement is therefore to refuse to give any general reply to a question whose form unfortunately invites such a response.

Theory without practice

When the legislature introduces new criminal sanctions and measures into the legal machinery it will not fail to claim all sorts of attributes for them: it will by its very nature be innovative, effective (at least, it is hoped) and promising, demonstration of this obviously being deferred. Evaluation requires distance; one has to wait for some time to elapse. Therefore the question "Does it work?" has a more mundane meaning during the phase when the sanction or measure is introduced. It usually means: "Is the criminal sanction and measure actually used?" "Are the judicial officials who have the power to do so using it in a significant number of cases?" At this level, the reply will be essentially quantitative in the most common sense of the term. For example, in France, between October 2000 (the beginning of the experimental phase) and 1 May 2002 – a period of 18 months – JAPs issued 175 electronic monitoring orders.[2]

---

2. Kensey, A., Pitoun, A., Lévy, R. and Tournier, P.V., *Sous surveillance électronique. La mise en place du "bracelet électronique" en France (octobre 2000, mai 2002)*, Ministry of Justice, July 2002.

Some 150 involved "sentences of less than a year" (type 1), 22 "remainders of sentences of less than a year" (type 2) and 3 "probationary measures following conditional release" (type 3). So one might say that type 2 electronic monitoring "does not work well" and that type 3 "does not work at all". But what is the threshold for saying that the figures are significant and promising?

In "SPACE II (Annual Penal Statistics of the Council of Europe) – Community sanctions and measures (CSMs)[3] ordered in 1999",[4] I proposed two indices for measuring the incidence of a particular sanction or measure: a global frequency index (GFI) obtained by finding the ratio of the number of sanctions or measures ordered to the number of prison sentences without full or partial suspension ordered the same year (figure per 100), and a specific frequency index (SFI) calculated as above but including only sentences of less than one year in the denominator. In 1999, the specific frequency index for community service orders was 4.7 per 100 in Moldova, 7.6 in Denmark, 28.7 in Sweden, 32.4 in the Czech Republic, 34.5 in France, 36.1 in Finland, 58 in Scotland, 74.6 in the Netherlands, and 88.4 in England and Wales. These indices will be more or less relevant according to the nature of the sanction or measure and, in particular, its more or less polymorphous nature. It is sufficient to remember here the different types of electronic monitoring orders in France.

But, setting aside the technical questions about the calculation of the indices, which will not be dealt with here,[5] the dissymmetrical nature of the interpretation of these figures is clear: if they are low, it can be said that they do not work and these practices can be neither good nor effective because, sociologically, they do not really exist. If they are high, however, saying that they work is to take, as it were, a short-term, productivist view which is inadequate without further information.

One sanction or measure may hide another

When a person who has not yet been on remand is placed under social and educational judicial supervision and is subsequently given a suspended sentence, it might be thought that the individual supervision order has really enabled him or her to escape prison. If this was the legislator's intention in creating the measure, one could say it works. But one might also say that the investigating judge would not have remanded the person concerned, if judicial supervision had not existed in law. The judge used a further safeguard available

---

3.   It should be recalled that in Council of Europe terminology a community sanction or measure is a non-custodial sanction or measure accompanied by supervisory measures, that is, aid, assistance, and supervision.

4.   "SPACE II (Annual Penal Statistics of the Council of Europe) – Community sanctions and measures (CSM) ordered in 1999", compiled by Tournier P.V., Council of Europe, *Penological Information Bulletin*, Nos. 23 and 24, 2002, pp. 131-154.

5.   Stock and flow indices, determination of the most relevant denominators, etc.

to him or her. If this is the case, such judicial supervision is not playing its part as an alternative to custody (a virtual alternative?) but is enabling the social supervision network to be widened. This is the net-widening theory. The same question may in fact be asked about virtually all alternatives to detention which enable entry to prison to be avoided.[6] Would such a person sentenced to community service have been sentenced to imprisonment without remission if community service had not been provided for in law? Would he or she not rather have been given a suspended sentence or even fined?

The question arises in rather different terms for alternatives which affect, not entries, but, the duration of imprisonment (second category alternatives). A prisoner who still has three years to serve in prison and is granted conditional release receives a genuine alternative. He or she will serve the remainder of the sentence outside prison. And yet ...

It is well known that conditional releases have become less and less common. The French Parliament and Government realised this and in the end embarked upon substantial reform of the procedures for granting it in the framework of the act of 15 June 2000. Let us suppose the desired revival of conditional release were effective. Would it not result over time in a compensatory increase in the length of sentences handed down by the courts, frustrated at seeing "their" sanctions so "eroded"? Thus a second category alternative perfectly real at "micro" level – the beneficiary can have no doubts about this – may become perfectly virtual at "macro" level.

With respect to third category measures, which reduce the time spent behind bars without changing the time spent on the prison register, a distinction has to be made between *ab initio* measures – taken at the beginning of detention – and the others. Let us take the example of an electronic monitoring order corresponding to the enforcement of a sentence of less than a year (type 1). Will the courts not now be encouraged to hand down prison sentences of less than a year without remission in cases in which they would previously have given a suspended sentence, knowing that the individual concerned will be able to escape prison thanks to an electronic tag? This is very risky reasoning since the following disastrous scenario is conceivable: a criminal court imposes a prison sentence of six months without remission, rather than a suspended sentence with probation, assuming that it will be enforced by electronic monitoring, but the JAP responsible for the decision refuses to order this. Far from being an alternative to a custodial sentence, electronic monitoring would then be fostering imprisonment.

---

6.   This is what I term "a first category alternative" in contrast to sanctions and measures that simply reduce the duration of detention, termed "second category alternatives", such as conditional release, for example. "Third category alternatives" are those that reduce the length of time spent behind bars, but not the time on the prison register (semi-liberty, for example). See Tournier, P.V., "Towards prisons without inmates? Re: the introduction of electronic monitoring in France", Council of Europe, *Penological Information Bulletin*, Nos. 23 and 24, 2002, pp. 3-6.

Electronic monitoring at the end of sentences (type 2) does not give rise to the same sorts of questions. Furthermore, probationary measures following conditional release are a special case: semi-liberty, external placement, type 3 electronic monitoring. They may favour the granting of conditional release by increasing the safeguards upon which the JAP may base his or her decision. But they may also delay conditional release. Without such measures, conditional release might have been effective from date t; with them, the prisoner is only released on t + t'; this is a virtual alternative because in reality its effect is to increase the length of imprisonment. Are criminal sanctions and measures in some way related to Janus?

Imposition does not equal enforcement

Let us suppose that an innovative criminal sanction or measure was imposed in a significant number of cases every year and, moreover, advisedly. Less pernickety analysts will, as we have seen, conclude that it works; others will be entitled to raise the question of the effective enforcement of those sanctions and measures. This is an extremely delicate question since what is understood by enforcement will be very different according to the particular type of sanction or measure, but also the analyst's expectations, which can be decisive.

Enforcement of a sentence may simply mean registration: this is the case with completely suspended sentences (with no follow-up) which are simply entered on the criminal record. The enforcing of a prison sentence without remission is more complex when the accused has left the trial a free man or woman: need in some cases for the police to look for the person, problem of time-limits, etc. On the other hand, there is no problem of definition in relation to enforcement: the individual will or will not be on the prison register.

Things are more complicated with respect to criminal sanctions and measures enforced in the community. Let us take as an example the community service orders introduced in France in 1983 in two forms: as the main sentence or as a condition of a suspended sentence with probation. Four stages can be identified in the enforcement of community service orders: (a) the individual's appointment with the JAP when he or she will be notified of the sanction; (b) the appointment with the probation officer with whom he or she will examine the practical conditions of enforcement; (c) the individual's first contact with the employer; and (d) the actual start of work (taking up of duties). For some individuals who are particularly maladjusted and/or drug dependent and/or have psychiatric problems and/or are homeless, this succession of appointments within deadlines set by the law may be equivalent to an assault course. Should the sentence be considered enforced once notification by the JAP has taken place or should we take a less strictly legalistic view and await the taking up of duties? This example shows that the assessment of enforcement of a sentence that works raises questions of definition.

Winning without risk

It is one thing for a criminal sanction or measure to be enforced in satisfactory material conditions and within an acceptable time, but will there be talk of good practice if things subsequently go wrong? What sorts of incidents will be considered benign, not calling into question the smooth enforcing of the sanction or measure? With what degree of indulgence or severity will the person in breach be assessed? Here, as elsewhere, the zero fault, not to mention the zero tolerance, policy may prove short-sighted. In order to show that an innovatory practice is a good practice, do those responsible for its application not run the risk of being obsessed with the question of incidents and failure to the point of deflecting the measure from its true objective? This takes us back to the previous question: in order for it to work, in other words, in order for enforcing to take place without incident, there is a risk that the measure will be imposed on persons who are easy to manage but for whom it was not really intended. As for the others, "the difficult ones", they will continue to be subjected to the good old methods that probably do not work. And the undemanding advocates of the new measure will be satisfied: the measure has been (1) imposed; (2) enforced; and (3) enforced without incident. What more could one ask? It is perfect. Others will want to ask further questions about what has become of the individual in terms of living conditions, reintegration and reoffending.

Post-sentence

The many functions of criminal sanctions and measures obviously include the idea that society can protect itself against any reoffending in the broadest sense of the term. At this level, a good practice is surely one that ensures zero reoffending or at least, to be more realistic, the lowest possible level of reoffending. Here we depart from the previous approaches with limited horizons to project ourselves into the future of individuals. Here again, however, there are many different approaches: what period of time will be taken into account with respect to "reoffending" and therefore to speak in terms of failure? A further conviction? A conviction of a certain degree of gravity? A particular type of offence? In order to assess the quality of criminal sanctions and measures, are we going to set a threshold above which we will say it does not work (1%? 10%? 20%? 50%?) or are we going to go down the slippery slope of comparing different measures?

If one looks at the public debate on the subject in France, one is struck by the lack of rigour on both sides of the argument, although the subject has been covered in a number of articles.[7] For example, new methods have been developed for comparing rates of return to prison[8] by persons sentenced to a term

---

7. Tournier, P.V., "'A chacun sa vérité', propos sur la récidive tenus à l'Assemblée nationale et au Sénat", *Cahiers de l'Actif*, No. 296-297, pp. 51-64.
8. A further custodial sentence.

of imprisonment according to whether or not they have been granted conditional release. As we know, the comparison is favourable to those released on parole rather than those simply released with no preparation at the end of their sentences.[9] This technique, known as "comparative rates", has been borrowed from demography and enables a distinction to be made in the difference in rates between the selection procedures for conditional release and what can be attributed to the measure itself: prepared, assisted and supervised release.[10] Generally speaking, it is not enough to compare the reoffending rate connected with sanction or measure A directly with the reoffending rate for sanction or measure B without taking into account the differences in structure between groups A and B according to variables which may directly or indirectly influence the reoffending rate. To put it another way, a good socio-demographic and/or criminal structure may be hiding behind a good reoffending rate, when one was hoping to recognise the effects of good practice.

How those much-discussed reoffending rates are interpreted then has to be examined, even when they are correctly calculated, even if account is taken – as far as that is possible – of the methodologies used to compare different sanctions and measures. Surveys of reoffending only take into account new acts or omissions brought to the attention of the criminal justice system. My colleague, Pierre Landreville, therefore prefers the term "resumption rate".[11] These rates may not give an accurate picture of the numbers of those who have again committed acts likely to be regarded as offences and, therefore, bias evaluation of the measure.

Cost-benefit

Does it work? Is it worthwhile/cost-effective?[12] Another commonly used expression, another area for concern in terms of evaluation. The great advantage of economic calculations is that here at least we know what accounting units are going to be used: euros. This makes it look easy: by introducing the number of persons subject to a particular sanction or measure and making the model a little more complex to take into account the length of time they are looked after, we should be able to get somewhere. The trouble is that we run the risk along the way of neglecting everything that cannot be expressed in purely monetary terms: for example, the price of freedom or the price of collateral damage[13] caused by prison on prisoners' families and friends. A comparison still

---

9.   Warsmann, J.-L., "Les peines alternatives à la détention, les modalités d'exécution des courtes peines, la préparation des détenus à leur sortie", report to the Garde des Sceaux, 2003.

10. Tournier, P.V., "La mesure de la récidive en France", *Regards sur l'Actualité*, No. 229, La Documentation Française pp. 15-23.

11. Landreville, P., "La récidive dans l'évaluation des mesures pénales", *Déviance et Société*, Vol. 6, No. 4, pp. 366-375.

12. A few years ago a French association for the assistance of prisoners' families, FARAPEJ, chose this as the title of a colloquy.

13. This very eloquent expression was suggested by a prisoner.

has to be made of these costs and benefits – and one comes back to the above points.

Many of these remarks are simply common sense. All of them probably deserve to be examined in more depth and from a more technical point of view. They do not challenge the need in a democracy to evaluate criminal and prison policies, just like all other public policies – on the contrary. I see them as an invitation to abandon, not the question "Does it work?", but the reductive responses of both the partisans and the denigrators of this or that innovation. There are no miracle solutions, and no solution respecting individual rights should be rejected out of hand.

Chapter 2

Long-term effects of heroin prescription on patients' offending behaviour[1]

Denis Ribeaud, Martin Killias and Marcelo F. Aebi

Following the adoption by the Swiss authorities of the federal decree on the medical prescription of heroin of 13 June 1999, medical prescription of heroin is now a recognised form of treatment for particularly serious forms of drug addiction. The main short-term aim of this type of treatment is to reduce the collateral problems linked to illegal consumption of heroin. These include certain infectious diseases such as Aids or various forms of hepatitis, economic and social problems (homelessness, unemployment) and, finally, crime. In the medium and longer term, the programme is designed to stabilise patients' psychosocial state, with a view to reintegrating them as fully as possible into society in terms of employment, housing and overall lifestyle.

Because it creates victims, crime is one of the collateral problems which impacts most directly on people with no particular links to the drug scene. As a result, this aspect has always been the focus of particular public interest in the debate on drug addiction. Accordingly, one of the main objectives in introducing this new form of therapy was to bring down crime levels.

The first phase of trials (see Killias and Rabasa 1997; Killias et al 1999 and 2002) revealed a substantial reduction in crime, and in particular property crime. The IPSC study showed a drop in offences linked to the acquisition of drugs (theft, receiving stolen goods, drug dealing, etc.) of between 50% and 90% depending on the type of measure and data. However, the findings related only to the short to medium-term effects, over one or two years, of heroin prescription. The data gathered for the purposes of the present study, meanwhile, cover a period of four years from commencement of treatment and include those persons who quit the project early. The findings set out below therefore provide the basis for conclusions concerning the long-term outcomes for patients who remain on the programme and also those who leave it after a certain time.

---

1. This project was supported by research contract No. 99.001149 (8151) of the Swiss Federal Pubic Health Agency.

Conduct of study/method

In conducting the first study, we made use of three types of data on crime: data gathered during standardised interviews conducted every six months with the participants in the programme (self-reported crime), data taken from police files in the cantons which had taken part in the trials (police reports) and, finally, data from the central criminal records (convictions).

It had emerged from the first study that participants tended not to deny their crimes when interviewed. In fact, the number of crimes admitted to in the course of those interviews far exceeded the number reported to the police. This openness was undoubtedly due to the fact that participants were guaranteed absolute anonymity. However, interviews have the drawback of always having to have the persons concerned on the spot. The difficulty is compounded by the fact that many patients no longer see any point in taking part in such interviews, which they were obliged to attend during the first evaluation phase. Furthermore, a number of participants dropped out of the trials after a while, making it still more difficult to contact them.

In order to obtain information on offences committed by the different groups of patients for the new series of data, therefore, we referred to police records and to the data held in the central criminal records, which have the advantage of being available without the need to interview patients. In addition, a study conducted by the IPSC (Aebi 1999) showed that the police data and the self-reported data gave a broadly similar picture of offending among participants. In other words, those participants known to the police, by and large, confessed to significantly more offences during the anonymous interviews than other participants (ibid., p. 172). Both types of data, therefore, may be regarded as a valid measure of offences committed.

During the summer and autumn of 2000, on this basis, the IPSC researchers gathered all the relevant data on the participants in the trials from the various police forces and the central criminal records. As a result, we now have a database covering a much longer observation period of four years following admission to the programme, allowing us to draw conclusions on the long-term effects of the heroin prescription programme. We will concentrate below on analysing the police data.

The figures set out in this article refer to incidence and prevalence rates. The incidence rate indicates the average occurrence of a particular event (offence, conviction, etc.) in a given population (patients). The incidence rate is important in assessing the trend in the volume of crime. An incidence rate of 1.3 indicates that, on average, each individual in the observed population committed 1.3 offences during the reference period. The prevalence rate, meanwhile, indicates the percentage of persons within a given population having committed a specific offence at least once during the reference period.

In all, our team gathered data relating to 947 persons treated with heroin under the PROVE trials. Of these, 428 (45.2%) remained on the programme for at least four years. Our analysis will concentrate initially on this group. The remaining participants left the programme before the end of the period, either because they switched to a different type of therapy (methadone, withdrawal, etc.) or because they resumed illegal consumption of heroin. We will then go on to examine outcomes depending on the length of participation in the programme.

Before we move on to the findings, it should be noted that the data were gathered using a procedure drawn up in agreement with the federal data protection authorities, the directors of the federal public health and police authorities and the cantonal and municipal chiefs of police. This procedure guaranteed participants in the PROVE projects the maximum degree of anonymity.

Findings

Trend for patients remaining on the programme for four years

Graph 1 sets out the trend in the annual prevalence rate for patients treated for at least four years under a PROVE project. As we can see, during the two years preceding treatment, over half (54% and 62%) of participants were the subject of at least one police report. From the first year of treatment, this rate falls sharply, with only 35% of persons being entered in police records.

Graph 1: Annual prevalence rate of police reports for participants in PROVE projects (N=248)

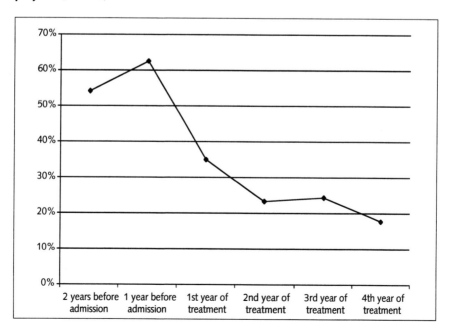

This positive trend is maintained in the second year of treatment, with the rate falling to 23%. In the following two years, the prevalence rate stabilises at around 20%, with a continuing downward trend.

Overall, the incidence rates (Graph 2) follow the same pattern as the prevalence rates. Whereas, before commencing treatment, participants were entered in police files on average 2.5 to 3.0 times a year, this falls to below 1.0 during the first year, and then stabilises at around 0.5 in subsequent years (continuous line: "overall incidence"). Of course, this fall is due to a large extent to the fact that, after commencing treatment, most of those treated were no longer being entered in police records (see Graph 1). However, as the dotted line (incidence per person questioned) shows, there is also a considerable reduction in the incidence rate among those who continued to be entered in the records, as the number of recorded interviews falls from almost 5 before treatment to around 2.5 during the 4 years of treatment. Hence, there is a sharp decline in the number of police contacts even amongst those still being apprehended.

Graph 2: Annual incidence rate of police reports for participants in PROVE projects (N=428)

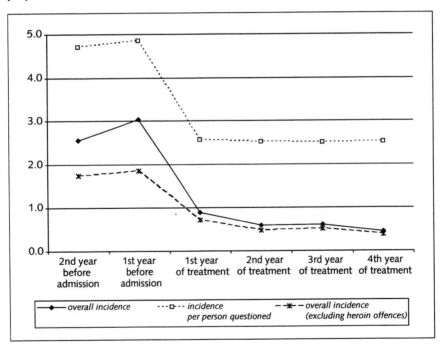

This drop in contacts with the police is also due in some measure to the simple fact that the participants in the projects, once they have been admitted, consume very little heroin purchased on the black market, as the drug is legally prescribed for them. As the third curve in Graph 2 – overall incidence excluding reports for possession/consumption of heroin – shows, the fall in the incidence rate is less pronounced, but still quite marked, if reports specifically linked to heroin consumption are excluded.

We examined in even greater detail the trend in relation to the type of offence committed. The corresponding incidence rates are set out in Graph 3. In order to maintain an overview, we confined ourselves to a few offences of particular relevance.

The most striking feature is the very sharp decline in reports for shoplifting, the corresponding rate for which falls from around 0.35 before treatment to around 0.1 throughout the treatment period, a relative decrease of 72%. The same is true of burglaries, which drop from an average of 0.13 before admission to the prescription programme to 0.03 after admission (-81%).

Graph 3: Annual incidence rate of reports for participants in PROVE projects (N=428) by offence type

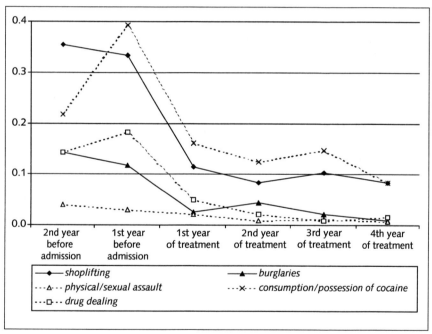

As we can see, there were very few incidents of assault before admission to the programme. Even here, however, there is a drop in the number of recorded incidents.

As regards cocaine consumption, there is also a significant decrease in the number of recorded incidents. The rate, which was 0.31 before the onset of treatment, falls to an average of 0.13 during treatment (-58%). It is important

31

to note at this point that this finding bears out the decrease in cocaine consumption found by Uchtenhagen (1997, p. 69) on the basis of a survey of participants. It suggests that participation in the heroin prescription programme has a positive impact on cocaine consumption, perhaps attributable to less frequent contact with persons involved in the drug scene (ibid., p. 79).

Furthermore, the figures show a sharp rise in police-recorded cocaine consumption during the year preceding treatment, probably as a result of heightened police activity on the drug scene. A great many of the participants in the PROVE programme embarked upon it following the closure of open drug scenes in the mid-1990s, accompanied by a heavy police presence. This thesis is borne out by the fact that a similar increase is observed in all offences directly related to the drug scene, such as cocaine or heroin consumption and drug dealing, which in practice are reported only by police officers. By contrast, other offences such as burglary or shoplifting, which are usually reported by the victim and the rates of which are therefore less dependent on police activity, do not show the same increase during the year preceding admission to the project.

Finally, a marked fall can be observed in reports of drug trafficking, with the average rate falling from 0.16 in the 2 years preceding treatment to 0.02 on average during treatment, a drop of 85%.

Trend depending on length of treatment

As we saw in the methodological section of the article, over half of participants dropped out of the programme after four years. This group breaks down into 159 patients (17%) who left after less than 6 months of treatment, 90 (10%) who left after between 6 and 12 months, 94 (10%) who left during the second year of treatment, 81 (9%) who left during the third year and, finally, 71 patients (8%) who quit treatment during the fourth year. The remaining 428 persons (46%) were treated for at least 4 years.

Since, before admission to the programme, these different groups all had broadly similar numbers of contacts with the police – either because they were really involved in more crime or because they frequented areas under close police surveillance – we calculated the average prevalence rate of police contacts in the two years preceding entry into the programme. The prevalence of contacts during treatment was then indexed in relation to this base level. Graph 4 below sets out the trend in the prevalence rate of police contacts for each of these groups compared with the rate prior to admission to the programme.

Graph 4: Trend in the number of police contacts for participants in PROVE projects according to length of treatment (annual indexed prevalence rates: average for period prior to treatment = 1)

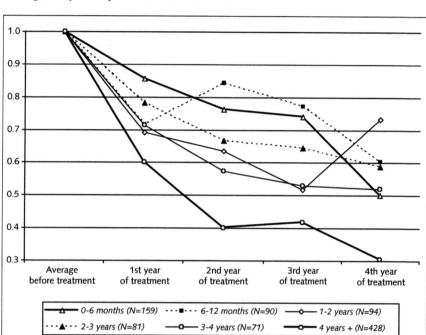

In order to make it easier to interpret the findings, the two extreme groups, namely those who left the programme after less than six months and those treated for over four years, are indicated by a bold line. As we can see, during the first year, the proportion of those apprehended by the police falls appreciably across all the groups. However, the reduction is less marked in the group of patients treated for less than six months. This may be explained by the fact that these persons were no longer receiving treatment for more than half of the observation period; it is very likely that many of them re-entered the drug scene and resumed their previous lifestyle. In fact, over 20% of this group dropped out of the programme without embarking upon alternative treatment (methadone, abstinence); for the other groups, the proportion is in the region of 10%. Subsequently, those in this group continue to have fewer contacts with the police.

The pattern for the second group, treated for between six and twelve months, is more typical. During treatment, the proportion of persons taken in for questioning falls sharply, but rises as soon as treatment finishes, suggesting that a number of these people re-entered the drug scene. However, this group also shows a subsequent reduction in the number of contacts with the police.

33

The next three groups, namely those who left the programme after between two and four years, fall between the two extremes, showing a steady fall in the number of contacts with the police, even after the end of the programme. The only exception is the group treated for between one and two years, where there is a marked resurgence in the number of contacts with the police during the fourth year following the onset of treatment. Overall, the graph shows that the treatment delivered benefits to all participants, with the exception of the group which dropped out of the programme almost immediately after admission. Particularly striking is the spectacular fall in the number of contacts with the police during the first year, which is almost identical for all those persons remaining on the programme for over a year. After this initial sharp fall, the rates tend to level off, even after the end of the programme. However, the fall is most pronounced and steadiest in the group treated continuously throughout the observation period.

Hence, the benefits of the programme for those who remain on it seem clear. However, the close resemblance between the different curves cannot be overlooked and raises a number of questions.

The first question is whether the reduction observed in the different groups is a direct consequence of treatment. If so, it would appear that even a brief period of treatment (two months on average in the first group) has a positive impact on offending behaviour. Even this short period, it seems, allowed some participants to alter their lifestyle and opt for an alternative form of therapy; 38% of the 159 persons who quit the programme soon after admission moved on to a course of oral methadone, and 22% even commenced withdrawal. Given that methadone treatment also leads to a significant reduction in offences committed by those treated (see Killias et al 1999 for Switzerland; Coid et al 2000 for the United Kingdom; and Bathsteen and Legge 2001 for Germany), and withdrawal even more so, as the pressure to finance the habit is removed completely, this would go some way towards explaining the reduction observed in this group.

An alternative theory, more critical of the efficacy of treatment, is that the different curves represent a "maturing out" effect, or a natural reduction in offending behaviour with age, a phenomenon well established by criminological research. This hypothesis is lent further weight by the fact that the average age of patients on admission to the programme was around 30.

Unfortunately, it is impossible to assess the specific impact of these two effects. However, the fact remains that the reduction is more pronounced for those who continued to be treated than for any other group. The level of criminal involvement before treatment, when the different groups were engaged in crime to a very similar extent, shows that the difference cannot simply be explained by a self-selection phenomenon, whereby the "good risks" remain on the programme while the others leave.

Discussion and conclusions

Overall, the police data analysed show that trials with heroin prescription contribute to an appreciable reduction in crime among patients even in the longer term. The effects noted in the first study (see Killias and Rabasa 1997) are therefore confirmed in the long term. Not only did a larger number of persons cease to be entered in police records: there was also a sharp reduction in the number of police contacts amongst those still being apprehended.

The reduction observed spanned all types of offences. Evidently, the greatest reduction was in the number of instances of police questioning for illegal consumption of heroin. However, a comparable reduction is observed for illegal cocaine consumption, suggesting that the treatment also has a beneficial impact on the consumption of other illicit substances. If we also take into account the reduction in the number of reports of drug dealing, we can conclude that prescribing heroin has had the effect of removing those treated from the drug scene. Moreover, the reduction in drug dealing offers hope that treatment may also prevent new users from becoming involved with hard drugs.

The fall in crime levels is not, however, confined to activities within the drug scene; it also encompasses property crime such as shoplifting, robbery and burglary.

In addition to the evident relief for potential victims, the fall in this type of crime is interesting in that it corroborates the theory of an overall reduction in crime linked to illegal consumption of narcotics. It could be argued that the reduction in the number of offences under the Narcotics Act is the result of the relaxing of police controls following closure of the open drug scene. This is made more plausible by the fact that this type of offence is almost invariably reported by police officers, and that offences under the Narcotics Act are probably less visible to the forces of law and order following the closure of these scenes. Property crime, on the other hand, is usually reported by the victim, meaning that the corresponding data are less dependent on police activity. As we also observed a significant reduction in that area, we can conclude that the fall in crime rates among patients is genuine and applies across the board.

Finally, the comparison between persons who discontinued treatment at different stages leaves a number of questions unanswered. It is unclear whether a brief stint on the prescription programme guarantees a long-term reduction in crime for a significant number of persons, or whether this reduction is simply the effect of "maturing out", a natural reduction in offending with age. The likely explanation is that both factors contribute to the reduction. However, generally speaking, the reduction is more marked the longer the period of treatment, suggesting an effect from the therapy independent of the age effect.

References

Aebi, M.F., *La validité des indicateurs de la criminalité*, IPSC, University of Lausanne, Lausanne, 1999.

Aeschbach, E., *Remise d'héroïne en Suisse*, Médecins Suisses contre la Drogue, Zug, 1998.

Bathsteen, M. and Legge, I., "Intendierte und nicht intendierte Folgen des Hamburger Substitutionsprogramms", *Monatsschrift für Kriminologie und Strafrechtsreform*, Vol. 84, No. 1, 2001, pp. 1-9.

Coid, J., Carvell, A., Kittler, Z., Healey, A. and Henderson, J., "The impact of methadone treatment on drug misuse and crime", *Research Findings*, 120, Home Office Research, Development and Statistics Directorate, London, 2000.

Killias, M. and Rabasa, J., *Rapport final sur les effets de la prescription de stupéfiants sur la délinquance des toxicomanes*, first edition, IPSC, University of Lausanne, Lausanne, 1997.

Killias, M., Aebi, M.F., Ribeaud, D. and Rabasa, J., *Rapport final sur les effets de la prescription de stupéfiants sur la délinquance des toxicomanes*, second edition, IPSC, University of Lausanne, Lausanne, 1999.

Killias, M., Aebi, M.F., Ribeaud, D. and Rabasa, J. (forthcoming), *Rapport final sur les effets de la prescription de stupéfiants sur la délinquance des toxicomanes*, third edition, IPSC, University of Lausanne, Lausanne.

Uchtenhagen, A. (ed.), *Rapport de synthèse PROVE*, ISF, Zurich, 1997.

Chapter 3

The Austrian Protection against Domestic Violence Act 1996[1]

Birgitt Haller, Christa Pelikan and Petra Smutny

The Austrian Protection against Domestic Violence Act came into force on 1 May 1997.

It is a body of special "targeted" legislation, comprising new or reformed sections of different realms of legislation, civil law – more specifically the Enforcement Code (*Exekutionsordnung*), and police (security) law, while criminal law in a narrow sense is not addressed. It focuses on the protection of actual and potential victims of domestic violence, protection from physical, sexual and psychological injury inflicted within the context of a household, and the intimate partnership and family relationships constituting it.

In the new legislation, the role of protection is assigned to the police with the "invention" of a new instrument devised to make this police intervention more adequately serve the purpose of immediate protection for the victim of violence. This new instrument provides for an eviction and barring order (*Wegweisung* and *Rückkehrverbot*) that can be extended by a civil law injunction (or restraining order) that keeps the person representing a threat to the physical and/or psychological safety of other household members from re-entering the premises or a wider defined area of safety (*Einstweilige Verfügung*).[2]

The Protection against Domestic Violence Act is characterised by: an unusual and remarkable genesis; a comprehensive and highly pragmatic construction; and its relative effectiveness.

The history of the Protection against Domestic Violence Act

The challenge

The challenge sprang from the women's movement, more specifically the shelter movement that became active and visible in Austria in the late 1970s,

---

1. As amended in 1998.
2. We are confronted with some confusion concerning the translation of the German legal terminology: the correct English term used for *Wegweisung* and *Rückkehrverbot* is eviction and barring order, more commonly it is called a "go-order"; the Austrian *Einstweilige Verfügung*, translated as "temporary injunction", corresponds to what is commonly called a protection or restraining order.

setting up and running a considerable number of shelters throughout the country (twenty-one shelters and four counselling centres in 1999). The shelter movement developed as a reaction to the increasing awareness of the actual existence of domestic violence and the need "to do something against it".[3] Over time, the protagonists of this movement changed their outlook and overall political aim from just providing help for battered women by harbouring them (reducing themselves to a social work perspective as it was perceived later on) to the fight for "gender democracy". The Austrian Minister for Women's Affairs Johanna Dohnal took a firm stance on this issue, and in the early 1990s came forward with a series of international conferences, the most prominent taking place in Vienna in 1992. Its title "Test the west" pointed already to the models that were to inform the politics of the women and the challenge implied. "The west" was the Domestic Abuse Intervention project (DAIP), the so-called "Duluth model", that became influential not only in Austria but also in Germany, for example, in Berlin.[4] It is a comprehensive model bringing together police intervention with a strong reliance on mandatory arrest, the state prosecutor regularly drawing up an indictment – rather unusual in a system that is marked by the principle of opportunity – and the court imposing orders for anti-violence training, which in the case of non-compliance are transformed into confinement orders. "This is what we want" was the message of "Test the west" and several years later, Rosa Logar, the head of the umbrella organisation of Austrian shelters, wrote: "The discontent and anger of women becomes a challenge to law and politics."[5]

In October 1993 a joint conference of the Minister for Women's Affairs and the Minister of Justice took place on the theme of "Women and the law", which resulted in a first proposal drawn up by the Minister of Justice stating his intention, "to provide help to the victim in a prompt and effective way and to offer the perpetrator – dependent on certain conditions – the possibility of therapy".[6] And he expressed his conviction that the implementation of this proposal would lead to co-operation among the various institutions and groups concerned. For this purpose a working group was to be constituted to further discuss how to proceed with efforts to achieve these goals.

---

3 . At this point one usually proceeds with information on the size and scope of the problem, the number of women and children being subjected to different forms and degrees of domestic violence, and the number of cases that remain hidden. We will refrain from this exercise, which leads quite rightly to the highly contested question of the definition of violence and the way violent acts are assessed and counted in the course of the large surveys that have been carried out in the US, Canada and the Netherlands. More recently attempts have been made to estimate the economic costs that arise for society as a whole as a consequence of domestic violence; presentation of these figures seems to carry the hope that they may even present a stronger argument for policy makers (for example, €200 million for the Netherlands and 400 million Swiss francs in Switzerland).

4. Duluth Project Team, "Duluth domestic abuse intervention project, 'Test the West'", Geschlechterdemokratie und Gewalt, Internationales Symposion, Vienna, 1992.

5. Logar, R., "Halt der Männergewalt – Wegweisende Gesetze in Österreich", *Streit*, 17, 1999, pp. 99-109.

6. Letter of invitation from the Minister of Justice of 2 November 1993, 4.214/26-I 1/1993.

The struggle

Innovative law-making

The unusual and truly innovative way of working towards a new piece of legislation consisted first of all in setting up a steering group that later distributed responsibility for different parts of the legislative package to different working groups on police law, civil (execution) law, criminal law and one dedicated to the design and establishment of the new *Interventionsstellen*, the intervention centres. These working groups consisted of civil servants from the relevant departments of the Ministries of Justice, the Interior and Family Affairs, and representatives of the police, judges and state prosecutors, attorneys, and shelters and other institutions working in the field of domestic violence. (Interestingly it is a setting and procedure that is to be found in international organisations – amongst others, the Council of Europe – when developing a new legal instrument.) Thus the working groups were neither restricted to professional law-makers, nor even to "jurists". That means that at a very early stage, the law-makers were forced into (or had the benefit of) confrontation – if not with the potential beneficiaries of the law and especially the victims themselves, at least with those who were immediately concerned with their plight.

During the subsequent three years and in the course of a number of group and plenary sessions, the new legislation – as well as the first new institutions, *Interventionsstellen*, designed to co-ordinate efforts for the protection and support of women – took shape and came into existence. It was also the result of remarkable co-operation. It was also the result of a struggle that was at times hard, even embittered, a struggle for demands and requests, needs and interests, rights to fight for and rights to protect. There were severe misunderstandings, there was often a lack of flexibility but there were also sincere efforts to understand and to recognise the concerns of others participating in the working group. As a matter of fact, this struggle or fight that had taken place inside the working group on criminal law was sometimes carried over to the plenary sessions.

Points of controversy

• The role of arrest

Within the Duluth project – as within other US initiatives – mandatory arrest had become an important instrument for setting in motion the process of "holding the perpetrator accountable". Without considering the stark differences that exist between the function and the inter-relation of different agencies of criminal law within a common law system and a continental European (civil law) system, a request was made to introduce a wider margin of discretion for the police when deciding whether to make an arrest when called to the scene of domestic violence. Naturally, one would say, this provoked objections from the criminal procedural law specialists at the Ministry of

Justice. An arrest in the Austrian system of law can only be made on very restricted grounds – the margin for police discretion being generally very narrowly circumscribed – namely, when there is danger of flight (*Fluchtgefahr*), obscuration (*Verdunkelungsgefahr*), or of the offence immediately occurring (*Tatbegehungsgefahr*). The latter is restricted to more serious offences, aggravated assault being the most relevant. Thus, there was much debate about whether to extend this condition to cases of minor assault. But it soon became clear that the jurists were almost unanimously opposed to this kind of extension. Consequently, this controversy served to endorse the search for other instruments that were already being made in the "police law" working group. Thus, the "go-order" – technically regarded as a less intrusive means (*gelinderes Mittel*) – became, as already stated, the essential core of the new legislation.

- • The role of victim-offender mediation (VOM)

Another topic on which controversy flared up was the role of victim-offender mediation (VOM) and more precisely its application in cases of domestic violence. Although this is not the place to go into this debate in more detail, it should be mentioned that since the instigation of the pilot project "VOM in general criminal law" in 1992, this new measure has been quite widely used (about a quarter of all VOM cases in the pilot project) by the state prosecutors co-operating with VOM services. From the outset, this practice met with the opposition of the women's movement who raised quite powerful arguments against it: namely, the potential lack of sufficient norm confirmation, the potential neglect of power imbalances inextricably present where violence has occurred, and the short-time character of the intervention, meaning that control and after-care were neglected. However, in the course of this controversy, the representatives of the shelter movement backed away from their initial request for a complete ban on the use of VOM in domestic violence cases. One has to perceive this development in the light of the reform of criminal procedural law that was under way at the same time. As with arrest, US models have also exerted their influence in the sphere of diversionary (or alternative) measures. Prosecutorial diversion dependent on the voluntary co-operation of the suspect was not deemed an appropriate criminal law response. A treatment order, imposed by the court and controlled by the judge, was preferred. The subject of such an order would also be liable to confinement in case of non-compliance. Although there was considerable support for the position of "the women", the model of "pure" prosecutorial diversion prevailed and took shape within the criminal procedural law amendment, a model emphasising the voluntary consent of the suspect.

Developments in this respect also took a course similar to those regarding the arrest question: the representatives of the shelter movement increasingly concentrated on negotiations concerning the establishment and financing of the intervention centres that were to provide counselling and immediate support for women who had obtained an eviction and barring order. Counselling in such cases would extend to explaining the advantages and disadvantages of going ahead with a criminal procedure, as well as the potential benefits and dangers of VOM. They also insisted – successfully – on making the instigation of a VOM procedure dependent on the consent of the victim; an obligation to contact the intervention centres in domestic violence cases remained a further request.

- The request for a more victim-oriented criminal procedure

The third line of controversy is closely related to the topic of VOM and domestic violence. It pertains to the attempt to make the criminal procedure more responsive to victims' needs in general. The criminal procedural law "experts" had mustered a lot of resistance to this demand, and had at the same time considerably enraged "the women". It appeared to boil down to a matter of principle: can criminal procedure be transformed at all to become more responsive to victims? What are the relations between procedural safeguards protecting the perpetrator from undue restrictions of his or her rights by state agencies, on the one hand, and the wider understanding of a human right to live free from violence, on the other? Perhaps a step toward achieving a more satisfying balance of interests has been struck by the new legislation.

Summarising this remarkable process of law-making, it might be argued that, on the one hand, the demands of the women's movement on the criminal justice system forced law-makers to scrutinise the array of traditional legal instruments and to invent new answers. On the other hand, the apprehensions of the conventional law-makers motivated those who had challenged "the law" to go beyond mere requests for a tighter grip of the law. The prime goal of immediate effective protection as well as of effective support that opens the road to empowerment came more clearly into view. From the background of a struggle that had touched upon far-reaching questions concerning the function and potential of (criminal) law interventions, an extremely pragmatic solution emerged.

The content of the Protection against Domestic Violence Act

In November 1996 the Austrian National Assembly passed the Federal Act on Protection against Violence within the Family, which entered into force on 1 May 1997. Some aspects of this legislation were amended and improved upon in January 2000. The Protection against Domestic Violence Act, as it is otherwise known, contained amendments to the Civil Code, the Enforcement Code and the Security Police Act, and was the first legal instrument of co-operation in this field to offer victims of domestic violence protection, security and support. As stated above, the special aim of this law is to assert a victim's right to protection from the offender in his or her living environment and social surroundings. This right may be granted by an eviction and barring order (commonly called a "go-order" and restraining order) issued by the police and/or by a temporary injunction (protection or restraining order) granted by the responsible district court.

The Protection against Domestic Violence Act rests on three pillars:

- eviction and barring orders as stipulated by the Security Police Act;
- longer term protection by means of a protection order (temporary injunction) as part of the Enforcement Code;
- so-called "intervention centres", offering free counselling and support.

The new measures of the Security Police Act

The provisions of the Security Police Act protect anybody living in the same household as a perpetrator: spouses, partners, children and other relatives, but also other lodgers. If a perpetrator threats one of those protected, the intervening police officers are required to evict that person from his or her home and its immediate surroundings and to bar that person from re-entering it – even if the perpetrator is the owner of the house or apartment. A precondition for issuing such an order is a dangerous attack on life, health or freedom and the perception that – due to certain facts, in particular, due to previous dangerous attacks – another dangerous attack is imminent.

An eviction and barring order is valid for ten days. The victim cannot influence this order and its duration in any way; this provision was deemed necessary, firstly, to stress that it is the state that condemns domestic violence and, secondly, to prevent the victim being put under pressure by the offender. During the first three days compliance with this order is controlled by local law enforcement authorities; even if the victim allows the offender to re-enter the home, this is considered a violation of the order and as such dealt with as an offence under the Administrative (Criminal) Law. In any case the police will send the offender away if he or she violates the eviction and barring order and he or she will be fined or – if there are repeated breaches of the order – placed under arrest.

Police authorities are obliged to inform the non-governmental "intervention centre". The intervention centre, on the one hand, provides advice and support for people – mostly women – subjected to domestic violence. On the other hand, in its special role under the Protection from Domestic Violence Act, the intervention centre acts as a link between the criminal law agencies, and the victim and offender in order to achieve effective prevention.

The temporary injunction (protection order) of the civil (district) court

If a barring order has been obtained and confirmed by the police, the victim may seek a "temporary injunction" through the responsible district court within ten days. The restraining order will thus automatically be prolonged for a total of twenty days; continuous "seamless" protection is thus to be provided until the local court has made its decision. However, an eviction order from the police is not a precondition for getting a temporary injunction through the court.

A temporary injunction can be issued by the court against a close, or a former close, relative after physical abuse, or after threats, or in case of psychological terror if this seriously impairs the victim's mental health and whenever these attacks make life with the violent person intolerable. The court requires evidence of acts of violence. Such evidence might include the testimony of the victim, the testimony of eyewitnesses, police reports, doctors', hospital or therapists' reports, photos etc. Information relating to previous violent attacks is also important. The evidence should be handed in to the court together with the application for the temporary injunction.

The offender can be ordered to leave the house and forbidden re-entry for a fixed period of time. The offender can also be banned from the immediate vicinity which could also include other defined areas, such as the route to the victim's workplace, schools, day nurseries, etc. Contact in any form can also be forbidden. However, the problematic condition remains of proving a recent joint household (or one that existed no longer than three months prior to the request for an injunction). Stalking, by ex-spouses or ex-cohabitees, is therefore difficult to counter.

The temporary injunction is valid for three months at the most. In some cases it can be prolonged, especially if the victim has filed for a divorce – in that case it remains in force as long as the proceedings last.

During this time the perpetrator is only allowed to come to the apartment if he or she is accompanied by a law officer, in order for example to pick up his or her belongings. The victim must be always previously informed. The court is obliged to inform the police of the protection order. The police have to hand over to the court the keys to the apartment the perpetrator had to leave: they are kept there for as long as the temporary injunction is in force. If the offender violates the order forbidding contact or enters any of the protected areas defined in the application, the victim can apply for a fine for contempt of court.

Evaluation of Austria's Protection against Domestic Violence Act

In 1999 the Ministry of the Interior commissioned the Institute of Conflict Research to conduct an evaluation study on the Protection against Domestic Violence Act.[7]

---

7. The main findings of the evaluation are published in: Dearing, A. and Haller, B. (eds.), *Das österreichische Gewaltschutzgesetz*, Vienna, 2000.

Police interventions

The frequency with which the Protection against Domestic Violence Act is applied by Austria's two security bodies varies considerably, the urban police being much more "active" than the rural police.[8] In 2001, nearly six out of ten "go-orders"/restraining orders were imposed by the police – but the urban police are responsible for approximately one third of the Austrian population, while the so-called "*Gendarmerie*" is in charge of two thirds. From May 1997 until the end of the year 2000, the total number of eviction and barring orders increased continuously; in 2001 it dropped slightly for the first time. In 2002 numbers seem to be on the increase. From May 1997 until July 2002, the new law was applied 13 835 times – or 7 times a day on average.[9]

Table 1: Eviction/barring orders

	1997	1998	1999	2000	2001
Federal police directorates	646 (47.3%)	1320 (49.4%)	1654 (53.8%)	1807 (53.9%)	1880 (57.3%)
Federal rural police (*Gendarmerie*)	719 (52.7%)	1353 (50.6%)	1422 (46.2%)	1547 (46.1%)	1403 (42.7%)
Total	1365 (100%)	2673 (100%)	3076 (100%)	3354 (100%)	3283 (100%)

Source: internal statistics of the Ministry of the Interior.

Table 2: "Go-orders"/restraining orders – Annual rates of growth

	1998	1999	2000	2001
Federal police directorates	+36.2%	+25.3%	+9.3%	+4.0%
Federal rural police (*Gendarmerie*)	+25.5%	+ 5.1%	+8.8%	-9.3%
Total	+30.5%	+15.1%	+9.0%	-2.2%

Source: in-house calculation based on 1997 figures extrapolated to twelve months.

Before the Protection against Domestic Violence Act came into force, the instrument most frequently used to respond to domestic disputes was that of "dispute settlement": the officers talked to the "conflicting parties", seeking to "calm"

---

8. There are still large local differences within the police.
9. See *Der Standard*, 31 July 2002, p. 8.

and "appease" them and occasionally suggested to the woman to seek refuge, for instance in a women's shelter. The idea behind the wish to "mediate" between victim and perpetrator was that violence in a personal relationship was regarded as a "private matter", and therefore the state and its authorities were not supposed to interfere. The instrument of dispute settlement is still available to police officers, along with "go-orders" and restraining orders. In 2001, it was used twice as often throughout Austria as the instruments of the Protection against Domestic Violence Act. It is striking that dispute settlement is still the method of choice used by the rural police reacting to family conflicts, and that the reason is a reluctance to "interfere" in family affairs.

According to an analysis of more than more than 1 000 police files (in the years 1997-98), "dispute settlement" was used in 52% of all cases, eviction/barring orders in 43% of cases and a charge was made in 5% of cases (most of them because of bodily injuries) without any other intervention.

Eviction orders are accepted to a large degree by the perpetrators. In 2000, 12.8% of proceedings under the Administrative (Criminal) Law were initiated because of a violation of an eviction order; in 2001, 15.4% of violations were charged by the police.[10]

Victims and perpetrators

These data refer only to the cases where "go-orders"/restraining orders were imposed by the police.

More than 80% of the interventions took place in partnerships: 50% against a spouse and 30% against a cohabiting partner. In 8% of all cases a former partner was concerned, and in 7% the conflict was an inter-generational one (the small number of female offenders appear mostly in this context).

The victims were female in nine out of ten cases. Nearly two thirds of them were between 25 and 44 years old and were employees or workers. Some 97% of the perpetrators were male. They were of the same age as the victims, and half of them were blue-collar workers. More than one quarter were unemployed.

A striking result is the over-representation of migrants among both victims and perpetrators. On average, about 9% of the Austrian population are migrants, whilst 20% of the victims and 25% of the perpetrators of domestic violence are migrants.

One quarter of the interventions led to a temporary injunction issued by the civil (district) court – sometimes combined with a divorce suit. Among the group of victims that went to court, migrants were under-represented.

---

10. But it has to be taken into consideration that not every violation becomes known to the police.

On the attitudes of police officers and victims of domestic violence[11]

Initially, police officers found it hard to meet their obligation to impose eviction/barring orders, especially when the victims opposed these measures. They were upset and occasionally complied with such requests, confining themselves to a "dispute settlement" role. Now it seems that these difficulties have been largely overcome.

There was a wide range of reactions expressed by the victims interviewed. Some women did not agree with the imposition of an eviction/barring order because they wanted to stay together with their partners and thought the police reaction inadequate and not at all helpful; although two years later, several of them stated in the course of follow-up interviews that they would never have succeeded in separating from their partners without the eviction order. Others judged this instrument very positively from the beginning; they perceived it as supportive in their attempt to leave their partner. In some cases the police intervention effectively shocked the perpetrators so that the relationship changed for the better. Some victims for whom "dispute settlement" had been considered sufficient were critical of this reaction: it had made their partners even stronger by reinforcing their conviction that nobody would stop their aggressive behaviour.

As regards diffusing situations, most of the victims were very satisfied with the police intervention. It is remarkable that gender-mixed teams were regarded as impartial whereas male officers were perceived to be partial in favour of women. It was only in rural areas that women complained about the *Gendarmerie* who often seemed prejudiced against women: they did not believe what the women had told them or blamed the women for their partners' aggression.

Summarising the results of the evaluation study, it can be stated that the Protection against Domestic Violence Act is widely accepted both by the police and by victims. It is important that discretion for imposing eviction/barring orders lies exclusively with the police: Firstly, because it is often very hard and even dangerous for a victim of violence to leave the relationship on her own initiative; victims need support to muster sufficient courage to take this step. Secondly, the new legal instruments signify a change of perspective: domestic violence being no longer perceived as a private "conflict", but constituting a ground for receiving protection from state agencies. The legitimate claim to live free from violence also inside one's home is thus confirmed.

---

11. A small random sample of police officers and victims at the research sites of Vienna, St Pölten, Salzburg-Land, Zell am See and Graz were approached and interviewed.

PART II
MEDIATION AND OTHER COMMUNITY SANCTIONS

Chapter 4

The impact of Council of Europe Recommendation No. R (99) 19 on mediation in penal matters[1]

Christa Pelikan

In April 1999, the Committee of Experts on Mediation in Penal Matters (PC-MP), in compliance with the terms of reference given to it by the European Committee on Crime Problems (CDPC) in 1996, drafted a recommendation entitled mediation in penal matters, which was subsequently adopted by the Committee of Ministers in September 1999 as Recommendation No. R (99) 19.

Three years later the Criminological Scientific Council (PC-CSC) decided to commission a study on the follow-up to this recommendation, which was to focus on the extent to which and the manner in which this recommendation had been implemented in different member states, and on the influence the recommendation had exerted in bringing about changes in the field of victim-offender mediation (VOM).

The PC-CSC thereby acknowledged (and there is growing awareness of this) that the following-up of the guidelines contained in recommendations drafted by committees of experts is, in itself, an important instrument for the further-ance of the Council of Europe crime policy.

The method of following-up the recommendation

The method chosen was a simple and practical one. In a way it was a continu-ation of the work carried out by the PC-MP, which met five times between November 1996 and April 1999 when the recommendation was finalised. Already in the course of the first session it was decided to gain an overview of developments in as many member states as possible, namely also in those countries not represented on the committee. For that purpose, experts were contacted by the members of the committee and asked to provide short reports on the situation in their respective countries.

I chose to repeat this procedure when compiling the present paper. A ques-tionnaire was sent out to the former members of the committee and to experts known through their work within the European Forum for Victim-Offender Mediation and Restorative Justice for the countries not represented. The list of the persons contacted is presented in Appendix II.

---

1. For the full text of Recommendation No. R (99) 19 see Appendix I to this chapter.

The questionnaire contained three main sections: the development of VOM in the respective country; the way the recommendation was adopted and implemented; and whether any of the changes mentioned could be traced to the influence of the recommendation (see Appendix III).

The answers received differed considerably, not only in content but also with regard to their form, that is, from only a general comment on the situation in a country and the influence of the recommendation to a detailed answer to each of the questions and sub-categories. For example, the Russian expert just wrote a letter containing an appeal for more help and support from the Council of Europe, whilst Anna Zairi from Greece stated in a letter that nothing had happened as regards VOM in her country.

Taken as a whole, the questionnaires that were received provided sufficient basis for preparation of a seminar that was planned as part of the programme of the Second Conference of the European Forum for Victim-Offender Mediation and Restorative Justice, which took place in Ostend from 10 to 12 October 2002.

In the course of the seminar a discussion took place on: (1) the diversity of developments regarding VOM in different member states; and (2) the overall course (or the direction) of the development of VOM.

However, there was no discussion of the third topic initially scheduled on the agenda – namely, the use and the usefulness of the recommendation, and what conditions are favourable or detrimental to the recommendation (or any other international document) becoming influential and supportive of other efforts?

To some extent, this chapter will therefore focus on finding an answer to this last question.

VOM development in Europe

The chapter will, however, begin with a presentation of what emerged as a consensus during the seminar and was expressed in the first of three statements presented to the participants: namely, VOM is spreading rapidly and continually in European countries.

Although considerable diversity can be found concerning this development as regards the scope of VOM – that is, the number of referrals or the range of offences to be included, the degree of its being grounded in legislation, its community or professional orientation – there has been (especially so during the last three or four years, 1998 to 2002):

- an upsurge in legislative activity;
- new activities in setting up VOM programmes or pilot projects, variously instigated by government agencies or NGOs;

- several training programmes and provisions for mediators as well as for magistrates and/or state prosecutors.

It can be said that these developments were part of a general movement that found its specific expression in the member countries; this "expression" was and is shaped by the specific features of the respective criminal justice systems and by the role played by groups of professionals, NGOs and individual actors.

Since it is not the purpose of this chapter to give an overview of the "state of the art" concerning VOM in different European countries (this is currently being done as part of a COST action led by Ivo Aertsen and Tony Peters at the University of Leuven), only brief mention will be made of relevant legislation, pilot projects and training programmes. The focus will be on the core question of this report, namely the influence the recommendation was perceived to exert on these developments, together with the categories or types of such influence.

The way the recommendation has influenced the development of VOM

An analysis of the replies to the questionnaire reveals different types or modes of influence:

The recommendation served as an important instrument in providing orientation and support, and even made its mark on developments in legislation

The following countries fall in this category: Belgium, Finland, Slovenia, Cyprus, Poland and, to some degree, Italy.

The Finnish experience will be presented in more detail; it provides an example of a country where there was specific VOM legislation and where the influence of the recommendation became explicit.

In Finland, a draft law on mediation in penal matters is pending. The government proposal was submitted in August 2002 following a report by Juhani Iivari, the government's rapporteur. The Ministry of Social Affairs and Health is responsible for drafting the text.

The scope of mediation according to this proposal will include all offences "where compensation for damages is possible and where the parties voluntarily agree to participate in mediation".

Finland has extensively used pilot projects for trying out VOM and it will now have mediation services all over the country, organised by the municipalities and staffed with lay persons who have received special training at general centres for adult training and education. The basic course takes thirty hours; additional specific "advanced" courses may follow; some municipalities provide for supervision.

The recommendation had been translated into Finnish and distributed to the relevant agencies. According to Juhani Iivari who served as the Finnish contact, the draft has included many of the elements of the recommendation; he explicitly points to Section II, "General principles"; the provisions in Section III concerning legislation and legal safeguards; Section IV on "The operation of criminal justice in relation to mediation"; Article 24 concerning the training of mediators; and to some of the articles referring to the "Handling of individual cases".

Slovenia offers another example that presents considerable insight into the processes and the means by which the recommendation becomes influential.

Slovenia implemented a nationwide programme of VOM in 2000 (following the establishment of a number of pilot projects). It is a diversionary measure with the state prosecutors being the referring agency; referral can take place at all stages of the criminal procedure until a conviction has taken place ("a judgment has been passed"), but it is restricted to petty cases. The instigation of a VOM procedure that is to take place with the help of a "neutral and independent" mediator needs the express written agreement of both parties. "The agreement must be in proportion with the seriousness of the committed offence and its effects on the victim". In her article in the *Newsletter of the European Forum for Victim-Offender Mediation and Restorative Justice*, Alenka Meznar has also stressed the personnel savings effect of VOM for the criminal justice system (837 court hearings less, which represent a caseload of almost 5 local court judges).

On the one hand, the role of the State Prosecutor's Office as the referring agency is strong and, on the other hand, Slovenia has opted for volunteer (lay) mediators (Norway has explicitly served as a model there). They undergo training covering a range of subjects and skills and lasting a few days. Interestingly, the State Prosecutor's Office is responsible for organising this training and it has also established an advisory board to supervise the work of the mediators. A degree of independence is guaranteed though by the Association of Slovenian Mediators, which was founded in December 2001 as an NGO.

In August 2002, the General Prosecutor's Office, with the financial support of the Ministry of Justice distributed a folder on "VOM in penal matters". "It was a big press conference with the media present. We are going to send a copy of this folder to each victim and offender who is to be invited to participate in the VOM process; copies are distributed to police units all over the country and many will be available at our district court," wrote Alenka Meznar.

The example of Cyprus bears some similarity to that of Slovenia – the main difference being the longer time span needed in Cyprus to get things moving. In January 2000 a committee was set up by the Ministry of Justice to look into policies followed in Cyprus in relation to the treatment of offenders. "This committee", Elena Zachariadou states, "is composed of the Director General of the

Ministry of Justice, who acts as chair, a senior judge representing the judiciary, the Director of the Prisons Department, a representative of the Welfare Department, an academic from the University of Cyprus, three representatives of the Ministry of Justice (two of them from the Department of Legal Research) and myself representing the Office of the Attorney General. As soon as I became a member of this committee, I informed its members of the recommendation and the work done in our committee of experts in Strasbourg. The members of the committee in Cyprus were provided with copies of the recommendation and also with copies of papers submitted by members of the committee of experts from countries where mediation in penal matters is already in place and working. The recommendation was positively received by all members of the committee and was seen in the context of introducing mediation in penal matters in Cyprus. The committee is now in the final stages of drafting its own recommendations to the Council of Ministers on action to be taken and I know that it will include action to be taken in relation to mediation."

By comparing the examples of Cyprus and Slovenia, another difference and another similarity become visible: in Cyprus, policies were mainly driven by the Ministry of Justice itself, who – by including Elena Zachariadou, a member of the Committee of Experts on Mediation in Penal Matters – deliberately established a link to the work of the Council of Europe. As with Slovenia, we see that for the influence of a former Council of Europe committee member to become relevant, it is not only necessary that he or she becomes active, but that there is interest shown, or at least a degree of acceptance, on behalf of the government – or, as in the case of Slovenia, on behalf of the criminal justice system professionals, namely the state prosecutors.

In can also occur where the efforts of an individual actor who has a good knowledge of the recommendation (as was the case with Juhani Iivari, who was also a member of the Board of the European Forum for Victim-Offender Mediation and Restorative Justice) coincide with a ministry's endeavours to establish VOM.

The history of the influence of the recommendation in Poland is again different and its success perhaps less pronounced than in the case of Finland and Slovenia. Changes to the Code of Criminal Law and the Criminal Procedural Law occurred as early as 1997 with a special regulation mentioning mediation added in 1998; mediation in juvenile cases was regulated in May 2001. It is the family judge who refers cases in juvenile matters, while the state prosecutors are the referring agencies for adult offenders. Mediation services in Poland are run by private organisations, the most important being the Polish Centre for Mediation. The majority of mediators are independent individuals (about 540 all over Poland) who have to be accredited to the courts of appeal or to the district courts.

Training is obligatory and regulated within the Law on Juvenile Justice; this law also contains quite detailed provisions concerning the way the mediation process is to be linked to the criminal procedure. The majority of mediators were trained in the course of special training sessions organised by the Polish mediation centre; training lasts four to five days. The first trainers were practitioners from Germany, although nowadays we find training for trainers carried out by Polish specialists and a group of sixteen mediators is now beginning to teach.

One has to mention that the Council of Europe has been very active in promoting VOM in Poland. Twice, in 1997 and in 1998, a seminar took place – including experts who were also members of the Committee of Experts on Mediation in Penal Matters – assembling quite a large number of criminal justice professionals. At an early stage, the principles and standards that had formed the basis of the recommendation were apprehended and discussed, thus influencing the VOM pilot project in juvenile cases that was evaluated by Beata Czarnecka-Dzialuk and Dobrochna Wojcik from the Institute of Justice.

The Polish Centre for Mediation, as well as the academics from the Institute of Justice that work closely with the Ministry of Justice (and of which it forms part), made use of the recommendation and of the arguments outlined in the explanatory memorandum to promote the cause of VOM. The Polish Centre for Mediation also used the recommendation to elaborate a code of ethics for mediators, as well as standards of good practice and standards for the training of mediators.

According to the national contact person for this paper, Beata Czarnecka-Dzialuk, acting together, these professionals proved quite successful as regards the regulations for VOM in juvenile justice. Commenting on the developments in Poland, she concludes that it seems much harder to achieve similar results in the field of mediation within criminal procedural law for adults. It is again the combined efforts of the Polish Centre for Mediation, academics from the Institute of Justice and a few judges that are pushing for an amendment of the legal regulations as they stand at present.

In Belgium, the recommendation was comparatively widely disseminated and followed. The influence of the recommendation became effective through two different channels. Firstly, there is a project by the Minister of Justice for a new Juvenile Justice Act, in which VOM plays a major role. In that project, mediation is presented as a *fil rouge*, an instrument to be used and given priority at the successive stages of the procedure involving young offenders. The lawmakers of the Ministry of Justice have referred to the explanatory memorandum of the recommendation several times to defend its legislative choices.

Secondly, the most important influence was exerted through Suggnomè, an NGO that has strong links with the Catholic University of Leuven, and the academics and researchers working there in the field of VOM and restorative justice. Suggnomè is working on a proposal for a global law on VOM oriented to the different types that exist in Belgium (juvenile VOM; VOM at police level;

"penal mediation" (the legal system within the Prosecutor's Office since 1994); "mediation for redress" (for more serious crimes, which will be prosecuted anyway); and VOM during the execution of the prison sentence).

Use is also made of the recommendation in the course of training programmes for mediators.

In Italy, VOM is still in its initial stages, with a few projects scattered all around the country. However, legislation providing for VOM is currently in a phase of rapid development. At the beginning of 2002, a Law on Criminal Proceedings before the Justice of the Peace was introduced.

A justice of the peace deals with minor offences only and can only impose fines, community service orders and a sentence obliging the offender to stay at home for a specified period of time. But a justice of the peace can also, during the first hearing, promote reconciliation between parties. For that purpose he or she suspends the hearing for a period not exceeding two months and may refer the case to mediation services. But he or she can also carry out mediation between the parties relying on his or her own skill. (Persons with legal education who pass an exam after a six-month training period become justices of the peace.)

Until now there exists in juvenile justice the possibility for the judge to suspend criminal proceedings and to give probation time; within this probation time that is monitored by social services, reconciliation and reparation to the victim can be one of the requirements the offender has to comply with. And it is the social workers that act as mediators and will write a sort of assessment of the "evolution of the offender's personality". Based on this report, the judge decides whether the case is to be dismissed or continue. A bill is currently being discussed in parliament that would amend these provisions. It is – according to the national contact person, Vania Patané – greatly influenced by the recommendation. This has occurred through the influence of members of parliament who used the document to design and support legislative initiatives.

The recommendation has mainly been read and subsequently used by NGOs and individual professionals outside the criminal justice system, and has thus exerted some limited influence

The Czech Republic was represented on the Committee of Experts on Mediation in Penal Matters by Jaroslav Fenyk of the Supreme State Prosecutor's Office. Since, due to his workload, he was not able to attend to the questionnaire, Helena Válková, as a member of the Criminological Scientific Council and someone intimately involved in the development of VOM in the Czech Republic, undertook the task of replying. There have been important legislative developments since 2000 when the Law on Probation and Mediation Service was adopted (it came into force on 1 January 2001). In addition, an amendment to the Criminal Procedural Law of 1 January 2002 opens up the possibility of referring cases to mediation even during the investigation phase. This legislation also deals in some detail with the mediation procedure and especially its relation to the criminal justice system. The Probation and Mediation Service is a government agency within the Ministry of Justice and consists of independent probation and mediation centres in each court district.

The training of mediators is organised by the Ministry of Justice in close co-operation with the Probation and Mediation Service. It is a professional service with high standards set for qualification as a mediator (twelve three-day sessions of training are required for so-called "officers" and six three-day sessions for "assistants").

The people who were active in the foundation of the Probation and Mediation Service were those who made use of the recommendation. According to Helena Válková, it has contributed to their understanding of mediation and its place in relation to the criminal justice system. It was little understood by judges and prosecutors, and not at all by the Ministry of Justice.

Albania, Bulgaria and the Russian Federation provide examples of countries where the influence of the recommendation was exerted exclusively via NGOs.

Together with the Czech Republic, Albania can be regarded as the most developed country in this group as regards VOM, since there exists a Law on Mediation in Conflict Resolution and Reconciliation of Disputes (adopted in March 1999), which deals with mediation in penal cases in several of its articles. Mediation is an optional procedure that can be started at the request of the injured party; referral is made by the police, the attorney's office or the court.

The Albanian Foundation for Conflict Resolution has been active since 1999 and it has established mediation centres that co-operate with the Prosecutor's Office and with the courts at district level. It has also set up training for mediators. In addition, mediation courses are now offered by the School for Magistrates where special attention is paid during training to the Council of Europe's recommendation (as well as the parallel recommendation on family mediation).

Rasim Gjoka has commented that "the most important thing is that the recommendation has sustained mediation in Albania, which is a volunteer activity carried out by NGOs. This is due to the fact that the recommendation reminds public institutions and the justice system of the necessity of the mediation process".

Of Bulgaria, Dobrinka Chankova, former member of the Committee of Experts on Mediation in Penal Matters, has written: "Many scientists in their research work insisted on introducing mediation into the Bulgarian criminal justice system; professors at the law faculty paid due attention to the recommendation in their lectures; foreign and Bulgarian experts during various fora commented on the possible positive effect of the recommendation; and the

Institute for Conflict Resolution grounded a lot of its initiatives in the recommendation." Although nothing has yet happened by way of legislation, except the launching of the "Promotion of restorative justice in Bulgaria" project and several proposals *de lege ferenda* made by academics, she states that, "all these small steps are inspired by the recommendation and by other relevant international instruments – as well as by numerous deficiencies in existing practice".

The case of the Russian Federation bears many similarities to that of Bulgaria. NGOs – notably the Centre for Legal and Judicial Reform in Moscow – are the primary advocates of the movement. (Interestingly its founding members were not jurists by training but had worked in close contact with lawyers and had a good knowledge of the Russian criminal justice system and of reform initiatives.) The centre developed and tested a training course on restorative justice in 2000; later the centre started to establish groups in eight cities; important co-operation was also established with the Prosecutor General of the Russian Federation. The centre has translated the recommendation into Russian and has published it in its newsletter. Mikhael Fliamer, the head of the centre and the contact person for this study, stated that after using the recommendation in a more general way "to add to our rhetoric about restorative justice, showing that VOM is a recognised practice in Europe and elsewhere in the world", the centre now intends to use it "in co-operation with officials of the Prosecutor's Office in order to elicit support for establishing a pilot project. We plan to organise activities exploring (analysing) the recommendation and compare it with the new Russian Criminal Proceedings Act and the Criminal Code (...). We are attempting to use this recommendation to change minds and practices".

He continues to implore the Council of Europe to provide additional help in this endeavour to influence Russian officials and government bodies; a request that was repeated in the course of the Second Conference of the European Forum for Victim-Offender Mediation and Restorative Justice. The forum is currently in the process of developing ways and means within the framework of the integrated projects to respond to this request.

The recommendation has contributed to and enhanced national policy establishing VOM

Within this group we find the majority of the countries of western and northern Europe, together with Germany and Spain. In some of these countries (France, Germany, Norway), the development of VOM practices and legislation had been taking place in the years – or even decades – prior to the adoption of the recommendation. They experienced an intensification of legislative initiatives.

A very rough outline and a few selected examples of the legislative activities that were reported are presented below:

Spain represents an example that could have also been placed in the first group. The recommendation's influence can be traced quite well; it became most evident in the setting up of the first pilot project for VOM with adults. This was due to an initiative of the Department of Justice and Home Affairs of the Catalan Government in co-operation with the Catalan Association for Mediation and Arbitration. Catalonia has been a pioneer in providing mediation services in Spain since the mid-1990s, establishing a tradition of international and bi-lateral contacts with associations (for example, the Austrian ATA) from the outset.

Spain's new Law on the Criminal Responsibility of Minors also bears the mark of mediation's influence, although not explicitly so. It is more a case of diversionary practices finding their way into juvenile criminal law – in a most advanced and well-designed way.

According to Jaime Martin Barberan, state prosecutors and judges working with juveniles, as well as the majority of other agencies working in the field of the treatment of young offenders, have taken notice of the recommendation and made use of it in developing and improving programmes and codes of ethics.

In France, significant developments have taken place in the field of legislation, introducing an array of clearly defined diversionary measures: such as *"la mediation entre l'auteur des faits et la victime, avec l'accord des parties"*. These diversionary measures are to be realised *"directement ou par délégation"*; such delegation to special agencies (or individuals) is increasingly prevalent. The *décret d'application* of 29 January 2001 provides for the placement of mediators and their relationship with state prosecutors. Another decree defines the conditions under which legal aid can be provided for VOM and for other alternative measures (*"la composition pénale"*).

A remarkable (36%) increase in the number of referrals to mediation services occurred between 1999 (when the new law was passed) and 2000. The offences included theft, family conflicts (ranging from domestic violence to non-payment of maintenance), brawls and assault, insult, bodily injury and environmental offences.

The state prosecutors exercise discretion as to whether to refer a case. VOM itself is carried out by individual mediators working "under" the state prosecutors (about 300 persons); a further 142 associations working together are accredited by the criminal justice system. They handle the majority of the cases where the prosecutor decides to use or try this measure. In general, offences of medium severity are regarded as suitable for VOM; there is a requirement to consider public order, the interests of victims and individual prevention/deterrence (to keep the perpetrator from further offending).

The recommendation seems to have exerted some influence on the development of guidelines and programmes for the training of mediators. Citoyen et Justice, one of the two big associations that co-operate with the criminal justice system in providing mediation services, mentions the work of the Council of Europe in its manual; and an "opinion" of the Economic and Social Council on mediation and reconciliation, adopted in the course of its meeting on 11 July 2001, also makes explicit reference to the recommendation.

Summarising, Maya Bartolucci (the successor to Nicole Planchon-Baranger, who was a member of the committee of experts) stated that the influence of the recommendation and strong national efforts for the reform of penal procedural law were contemporaneous and effective in the same direction.

The general outlook in Germany is quite similar: the reply received from Martina Hemmersbach of the Ministry of Justice (the former members of the committee of experts, M.K. Hobe and Horst Viehmann having retired) starts with the statement that "the main development in the area of mediation in penal matters has already been extensively implemented" and that this happened "prior to the timeframe indicated in the questionnaire (the past three to four years)".

Notwithstanding the above, legislation was enacted on 20 December 1999 that was intended to enhance further the already existing role of VOM in criminal procedural law. "Public prosecution offices and courts are expressly charged with the duty of examining, at every stage of the proceedings, whether it may not be possible to arrive at a mediated settlement between the accused and the victim of a crime. The conditions for a termination of proceedings have been specified and enlarged."

Training and further training of mediators is organised to a large extend by the TOA Servicebüro, which is also engaged in elaborating quality and qualification standards for mediators – they can be assessed as professional standards – with volunteer mediators playing only a very limited role.

With regard to the perception of the recommendation, the representative of the Ministry of Justice commented that "a reliable statement on the general degree of awareness and breadth of application of the recommendation cannot be made. It has found its way into the series 'recht' published by the Federal Ministry of Justice in co-operation with the Deutsche Vereinigung für Jugendgerichte und Jugendgerichtshilfen e.V (...) this is an annotated compilation of relevant United Nations and Council of Europe documents that is designed to evoke broader awareness on the part of those working in that area of criminal law relating to young people".

In answering the question concerning the influence of the recommendation visible in any of the changes outlined, the reply states that, "Due to the 'parallel course' of the recommendation and this legislation, the influence of the recommendation alone on the VOM situation in Germany cannot be gauged. However, the discussion in Europe on mediation in penal matters has unquestionably positively fuelled the corresponding discussion in Germany."

The case of the United Kingdom is different:

The answer David Miers (replacing Tony Marshall, who had served as a scientific expert to the committee of experts and is now retired) provided contains a note of caution, pertaining to the fact "that within the United Kingdom the preferred official designation is 'restorative justice', of which VOM is but one method". Bearing this in mind, the following picture emerges with regard to restorative justice developments and the influence exerted by the recommendation:

In 2001, "The review of the criminal justice system" (the Auld report) recommended the "development and implementation of a national strategy to ensure consistent, appropriate and effective use of restorative justice techniques across England and Wales". The review identifies six stages at which restorative justice might be applicable within the conventional criminal justice process.

In 2002, *Justice for all* (Home Office 2002) confirms that the Home Office is developing a national restorative justice strategy. It will consider the availability of restorative justice across all age-groups and at all stages of the criminal process: pre-crime, especially with juveniles, pre-charge, post-conviction, pre-sentence and post-sentence.

A direct influence of the recommendation is not discernible though.

NGOs, especially Justice and the Restorative Justice Consortium, have been using the recommendation to make policy demands and to support new initiatives; in so far as these play an important role in the movement for restorative justice, the recommendation has also made a contribution in the United Kingdom.

Norway ought to be especially mentioned since – as a forerunner in VOM development – it was not expected to pay much attention to the recommendation, preferring rather, as in the case of Austria, after having contributed substantially to the drafting of the recommendation, drawing on its longstanding national experience, to continue its development of VOM with only a few changes made independently of the recommendation's content. However, the setting-up of a VOM pilot project concerning more serious offences can clearly be seen as having been influenced by the involvement of the Norwegian representative, Siri Kemeny, on the committee of experts. This influence seeped through to the working party responsible for preparing the project within the Ministry of Justice.

There is also an interesting instance of the influence the recommendation had on preventing a particular development: there was a debate in parliament in spring 2001 concerning a proposal to introduce compulsory mediation for offenders under the age of criminal responsibility where the proposal was rejected by pointing to the principles set out in the recommendation.

It can be seen in Norway, as in the countries mentioned above, that although the influence of the recommendation was scarcely visible, one can detect a general trend similar to the one that prevailed in the committee of experts.

The recommendation has contributed to the introduction of VOM

The Netherlands, Sweden, the Republic of Ireland and Portugal are included under this heading.

It must be said that the Netherlands has a very specific approach to VOM. Having lagged behind in this field for some time, a great deal of serious experimentation – well designed and well researched – is currently under way. In addition to the police-driven HALT project that focuses on material reparation, there is family conferencing with juvenile offenders, so-called "restorative mediation" in both juvenile and adult cases, experiments with restorative mediation in relation to very serious offences, and mediation in the context of the justice in the neighbourhood bureaux (Justitie in de Buurt). At the end of this year, the results of the evaluation of several of these projects should be available and the Ministry of Justice will then decide which type, or types, of mediation will be implemented.

Although there was no active dissemination of the recommendation amongst public prosecutors and judges, Lodewijk Tonino of the Ministry of Justice points out that it is easily found. NGOs (victim support services) took notice of it.

Another important Dutch tradition is the attention academics have paid to the recommendation – as well as to other international documents. Marc Groenhuysen, professor at the University of Tilburg, has given one of the most exhaustive analyses of the recommendation.

Lodewijk Tonino sums up the recommendation's influence thus: "Although the recommendation is not followed by the letter, VOM (in the Netherlands) follows at least the intention of the recommendation."

Sweden introduced a new law on 1 July 2002. Various pilot projects and evaluation efforts had preceded this development and a government commission had been set up to report on the possibility of establishing VOM in Sweden. The recommendation was one of the documents the commission paid attention to and informed the government of. The Department of Justice also drew on the recommendation when outlining its arguments with respect to VOM.

"The recommendation", writes Christina Nehlin of the Swedish National Council for Crime Prevention, "has contributed to the discussion of VOM and has given the practice a greater credibility. It has also given moral support to practitioners".

The Republic of Ireland may also be placed in this group. Up to now VOM has only found its way into the new Children Act 2001. Here, VOM is available at police level in the shape of "restorative cautions" or "family conferences"

(although these terms are not used in the act) and as a court-based pilot programme that is being tried out in Dublin and a rural area (the Nenagh programme). These two programmes receive funds from the Department of
Justice, Equality and Law Reform and are processed through the Probation and
Welfare Services. Both can be regarded as pre-sentence diversionary models
with referrals coming from the courts and reports going back to the judge.
According to Denis Griffin, the national contact person, the Dublin-based programme works with trained mediators who facilitate the mediation procedure
involving victims and offenders; the Nenagh programme, operated by specially
trained probation and welfare officers, concentrates on interventions between
the offender and community representatives.

It is difficult to assess whether the recommendation has contributed in any
manner to the provisions in the Children Act 2001. According to Denis Griffin,
the setting-up of the two pilot projects has been influenced by the recommendation and this seems plausible because Ireland was represented on the committee of experts (in the beginning by Michelle Shannon of the Department of
Justice and then by John O'Dwyer of the Probation and Welfare Services from
the same ministry). It is especially interesting to note that the principles set out
in the recommendation are reflected in the two schemes that provide for VOM
at the police stage, most markedly the principle of voluntariness.

Another latecomer is Portugal.

The fact that Portugal appeared reluctant to adopt any diversionary measure,
including VOM, can to some degree be explained by the adherence of its
judicial system and its protagonists – the prosecutors and the judges – to the
principle of legality, with the opportunity principle gaining ground only slowly.

As is the case of the Republic of Ireland, the only VOM measures that have
been introduced following the recommendation concern juveniles. In Portugal
this happened with the Educational Guardianship Law (*Lei Tutelar Educativa* –
Law 166/99 of 14 September). The act applies to young persons aged 12-16
years. The judicial authorities (state prosecutors or judges) act as the referring
agency and the organisation operating the new mediation programme is the
Social Rehabilitation Institute. This institute, characterised by the national contacts, Joao Lazaro and Federico Marques, as an "auxiliary body in the administration of justice", acts on the basis of a "despatch of its president" dealing
explicitly with the implementation of mediation within the educational
guardianship process.

The VOM model that has been adopted provides for direct victim-offender
mediation. Its potential outcomes are an apology and/or reparation and financial compensation to the victim but also community service or donations to
charitable organisations.

In Portugal, besides the Ministry of Justice, it was mainly the Portuguese
Association for Victim Services that took notice of and started to use the rec-

ommendation to support the goals it had set itself. The Social Rehabilitation Institute also used the content of the recommendation to justify practices it considered appropriate. One has to be aware though that in Portugal, due to the placement of VOM in the Educational Guardianship Law, mediation is bound to the educational goals that this law considers essential – or, to put it differently, it is mainly perceived as a rehabilitative and educative measure.

The recommendation has not been paid much notice or has even been neglected

Earlier in the course of the analysis, several countries had been placed within this group: Besides Austria, the United Kingdom and Denmark, also France, Germany and Norway – namely, those that had already gone quite far in establishing VOM practice and legislation. However, the replies to the questionnaire received from France and Germany meant that they should really be placed in the third group. Norway presents, as explained earlier, a special case.

This leaves us with Austria.

Very little attention was paid to the recommendation – due to the fact that Austria was supposed to serve as a model for European development and as a leading country, especially so in the field of legislation. However, this conviction prevented professionals as well as the representatives of the nationwide VOM service from recognising the existence of potential areas of further application of VOM: Article 4 of the recommendation, "Mediation in penal matters should be available at all stages of the criminal justice process", was simply neglected.

I must bear a certain responsibility for this since, in so far as much depends on individuals becoming active in the promotion of VOM and in ensuring that it is available "at all stages of the criminal justice process", I should have drawn attention to these deficits. (However, the Second Conference of the European Forum for Victim-Offender Mediation and Restorative Justice has been an attempt to do so.)

Finally, one is left with the last (sub-)group that did not pay attention to the recommendation although there was, and still is, practically no evidence of VOM practice. The most notable case is that of Greece. According to Anna Zairi, attempts to introduce some kind of VOM procedure met with resistance, particularly from lawyers' groups. What seems lacking in Greece is an NGO that is interested in promoting an alternative perspective such as VOM.

Denmark has had very little experience with mediation until now. Experiments took place in the police districts of Glostrup, Roskilde and Ringsted. The duration of these experiments was supposed to be three years, but was prolonged until the end of 2002. VOM is perceived as an action guided by the government's intention to strengthen the position of victims.

VOM in Denmark is a supplement to ordinary prosecution and does not replace it. Only in a very few cases has a suspended sentence been passed by a judge taking into account an agreement reached through VOM. The eight mediators presently at work have received five days' training.

A promise is contained in the reply from Denmark: "The ministry has taken notice of the recommendation. It will be taken into account in the future work with VOM in Denmark."

On the use and usefulness of the recommendation: or which conditions are favourable to taking conscious notice of and making use of an international document?

One should perhaps begin with what might seem a triviality (or even a tautological statement): a document becomes influential – and thus useful – when it is made use of. In other words, when people dedicated to a "cause" perceive a document as supporting and promoting their arguments, they will use it. The expertise that went into drafting the document becomes an argument that gives additional weight to their demands. Or, in the words of Ivo Aertsen from Belgium, a member of the Committee of Experts on Mediation in Penal Matters: "The recommendation is an effective instrument when you have people in a country picking it up and working with it effectively."

There are, however, different ways to start action and a movement, and to have people drawing on the recommendation for support.

These users and proponents can be individuals who stand in close relationship to the government and/or are representatives of criminal law professionals, for example state prosecutors

The countries in the first group provide ample evidence of this type of usage and influence. There the engagement of individuals dedicated to the cause of mediation has played an important role. It is, of course, individuals with a certain organisational affiliation: either with the relevant ministry (Finland), or within one of the professional groups of the criminal justice system (Cyprus and Slovenia).

The size of the population of a country might make a difference: there seems to be a better chance for this strategy to bear fruit in a small country. Both Cyprus and Slovenia belong to this category. Poland and Finland are bigger but it appears not too difficult to make a mark on the legal and criminal policy structure of theses countries. Looking more closely, it is rather these structures and their complexity that might be decisive for the outcome of any attempt to find an inroad for the recommendation to leave its mark on national criminal policy. These structures have to be sufficiently transparent and accessible for the proponents of VOM to find the ear of decision makers.

The influence of individuals being both close to the government and aware of the potential of the recommendation is also discernible in Sweden, where VOM was introduced only recently. In the Netherlands it was probably the strong tradition of academic internationalism that influenced policy makers.

The challenge of NGOs

Turning to the second group of countries, it was NGOs advocating VOM who have had recourse to the recommendation. In this way the content of the recommendation yielded some influence on the way of establishing VOM programmes and designing practice and training. The examples of Albania, Bulgaria and the Russian Federation (and to a certain degree, the Czech Republic) impart an ambivalent message: in these countries – at least on the surface – a European document is, on the one hand, highly valued and carries considerable weight but, on the other hand, it is obvious that the combined voice of a few academics commenting on the document is not sufficient to have an impact on decision makers; they are easily pushed aside and neglected. NGOs adopting the policy recommended might remain equally marginalised. They are left with too few resources to make real headway. However, Helena Válková's statement that the recommendation has influenced a better understanding of all those involved in mediation practice, policy and education, but not exerted any influence on the "experts" of the criminal justice system can also be read with a less resigned angle to it: by emphasising that there was indeed an influence on the concrete practice of VOM – not on the side of the referring agencies but on the side of the VOM practitioners – and this might indeed be important.

NGOs using the recommendation were also influential in Portugal.

The recommendation in eastern European countries

Poland and the Czech Republic can be placed between the groups above: NGOs challenged national criminal policy and it was again the recommendation that provided them with a viable instrument to press their point. But the example of these countries also illustrates difficulties in making the new perspective contained in the recommendation, albeit in a very pragmatic and "realistic" way, understood and taken on board by the agencies of the criminal justice system and its representatives.

There is one feature shared by the two groups, namely the willingness voiced by governmental agencies or by NGOs to tread new paths in the field of criminal justice, and to join in a movement for a kind of justice that better and more effectively attends to victims' needs. Simultaneously, these agencies can rely on European standards and values as enshrined in the documents of the Council of Europe as carrying some political weight in themselves. There is an urge (or maybe rather a need or a necessity) to belong to this Europe and therefore to live up to these policy orientations.

Taking this into account, it should be mentioned that what has been seen in eastern European countries with regard to setting up practices of VOM and inserting or attaching them to their criminal procedures is not just superficial compliance with a certain strand of European criminal policy; without people and groups really identifying with the aims and the spirit of VOM, the developments described would not have been possible. They are the result of conscious effort, a struggle even, and the struggle is far from won – but this holds true for the rest of Europe as well.

The recommendation as reinforcement of national developments

The influence of the recommendation as observed in the United Kingdom, France, Germany, Austria, the northern European countries, Spain and – with considerable delay – the Republic of Ireland and Portugal is of a different nature. If the recommendation has had any influence, it is as a reinforcement of the general movement that has just mingled with and added to more specific national developments. These developments had been taking place during the last decades in Austria and Norway, and have become intensified during the last three to four years in France, Spain and Belgium and more recently in Sweden, the Netherlands and Portugal.

As already stated, the impact of this type of influence cannot be gauged. But the developments observed and reported point to a specific quality of work in a European, and international context. It points to the potential of discourse and exchange to seep through in a general (or subconscious) way into national and local discourse.

One might venture that the document in order to exert an influence has to become part of an ongoing discourse, or that the power of the discourse that took place in the course of creating the document is revived and fuelled in the national discourse.

The recommendation and the UN basic principles

The same kind of influence is seen in the international context. The recommendation had a marked influence on the work and the final draft of the United Nations Basic Principles on Restorative Justice. This was as a result of co-operation, deliberately sought and established, between members of the Committee of Experts on Mediation in Penal Matters and the NGO Drafting Group of the ECOSOC (Economic and Social Council) within the UN, in the person of Dan van Ness from the NGO Prison Fellowship International. There was an exchange of ideas and considerations that became manifest in the UN basic principles following to a large extent the provisions laid down in the recommendation – with those modifications that were deemed necessary to take account of the wider and more general notion of "restorative justice" (of which VOM is to be seen as only one of a number of potential instruments and procedures). At the meeting of experts in Ottawa in October 2001, it became obvious though that consequently a Eurocentric orientation marked the draft that was criticised by representatives from African and North American countries. In particular, the provisions regarding the training and qualification of facilitators were accordingly revised. The effort proved to be quite interesting and produced fruitful co-operation between the Council of Europe and UN bodies.

It should also be mentioned that two Canadian experts, Ezzat Fattah, professor emeritus at Simon Fraser University in Vancouver, and David Daubney from the Canadian Ministry of Justice, took part in most of the meetings of the committee of experts. As observers and guests they made valuable contributions. Canada later not only hosted the expert meeting that revised the first draft of the basic principles but acted as a promoter of the UN basic principles at the eleventh session of the UN Commission on Crime Prevention and Criminal Justice in Vienna in April 2002, where the basic principles were "taken note of" and member states were urged to implement restorative justice programmes following the principles laid down in the document. Meanwhile, Canada is following a proactive strategy of disseminating and using the basic principles for supporting its national criminal policy. According to David Daubney, departmental principles and guidelines have been drafted. He states, "We have been using this as a basis for conversation with Canadians interested in a national statement of principles. This will be intensified soon with online dialogue due to begin later this month" (personal communication, September 2002).

The recommendation and the European Forum for Victim-Offender Mediation and Restorative Justice

Finally, mention should also be made of the foundation of the European forum. It is clear that the creation of a network is a pivotal instrument in disseminating an international/European document. But one has also to be aware of the fact that the foundation of the forum depended on very specific circumstances, not easily repeatable with regard to other Council of Europe documents. It is only new instruments that do not remain isolated and piecemeal but have become part of an innovative perspective, even a new paradigm, that have a chance of getting people to rally under their flag and to make a conscious effort. If this happens, promoting a recommendation becomes an important and relatively powerful instrument, and it is precisely this kind of association/organisation that stands in need of documents of this nature – for providing guidance and coherence.

Using Council of Europe recommendations

It needs people coming together voicing a need and an interest and making use of international documents to promote a policy that attends to these needs.

The initiatives and leadership of an individual often prove important but he or she must not stand alone. The challenge by professional groups within the criminal justice system and/or of NGOs is indispensable. A process has to be set in motion. In the course of this process, Council of Europe instruments might be used as an important and "convincing" tool.

In a way it means continuing the process of drafting through to implementation – in member states and, as in the case of the European Forum for Victim-Offender Mediation and Restorative Justice, at the level of networking.

It has been said that, as with all Council of Europe work, it is processes more than outcomes that bear relevance and contribute to change. Following up on recommendations is probably a way to continue these processes and to make the changes envisaged more real and sustainable.

Appendix I – Recommendation No. R (99) 19 of the Council of Europe Committee of Ministers on mediation in penal matters

Adopted by the Committee of Ministers on 15 September 1999 at the 679th meeting of the Ministers' Deputies

The Committee of Ministers, under the terms of Article 15.*b* of the Statute of the Council of Europe,

Noting the developments in member states in the use of mediation in penal matters as a flexible, comprehensive, problem-solving, participatory option complementary or alternative to traditional criminal proceedings;

Considering the need to enhance active personal participation in criminal proceedings of the victim and the offender and others who may be affected as parties as well as the involvement of the community;

Recognising the legitimate interest of victims to have a stronger voice in dealing with the consequences of their victimisation, to communicate with the offender and to obtain apology and reparation;

Considering the importance of encouraging the offenders' sense of responsibility and offering them practical opportunities to make amends, which may further their reintegration and rehabilitation;

Recognising that mediation may increase awareness of the important role of the individual and the community in preventing and handling crime and resolving its associated conflicts, thus encouraging more constructive and less repressive criminal justice outcomes;

Recognising that mediation requires specific skills and calls for codes of practice and accredited training;

Considering the potentially substantial contribution to be made by non-governmental organisations and local communities in the field of mediation in penal matters and the need to combine and to co-ordinate the efforts of public and private initiatives;

Having regard to the requirements of the Convention for the Protection of Human Rights and Fundamental Freedoms;

Bearing in mind the European Convention on the Exercise of Children's Rights as well as Recommendations No. R (85) 11 on the position of the victim in the framework of criminal law and procedure, No. R (87) 18 concerning the simplification of criminal justice, No. R (87) 21 on assistance to victims and the prevention of victimisation, No. R (87) 20 on social reactions to juvenile delinquency, No. R (88) 6 on social reactions to juvenile delinquency among young people coming from migrant families, No. R (92) 16 on the European rules on community sanctions and measures, No. R (95) 12 on the management of criminal justice and No. R (98) 1 on family mediation,

Recommends that the governments of member states consider the principles set out in the appendix to this recommendation when developing mediation in penal matters, and give the widest possible circulation to this text.

Appendix to Recommendation No. R (99) 19

I. Definition

These guidelines apply to any process whereby the victim and the offender are enabled, if they freely consent, to participate actively in the resolution of matters arising from the crime through the help of an impartial third party (mediator).

II. General principles

1. Mediation in penal matters should only take place if the parties freely consent. The parties should be able to withdraw such consent at any time during the mediation.

2. Discussions in mediation are confidential and may not be used subsequently, except with the agreement of the parties.

3. Mediation in penal matters should be a generally available service.

4. Mediation in penal matters should be available at all stages of the criminal justice process.

5. Mediation services should be given sufficient autonomy within the criminal justice system.

III. Legal basis

6. Legislation should facilitate mediation in penal matters.

7. There should be guidelines defining the use of mediation in penal matters. Such guidelines should in particular address the conditions for the referral of cases to the mediation service and the handling of cases following mediation.

8. Fundamental procedural safeguards should be applied to mediation; in particular, the parties should have the right to legal assistance and, where necessary, to translation/interpretation. Minors should, in addition, have the right to parental assistance.

IV. The operation of criminal justice in relation to mediation

9. A decision to refer a criminal case to mediation, as well as the assessment of the outcome of a mediation procedure, should be reserved to the criminal justice authorities.

10. Before agreeing to mediation, the parties should be fully informed of their rights, the nature of the mediation process and the possible consequences of their decision.

11. Neither the victim nor the offender should be induced by unfair means to accept mediation.

12. Special regulations and legal safeguards governing minors' participation in legal proceedings should also be applied to their participation in mediation in penal matters.

13. Mediation should not proceed if any of the main parties involved is not capable of understanding the meaning of the process.

14. The basic facts of a case should normally be acknowledged by both parties as a basis for mediation. Participation in mediation should not be used as evidence of admission of guilt in subsequent legal proceedings.

15. Obvious disparities with respect to factors such as the parties' age, maturity or intellectual capacity should be taken into consideration before a case is referred to mediation.

16. A decision to refer a criminal case to mediation should be accompanied by a reasonable time-limit within which the competent criminal justice authorities should be informed of the state of the mediation procedure.

17. Discharges based on mediated agreements should have the same status as judicial decisions or judgments and should preclude prosecution in respect of the same facts (*ne bis in idem*).

18. When a case is referred back to the criminal justice authorities without an agreement between the parties or after failure to implement such an agreement, the decision as to how to proceed should be taken without delay.

V. The operation of mediation services

V.1. Standards

19. Mediation services should be governed by recognised standards.

20. Mediation services should have sufficient autonomy in performing their duties. Standards of competence and ethical rules, as well as procedures for the selection, training and assessment of mediators should be developed.

21. Mediation services should be monitored by a competent body.

V.2. Qualifications and training of mediators

22. Mediators should be recruited from all sections of society and should generally possess good understanding of local cultures and communities.

23. Mediators should be able to demonstrate sound judgment and interpersonal skills necessary to mediation.

24. Mediators should receive initial training before taking up mediation duties as well as in-service training. Their training should aim at providing for a high level of competence, taking into account conflict resolution skills, the specific requirements of working with victims and offenders and basic knowledge of the criminal justice system.

V.3. Handling of individual cases

25. Before mediation starts, the mediator should be informed of all relevant facts of the case and be provided with the necessary documents by the competent criminal justice authorities.

26. Mediation should be performed in an impartial manner, based on the facts of the case and on the needs and wishes of the parties. The mediator should always respect the dignity of the parties and ensure that the parties act with respect towards each other.

27. The mediator should be responsible for providing a safe and comfortable environment for the mediation. The mediator should be sensitive to the vulnerability of the parties.

28. Mediation should be carried out efficiently, but at a pace that is manageable for the parties.

29. Mediation should be performed *in camera.*

30. Notwithstanding the principle of confidentiality, the mediator should convey any information about imminent serious crimes, which may come to light in the course of mediation, to the appropriate authorities or to the persons concerned.

V.4. Outcome of mediation

31. Agreements should be arrived at voluntarily by the parties. They should contain only reasonable and proportionate obligations.

32. The mediator should report to the criminal justice authorities on the steps taken and on the outcome of the mediation. The mediator's report should not reveal the contents of mediation sessions, nor express any judgment on the parties' behaviour during mediation.

VI. Continuing development of mediation

33. There should be regular consultation between criminal justice authorities and mediation services to develop common understanding.

34. Member states should promote research on, and evaluation of, mediation in penal matters.

Appendix II – National contacts

Albania: Rasim Gjoka (Albanian Foundation for Conflict Resolution)

Austria: Christa Pelikan (Institute of Sociology of Law and Criminology)

Belgium: Ivo Aertsen (Catholic University of Leuven)

Bulgaria: Dobrinka Chankova (Institute for Conflict Resolution)

Cyprus: Elena Zachariadou (Attorney General's Office)

Czech Republic: Helena Válková (University of West Bohemia, Pilsen)

Denmark: Dagmar Rasmussen (Crime Prevention Council) and Thomas Stenfeldt Mathiasen (Ministry of Justice)

Finland: Juhani Iivari (National Research and Development Centre for Welfare and Health)

France: Maya Bartolucci (Ministry of Justice)

Germany: Martina Hemmersbach (Ministry of Justice)

Greece: Anna Zairi (Attorney General's Office)

Ireland: Dennis Griffin (Prisons Policy Division) and Kieran O'Dwyer (Garda Research Unit)

Italy: Vania Patané (University of Catania)

Netherlands: Lodewijk Tonino (Ministry of Justice)

Norway: Torunn Bolstad (Ministry of Justice)

Poland: Beata Czarnecka-Dzialuk (Institute of Justice)

Portugal: Joao Lazaro and Federico Marques (Portuguese Association for Victim Support – APAV)

Russian Federation: Mikhael Fliamer (Centre for Legal and Judicial Reforms)

Slovenia: Alenka Meznar (Higher State Prosecutor's Office)

Spain: Jaime Martin Barberan (Department of Justice)

Sweden: Christina Nehlin (Crime Prevention Council)

United Kingdom: David Miers (Cardiff Law School)

Appendix III – Questions to follow up Recommendation No. R (99) 19 on mediation in penal matters

I. What developments have occurred with regard to mediation in penal matters in your country during the last three to four years?

1. In the field of legislation;

2. Concerning the practical use of mediation in penal matters:

   a. the scope, namely the number and type of cases dealt with;

   b. the number and types of programmes available;

   c. the procedure of mediation and its connection to the criminal justice system;

   d. the recruitment and training of mediators.

II. Who took notice of the recommendation?

   • the Ministry of Justice;
   • parts of the criminal justice system: state prosecutors, judges;
   • social services associated with the criminal justice system;
   • existing mediation services;
   • other interests groups, NGOs, etc.

Who used it for:

   • supporting new initiatives;
   • making policy demands;
   • justification of existing practices;
   • a critique of existing practice;
   • in any other way.

Who commented on it and in which way?

III. Could you trace any of the changes mentioned to the influence of the recommendation?

(Please, explain in detail)

Chapter 5

Victim-offender mediation with serious offences

Ivo Aertsen

The challenge

Developing mediation and mediation programmes in cases of serious crimes can be seen as a challenge for several reasons.

The desirability and practical feasibility

Victim-offender mediation became widely accepted as a method for dealing with less serious offences, often in the sphere of small property or violent delinquency, committed by young offenders who do not have a marked criminal record. Although regulation at a supranational level, on the one hand, does not exclude mediation for different types of cases at all stages of the criminal justice process,[1] it might, on the other hand, formulate guidelines rather cautiously in this respect.[2] Nevertheless, comparative research confirms the minor degree of seriousness of offences in victim-offender mediation in most European and other countries (Lauwaert and Aertsen 2002; European Forum for Victim-Offender Mediation and Restorative Justice 2000). Whether an offence is considered to be "serious" can depend on different criteria, such as the legal qualification, sentencing policies and jurisprudence, the violent character of the facts, the consequences for the victim and the (expected) reaction by public opinion. The general feeling of reluctance towards the idea of mediation in serious cases refers to the character of "a favour" which is often given to this measure. It can be observed in judicial decision making after a failure in mediation, where the prosecutors tend to issue a summons although often not legally required. However, mediators witness that participation in a mediation process is not at all a soft option, not even for minor crimes. And they also refer to the needs of the victim as a starting point for mediation, whatever the legal qualification or judicial stage of the case might be. One could even expect a more

---

1. Committee of Ministers Recommendation No. R (99) 19 on mediation in penal matters, Articles 3 and 4.

2. European Council Framework Decision of 15 March 2001 on the standing of victims in criminal proceedings, *Official Journal*, L 82, 22 March 2001. Article 10 states that: "1. Each member state shall seek to promote mediation in criminal cases for offences which it considers appropriate for this sort of measure; (...)".

important need for victims in cases of serious crimes, hoping to receive information and explanation from the offender.

Together with the assumption of a limited scope for victim-offender mediation, many wonder whether a sound mediation method for serious crimes, for example in cases of severe violence, can be developed. Issues arise as to whether such (repeat) offenders can be motivated in a non-opportunistic way, whether a safe environment can be created and whether victims will not be harmed emotionally. It is clear that mediation in these cases will require special mediation skills.

The relation to criminal justice

The fact that it is mostly minor crimes which are involved in mediation means that many cases take the form of a diversionary measure. Most referrals to mediation are indeed made by the Public Prosecutor's service or the police. If there is a positive outcome – if an agreement is reached with the victim – the mediation will result in the dismissal of the charges by the Public Prosecutor. Mediation – especially with more serious crimes – can also be organised parallel to prosecution, the final result then being taken into consideration by the sentencing judge. A final possibility is that mediation is instigated at the sentencing level or occurs after a sentence has been pronounced.

At the sentencing level, judges may feel rather uneasy after a successful mediation process in the case of a serious crime. In these cases, the role of punishment can be questioned: what could be the added value of a punitive element after the parties reached an agreement and commonly declared that the problem according to them and their surroundings found a constructive and reasonable solution.

Apart from the question of how a mediation outcome would be taken into account, one clearly feels the need for protection and legal safeguards for all parties involved. Although many of these concerns can be met by using mediators' recognised practice standards and through good training and supervision, the role of the legal system is obvious. Certainly for more serious crimes, where one can expect a possible impact of mediation on judicial decisions, there is a need for control or judicial supervision of both the mediation process and the outcome.[3]

The theoretical underpinnings

When victim-offender mediation is conceived as an alternative measure or sanction, reference can be made to legal and/or criminological theory, for example that related to the principles of legal subsidiarity or community

---

3. Council of Europe, *Mediation in penal matters – Recommendation No. R (99) 19 and explanatory memorandum*, Council of Europe Publishing, Strasbourg, 2000, p. 13.

involvement. When mediation in criminal cases is not merely a diversion measure, but offered parallel to prosecution and sentencing, a theoretical framework for this relationship is not immediately available. Two different, apparently contradictory, rationalities have to been conciliated: a horizontal, inter-individual, consensual one with a vertical, state-based, authoritarian one. It is not always very clear in mediation practices for more serious crimes how the experience at the personal level can meet the more universal or societal norms, and how this confrontation should play at the legal forum, if necessary at all.

But even in the case of diversion, we find a paradoxical development in practice with implications at policy and theoretical level. On the one hand, community sanctions and measures have been differentiated and put into practice in a increasing way in most or our countries over the past fifteen years. On the other hand, the use of the prison sentences and prison populations are not decreasing, quite the contrary. A two-track or "dualistic" development can be observed: more community sanctions are applied for minor crimes, whereas the prison sentence is the ever more preferred sanction for so-called "serious crimes". The net of social and judicial control is widening, and one can ask whether recent developments bring about a *"socialisation du pénal"* or rather a *"pénalisation du social"* (Mary 1997).

This kind of criticism of the functioning of the criminal justice system as a whole, together with the (re-)discovery of the victim and the influence of the victim movement, has been the impetus for criminologists and others to search for a fundamental new approach and new definitions of crime and criminal justice. Theorists maintain that as long as we do not change the underlying paradigm, we will never be able to cope with the considerable deficiencies of the system, such as the excessive use of a prison sentence and the weak position of the victim (Fattah 1992). Others reject a pure paradigmatic approach and believe in a more pragmatic and phased strategy (Groenhuijsen 1999). For many, a new approach is found in the general framework of "restorative justice". Victim-offender mediation and family group conferencing are the dominant methods in this new way of thinking. A central question is not whether these methods are realisable as such, but – certainly when applied to more serious crimes – to which extent are they able to interact with, and to re-orient or influence at least in the long run, some of the basic principles of our current retributive criminal justice system.

The practice

What follows are concrete examples of victim-offender mediation programmes for more serious crimes. The first type occurs parallel to prosecution, the second one after sentence – more precisely within a prison context. The examples come from Belgium, where efforts are made to develop mediation and other restorative justice programmes in a co-ordinated way at the subsequent stages of the criminal justice process, both for young persons and for adults (Aertsen 2000). References are made to similar programmes in other countries as well.

Mediation parallel to prosecution

The context

The Flemish project "Mediation for redress" started in Leuven in 1993 out of a partnership between the Research Group on Penology and Victimology of the Catholic University, the Public Prosecutor's Office and a private service for forensic welfare work. From the outset it was decided that the programme would be reserved for adult offenders and more serious types of crime, that is cases in which the Public Prosecutor had already decided to prosecute. Thus, the objective of the project was not situated outside the process of criminal justice, but it was organised in the perspective of promoting and introducing restorative actions and thinking within the system. Nevertheless, the mediation itself would be done at a non-judicial level, by an independent mediation service.

After an experimental period of three years, the project took on a more definitive status at the beginning of 1996. At that moment, a mediation project with juveniles joined and a new mediation project at the police level was started. The three projects together constituted the Leuven Mediation Service, with one common team of professional mediators and the support of one steering group, consisting of representatives of eight judicial and non-judicial partner organisations. Within this mediation service, two full-time mediators were (and still are) responsible for the mediation for redress programme concerning more serious crimes. This programme was extended in 1997 to other judicial districts in Belgium (eight in Flanders and four in Wallonia at the beginning of 2003) – the Flemish ones all based on the same mediation methodology and inter-agency approach. The programme is financed by the Federal Ministry of Justice, via subsidies to the Flemish NGO Suggnomè and the Walloon NGO Médiante (both are support structures for the implementation of mediation services and restorative justice). Besides mediation for redress, mediation for juveniles has been implemented in almost all judicial districts of Flanders and in some of those in Wallonia, mainly in a hybrid combination with community service and training orders (which are all called "restorative measures"). Finally, mediation at the police level has been started in eleven municipalities in the Brussels region and in Flanders. In the following, only the mediation for redress programme is discussed.

The mediation process

Mediation for redress is a free service for both the victim and the offender, offering the parties support to reach a personal settlement focused on reparation or conflict solution through a process of mutual communication. A neutral, third party guides mediation following a structured process.

78

Cases for mediation are selected at the Prosecutor's Office, according to well-defined criteria and a selection procedure. However, referrals can also be initiated by the investigating judge (*juge d'instruction*), a practice that happens in about half of all cases (in Leuven). As is the case for many new mediation programmes, finding a good method for selecting appropriate cases required a lot of time and experience. It soon became clear in the case of the Leuven programme that a proactive selection procedure should be developed. Simply leaving the initiative to refer cases to the mediation programme to the deputy prosecutors did not work, not even when instructed by the chief prosecutor. A liaison magistrate was installed, which resulted in referrals being made in a more systematic way and in more permanent and effective co-operation in general. Later, a jurist within the Prosecutor's Office became responsible for the selection of cases, which proved to be very effective as well. Nevertheless, the proposals for selection are always discussed with the mediators, and the latter can refuse when they feel that the case is not an appropriate one for mediation. The direct and regular contacts between mediators and the liaison magistrate (or jurist) at the court have a stimulating effect on the ongoing reflection about the objectives and principles of the programme. This relationship is an open and trustful one with a mutual desire to explicitly formulate objectives and concerns. Mention should be made of the independent status of the mediators in this programme: they are hired by a private association (the NGO Suggnomè), and they have their local offices in a public, municipal building, together with colleagues from the Leuven Mediation Service. This leads to a continuous need for communication between the partners involved in the programme.

One requirement for the case to be accepted for mediation is that the offender admits the crime. It is not always easy to see – and it provokes strong discussions with positivist lawyers from time to time – that this is not necessarily the same as admitting guilt in a legal way or assuming full responsibility. It is precisely through the dialogue between the conflict parties in mediation that notions of responsibility and guilt can become subject to interpretation. The types of cases selected for "mediation for redress" refer mainly to physical assault, robbery, burglary, theft and sexual offences.

Once a case is selected, the prosecutor sends out a letter to the victim and to the offender, with the offer to participate in mediation. In the experience of both victim and offender, it has a special meaning to know that a judicial authority took the initiative: it offers recognition of the needs of the victim and a clear and constructive approach to the offender. It also clarifies the mandate of the mediator. The way in which the letter to the parties is formulated and the offer explained by the mediator at the next stage are of the utmost importance. From research it has been shown that the willingness of victims to take part in mediation depends largely on how the role of the parties is presented, on their familiarity with mediation (programmes) and on their experience with victim support (Aertsen 2004, pp. 141-145).

The mediator first contacts both parties separately for one or several individual meetings. A home visit is offered. The conventional practice in the Leuven programme is to contact the victim first. But, as to which of the parties to contact first, practice differs according to the type of programme and national preferences. There are pros and cons to either decision.

During separate meetings, the mediator focuses on individual needs and questions. He or she carefully listens in order to learn more about the victim's personal experience and the backgrounds of those involved. The creation of a good rapport and an empathetic climate are essential. The mediator has to show recognition and respect for the victim as well as for the offender. Special (practical) help and information is given. When talks progress, emphasis is on the information exchange between the parties. Mutual meanings, questions and expectations are communicated and reformulated indirectly through the mediator. This process of indirect mediation (where parties do not meet physically) may, by itself, lead to agreement. But it can also proceed to a direct, face-to-face meeting between the victim and the offender.

In the communication process, indirectly or directly, the following elements are often evoked by the parties:

- a discussion on what happened, how the offence occurred and the context thereof;
- the background and the origins of the offence;
- the personal meaning given to the offence and the consequences for both parties;
- the personal, family and social impact on other persons indirectly involved;
- the material and immaterial harm caused to the victim;
- each party's perception of, and attitude towards, the other;
- the issues and possibilities of redress or compensation;
- the reaction expected or preferred by the court.

An exchange of these feelings, attitudes and opinions is, of course, much more powerful in a direct meeting between victim and offender. In a personal meeting, parties put a face to each other. The background of the offence, its consequences and the respective needs become much more concrete, and both victim and offender have to leave their personal stereotypes behind.

In about 50% of cases, mediation results in a written agreement. This contains much more than a financial settlement for the material or moral damage; it is a report about the preceding talks and meetings. Thus the written agreement refers to the meaning and consequences of the offence, both at the personal and social levels. Excuses are formulated and may be accepted. Commitments are agreed upon. It often happens that the victim drops his or her complaint (symbolically) or does not introduce further claims for indemnification. In the majority of cases, the written agreement also expresses a point of view concerning the desirable penal outcome (the mediator frequently asks the question: "What would you decide if you were the judge in this case?").

The written agreement is transferred to the Public Prosecutor and attached to the judicial file. When there is no agreement, the mediator communicates this to the Public Prosecutor without further details. It must be mentioned that the non-communication of the reasons why no agreement could be reached is a recurring issue in discussions with the Public Prosecutor. Be this as it may, reaching an agreement cannot be seen as the decisive criterion in calling the mediation process a success. Evaluation of the programme shows that more than the agreement, the proposal of mediation and the communication between parties have a meaning in their own right and are very much appreciated by those involved.

Communication between parties about further judicial intervention is an important element in the process of mediation for redress. This is a consequence of the fact that, given the seriousness of the offences, the cases are referred to a penal judge. This is clear to both parties at the beginning of mediation. With discussion of the judicial outcome, one transcends the inter-individual level of the conflict, putting it into a societal context. It gives the victim, the offender and their direct social network the opportunity to reflect on what is socially acceptable and unacceptable. Expressing and transferring their commonly and fully discussed opinion on the penal reaction gives both parties the opportunity to play an active and constructive role in the criminal justice decision-making process, without themselves deciding on the final outcome. Stated this way, mediation for more serious crimes not only produces horizontal dialogue between the offender and the victim, but also results in vertical communication between the parties, on the one hand, and the court, on the other. The judge also learns from the parties.

Mediation within a prison context

From both practice and research, it is evident that prison is not the best place to teach people to take responsibility or to repair the harm done. Inmates develop psychological coping mechanisms oriented more to rationalisation and denial. For their part, victims of serious crime often still suffer after the sentence has been passed. They are struggling, for example, with unanswered questions on the nature of the offence and the reasons why it happened. They feel the need to express themselves to the offender. Or they find it extremely difficult to accept how the inmate is accommodated in prison or that early release is anticipated. All these are good reasons to conceive a programme of victim offender mediation at this level.

The above-mentioned NGO Suggnomè assumed responsibility for initiating such a programme. With the financial help of the Flemish Community, an experimental victim-offender mediation programme was set up at the beginning of 2001. The project operates in three prisons: one open institution for less serious crimes, one prison for remand custody and short-term punishment, and one prison for long-term inmates, namely offenders convicted to at least three years' imprisonment. It is mainly the experience in this last prison, the Central Prison of Leuven (about 220 inmates), that is being reported here (Eyckmans 2002; Buntinx 2003).

The mediator in this pilot project (the Leuven part) is employed full time and is part of the Leuven Mediation Service. In the years 2001-02, a total of fifty-five applications for contact with the other party were received. It is the offender or the victim who must take the initiative to contact the mediator. Most applications came from offenders (which is understandable in the first period of the project, because it is much easier to make this service known in a prison than to a dispersed group of victims or victim agencies). About half of the applications relate to cases of homicide (passionate crimes, robbery with murder, parenticide, kidnapping with murder). About one out of five are sexual offences (rape, incest, sexual assault). Other cases are armed robbery, arson, physical assault, threat, theft, car jacking and fraud.

The mediation process in this programme is similar to that of "mediation for redress". The same principles apply: voluntariness, confidentiality and neutrality. In a first, exploratory meeting with the applicant, the offer and method of mediation are explained, the applicant's motivation is discussed and checked, as well as his or her suitability for mediation. Sometimes, a relevant third person is consulted. Then the other party is contacted, sometimes through an intermediate person or service, for example a victim support scheme. The parties decide, with the help of the mediator, what steps they would like to take and at what pace. In case of direct mediation, the meeting will be organised in the prison and the parties can propose support persons to bring along. In this kind of mediation – compared to "mediation for redress" – the emphasis is more on communication than reaching an agreement.

Out of the fifty-five applications made, twenty did not progress. Most applicants withdrew, or postponed their decision, after the first exploratory talk with the mediator. Others were refused by the mediator because of, amongst other reasons, an unclear motivation, an offender denying the offence, the strictly legal character of the request, or the total lack of financial resources where restitution was the offender's only motive.

Other cases were started, but not concluded, for example because one of the parties preferred to stop the mediation process. But, here again, this should not be considered a failure. For many, taking the initiative and reaching out to the other party is extremely meaningful and beneficial in a psychological way. But it must also be said that victims found it hard and disappointing to accept a refusal from the offender to enter into a mediation process.

Comments

Offering mediation in cases of serious crimes is not self-evident. The mediator in the Leuven project with prisoners reports that the impact of the crime is still sometimes too strong to avoid polarisation. The trauma can still be overwhelming, and in general, the consequences of the crime for both sides are tremendous. Strong emotions occur during the meetings. Therefore, cases should be selected extremely carefully. Above all, high demands are put on the mediator. The work affects the mediator as well, who will not deal with too many cases at the same time. As is the case in "mediation for redress", support from fellow mediators, good supervision and continuous training are essential. In mediation, it is the task of the mediator to create an open and respectful atmosphere, but also – at least in these types of cases – to stimulate in an active way the mediation process. The mediator ensures a safe environment for the meeting and that imbalances in power do not disturb the process. Maybe it is therefore important to mention the personal background of the mediators in the two Leuven mediation programmes: they are social workers, criminologists or jurists, all with at least five years of previous experience with victims and/or offenders.

Mediation for the most serious crimes often takes the character of a therapy process for both parties. Reference in this regard should be made to experiences in Langley (British Columbia, Canada), Texas and New York (Aertsen 1999; Umbreit 2001). In these programmes, mediation – even on death row – is prepared in detail and easily takes up more than a year. The cultural context, and sometimes strong religious motives, should be taken into account when looking at these initiatives. Less extreme examples of mediation programmes with serious crimes can be found in Europe, for example the Leeds Mediation and Reparation Service (UK) or Herstelbemiddeling in The Hague and 's Hertogenbosch (Netherlands).

Indirect mediation is more prevalent than direct mediation in cases involving serious offences. This is true for the two mediation programmes in Leuven ("mediation for redress": only 25-30% direct mediation), and also for similar programmes in other European countries. The relative merits of indirect and direct mediation offer ground for debate. In this regard, the Leuven mediation for redress project has been criticised because of its overprotective attitude towards the parties (Marshall 1994). The mediator was believed to have adopted too hesitant an attitude, rather than moving quickly and more frequently to direct mediation. This criticism could apply especially to mediators with a counselling, social work or therapy background.

Mediation programmes for serious crimes reveal the necessity to foresee a service of mediation at all stages of the criminal justice process. It is clear that the timing (offering) of mediation should mainly be determined by the needs and possibilities of the parties. The work done in one phase should not be neutralised in the next, where there is no room for reparative actions. Neither should mediation be provided at the end of the prison sentence, just before conditional release, without mediation or victim-oriented actions having been offered before. Implementing mediation at the different stages requires a general framework that should provide the theoretical, organisational and legal context. These developments also presuppose a change of attitudes and the introduction of specific skills at all levels. Sensitisation and training of the personnel involved is required.

A good example of how victim-offender mediation should be conceived as part of a larger whole is the Belgian "Restorative justice in prisons" programme. After an experimental period of three years, this programme had been introduced in all prisons by the end of 2000. A "restorative justice adviser" has been employed in each prison. His or her role is not to offer mediation or work at the individual level with the inmate or the victim, but to launch new initiatives, to create new structures and networks, and to support a culture in and around the prison oriented to victims and to different forms of reparation (Robert and Peters 2003).

References

Aertsen, I., "Mediation bei schweren Straftaten – Auf dem Weg zu einer neuen Rechtskultur?", in Pelikan, C. (ed.), *Mediationsverfahren: Horizonte, Grenzen, Innensichten (Jahrbuch für Rechts- und Kriminalsoziologie)*, Nomos Verl.-Ges., Baden-Baden, 1999, pp. 115-138.

Aertsen, I., "Victim-offender mediation in Belgium", in European Forum for Victim-Offender Mediation and Restorative Justice (ed.), *Victim-offender mediation in Europe. Making restorative justice work*, Leuven University Press, Leuven, 2000, pp. 153-192.

Aertsen, I., *Slachoffer-daderbemiddeling: een onderzoek naar de ontwikkeling van een herstelgerichte strafrechtsbedeling*, Leuven University Press, Leuven, 2004.

Buntinx, K., "Bemiddeling in de fase van de strafuitvoering, twee jaar later", unpublished, Bemiddelingsdienst Arrondissement Leuven, Leuven, 2003.

European Forum for Victim-Offender Mediation and Restorative Justice (ed.), *Victim-offender mediation in Europe. Making restorative justice work*, Leuven University Press, Leuven, 2000.

Eyckmans, D., *De uitbouw van een herstelgericht aanbod aan gedetineerden vanuit de Vlaamse Gemeenschap. Eindrapport oktober 2002*, Slachtoffer in Beeld – Suggnomè vzw Forum voor Herstelrecht en Bemiddeling, 2002.

Fattah, E.A., "Beyond metaphysics: the need for a new paradigm – On actual and potential contributions of criminology and the social sciences to the reform of the criminal law", in Lahti, R. and Nuotio, K. (eds.), *Criminal law theory in transition*, Finnish Lawyers' Publishing Company, Helsinki, 1992.

Groenhuijsen, M., "Victims' rights in the criminal justice system: a call for more comprehensive implementation theory", in Van Dijk, J., Van Kaam, R. and Wemmers, J. (eds.), *Caring for crime victims. Selected proceedings of the 9th International Symposium on Victimology*, Criminal Justice Press, Monsey, 1999, pp. 85-114.

Lauwaert, K. and Aertsen, I., "Restorative justice: activities and expectations at European Level", *ERA-Forum – Scripta Iuris Europaei*, 1, 2002, pp. 27-32.

Marshall, T.F., *The search for restorative justice: reflections on the Leuven mediation project*, unpublished, Koning Boudewijnstichting, Brussels, 1994.

Mary, P., "Le travail d'intérêt général et la médiation pénale face à la crise de l'état social: dépolitisation de la question criminelle et pénalisation du social", in Mary, P. (ed.), *Travail d'intérêt général et médiation pénale. Socialisation du pénal ou pénalisation du social?*, Bruylant, Brussels, 1997, pp. 325-347.

Robert, L. and Peters, T., "How restorative justice is able to transcend the prison walls: a discussion of the 'restorative detention' project", in Weitekamp,

E.G.M. and Kerner, H.-J. (eds.), *Restorative justice in context. International practice and directions,* Willan Publishing, Cullompton, 2003, pp. 95-122.

Umbreit, M., *The handbook of victim-offender mediation. An essential guide to practice and research,* Jossey-Bass, San Francisco, 2001.

Chapter 6

Community service as a means of restoring civic dialogue after offending

Vincent Delbos

The purpose of this paper is to describe a local experiment which tried to give some meaning to the enforcement of non-custodial sentences – or even the serving of a prison sentence – by re-establishing, on a small scale, the elementary foundations of life in society, the conditions for learning some of the rules for living peacefully in the community. It may well be an example of "1+1+1" promoted by Alexandre Jardin: "I am not interested in the colour of the ballot papers of all these committed people, but whenever a man – or a woman – demonstrates their responsibility as a citizen through their actions, it really does something for me. So politically, I am on the side of sincere republicans who participate by getting involved."

The "Civic dialogue" project began in late 1999. The experiment was conducted in the Yvelines district to the west of Paris, an area of contrasts where very wealthy and very poor districts exist side by side. It is an area that well illustrates Vincent Cespedes' Aphélie,[1] namely one of conflict and so-called "urban" violence. Associations, public institutions, local partners and inhabitants all complained of being unable to perform their duties or live in security: for example, the Post Office was no longer able to distribute the mail because vehicles disappeared on every round; caretakers of buildings were attacked if they asked children to stop damaging letter boxes; and firefighters had to work under a hail of stones – the litany of urban violence caught between the feeling of insecurity and impunity, the visible expression of relegation.

The criminal justice system became involved after the act, trying and punishing, without having any real impact on the situation, without really changing how offenders saw their acts, although victims saw the aggression they had suffered or how the authorities viewed the possibility of being able to rectify the situation. In particular, non-custodial sentences did not seem to be producing results or having any perceptible effect on offenders. The most frequently

---

1.   Cespedes, V., *La cerise sur le béton, violences urbaines et libéralisme,* Flammarion, Paris, 2002. The author describes Aphélie as "the land of society's rejects, whose iris will never be dilated by the gleam of freedom and power".

imposed non-custodial sentence was community service, working without pay for a public body or association. Data collated in 2000 showed that about 100 of the 700 people sentenced to community service each year had been convicted of so-called "urban violence", damage to public property (for example, spray-painting or vandalising bus shelters), insulting public servants (insulting police officers), obstructing police officers in the execution of their duty, verbal or physical violence on public transport and even offences committed in circumstances suggesting lack of public spirit (for example, thefts committed during the last storm in late 1999, taking advantage of the disarray of the public services).

At the outset it was fairly clear that the people responsible for such acts were completely cut off from everything and everyone, even from their own families, and that it might be more useful to bring them together in a single room in order to end their isolation and get them to talk so as to prevent reoffending. Hitherto, they had been sent to work for a certain number of hours, often alone, in one organisation or another, without anything being done to try to understand what had happened. This situation was all the more worrying since commission of the offences often revealed that the law or social code violated had never been explained, turning the offenders into victims of the criminal justice system and the people they "attacked" into perpetual targets, without there being on either side any room for explanation which might have disengaged, at least partially, the two-way mechanism by which the offender felt a victim and the victim powerless to obtain compensation. The enforcement of such sentences demonstrated – above all from the point of view of crime policy – a lack of understanding of the role, objectives and missions devolved upon local public organisations and others, a lack of intercommunication and, in a sense, a disturbance of civic dialogue.

The people who had complained of the problems in their neighbourhoods, at work and in their daily lives, were contacted and asked to become involved in the construction of such a dialogue. Between December 1999, when the first session was held, and December 2001, 110 offenders took part in the experiment. Most of them were young people aged between 18 and 24 who had been sentenced to between 40 and 240 hours' community service.

The jobs to which offenders sentenced to community service were assigned did little to address their lack of public spirit. This meant that sentences intended as reparation were not meaningful and had little impact on reoffending. In order to make community service meaningful some collective time needed to be organised. One of the theories is that community service is particularly appropriate to these sorts of offences. There are a number of reasons for this: it is by definition shared and enables potential for local partnerships to be mobilised; it may foster the pooling of very diverse types of local resources channelled towards the suppression of a type of crime the public strongly perceives as being symptomatic of the ineffectiveness of public institutions and revealing the feeling many people have that they are neglected. Community service orders therefore seem to be underused and, above all, too seldom imposed because the tasks assigned are not adapted to offences involving "urban violence".

The "Civic dialogue" project was developed on the basis of these observations.

Objectives

There were a number of parallel objectives. The first was to show the young people sentenced for offences symptomatic of a breakdown in community life that there are other ways of dealing with public institutions.

It was also a case of making time for the formation of more responsible, more "civic" behaviour. Learning about relationships based on respect and dignity and the dialogue that should be preferred to violence requires preparation, negotiation and mediation. It is not easy, either for offenders or people working for the various institutions. As one of the people sentenced to community service said at the end of one session, "We are ambassadors", a particularly apt comment.

Like all sentences, community service orders indicate a degree of gravity in the breakdown of public order. They should also be a means of reconstituting the rules of community life, breaches of which have been sanctioned. Once the trial and sentencing phase are over, they should also facilitate the reconstruction of those rules together with reconciliation.

The aim was to create the conditions for dialogue between offenders and the public officials who had been their victims and devote eighteen hours of the sentence to it. The speakers were willing to lead the activity and build this often complicated dialogue. The offenders also agreed to take part, in many cases because "they had things to say". However, failure to participate was regarded as an incident in their community service. This time spent together also made it possible to introduce time for individualisation before individual appointment to specific posts (with the fire service, public transport companies, in police stations, etc.).

In this way a sentence to fit the offence, the offender and his or her social and institutional environment was created, which also helped to prevent crime and reoffending and "reconcile" young people and institutions to some extent.

Methodology

The offenders were together for 3 days – 18 hours out of a total of between 40 and 240 hours. This meant, in particular, that once those eighteen hours were over, the majority of the sentence still remained to be served.

From a legal point of view, the "Civic dialogue" community service was authorised as one of the community service jobs on the list of the Versailles Regional
Court. The content of the sessions was decided upon during some ten meetings between the judge responsible for the enforcement of sentences, probation officers and prospective speakers.

The sessions took place over three days. On the first day, the young offenders'
rights and duties were explained. Day two was devoted to exchange and dialogue and the last day to work on the individual in the group. It is important to
understand that most insulting behaviour is perpetrated by people who are
members of a group but often have difficulty finding their place in it. Work on
gesture and language, as well as role-plays, are required to help the young
people express themselves.

A group usually consisted of about twelve people. One of the working principles when forming groups was to bring together people from all parts of the
area and every type of sociological background. The meeting of people from
different backgrounds can be difficult, since it sometimes creates a confrontation between people from completely different worlds. In practice, however,
most were young (the average age was 23) and from social housing neighbourhoods. They had to learn to get about as the group met in at least three
different places. In many cases this was no mean task since the offenders had
real problems leaving the confines of their estates. The midday meal and breaks
were also a factor in the formation and balance of a group.

There was also a principle that groups should be mixed, but girls and young
women were very much in the minority. In reality, therefore, most groups were
not mixed: in ten groups there was a total of only two women. And yet it was
they who entered most into the spirit of things. H, aged 22, a young woman from
Les Mureaux found guilty of insulting a judge, was delighted by her experience:
"When I go back to the estate, I am going to tell everyone I met a guy from the
Crime Squad who was as gentle as a lamb. It is true! I cannot believe it!"

Since the sessions were part of the enforcement of a sentence, real involvement
by the young people concerned was always sought, even when they were
unwilling. It was essential that they should examine what they had done. There
is therefore no question of doing community service without thinking about
what has been done.

After about ten sessions a sort of pattern emerged which was then used to
structure the period of dialogue.

For the first half-day, the session programme and the role of the Maisons
de Justice et du Droit[2] were presented: being a citizen of one's town and

---

2. Maisons de Justice et du Droit are local utilities, based on partnerships between local
authorities, the courts and various actors, which offer information on law. In some cases, also,
alternative dispute resolution can take place there.

neighbourhood, rights and duties. The partners and speakers varied widely. Instructors from the courts of the Val de Seine and Saint-Quentin-en-Yvelines played an active, decisive role. The Maison de Justice et du Droit – the major link in a public justice system close to citizens – was of great importance here. Fatia Mekerri,[3] Director of the Maison de Justice et du Droit of the Val de Seine, located at the heart of the Les Mureaux housing estates, took part in most of the sessions. She explains:

> "At first, the young people often wonder what is going to happen during the ses-sion, so we lay down ground rules. Our aim is to create an atmosphere of trust, above all to avoid their seeing us as a second court. The young people often ask to step outside the work context – which reassures them since we all have the same problems as they do. The rules are applicable to everyone because rights and duties are valid for everyone. Then, we talk about citizenship (which is not an ethics lesson). We discuss offences, families and personal situations. Once these foundations have been laid, it is also important to realise that silence has its part to play. When we start, we do not know what offences the young people have committed. It is only later that there might be a confession. Next we talk about violence, discontent and the emotional problems young people suffer. The parents seem to be patently lacking in affection. In the long run, offenders sen-tenced to community service have to realise that violence is not the only way of expressing oneself (for example, charity work and the vote are also modes of expression) and that their offences are not decisive for their lives – the young offenders think that once they have made one mistake they are stigmatised for life. It is also important to develop the skills of the young people we meet. The sessions are, moreover, particularly relevant when those involved (firefighters, police officers, elected representatives, etc.) transmit a consistent message. The young people have to learn to understand each other, which in particular helps them to develop, and fight against preconceptions. These young people feel that we are afraid of them. It is not an easy situation to manage. We have to learn to communicate and be able to communicate. One can of course negotiate without hesitating to apply the rules, if necessary, and interrupt the negotiation. Discussion and transmission of knowledge are perhaps the two most important aspects of the sessions."

The second half-day of the session was devoted to explaining what citizenship and community mean in practical terms and involved speakers from the fire and public transport services, and the contact, emergency, assistance and commu-nications services, all of which are among the prime targets of aggression. As one speaker said:

> "Every day I catch a bus that goes through Les Mureaux. The driver never asks me to show my ticket. One day, he did not ask the young people who got on to show theirs either. But suddenly, at the Les Mureaux stop, he asked a young man

---

3. The people quoted took part in a regional "Justice and the city" meeting in Les Mureaux (8 June 2001) on the theme of mobilising civil society against offending.

who got on for his ticket. I asked him why he had asked that young man and not the others. He said that the bus was already paid for by the local authority, so usually there was no need to check tickets but occasionally he wanted to remind people that, as a bus driver, he had certain prerogatives; so, when he saw a youngster he 'did not like the look of', he asked him for his ticket."

The firefighters played an essential role in the partnership. Usually, two fire-fighters spoke during these sessions. The first question is: why is the fire service subjected to violence (stone throwing, fires, etc.)? On the whole, the young people have nothing against firefighters, but they wear a uniform and there-fore represent the state; in other words, a form of repression. The discussion then moves on to other things because the young people want a broader dia-logue – on life, their future, relationships, etc. Justifiably, the firefighters also emphasise public-spiritedness, respect for the law, attitudes in the street and so on. The youngsters are open to such discussion. The most important things for them are to have a real family life with children and to be respected. Community service also takes place in fire stations and emergency services cen-tres. It was noticed during the experiment that some of the offenders volun-tarily came back to say that the time they spent there was quite pleasant, so the message can even be transmitted in problem areas.

Half a day is spent on the role of the police. The reason a "police session" was included in the "civic dialogue" module is that most offences are connected with urban violence of which public servants, especially the police, are the main targets. Urban violence consists by its very nature of acts that disrupt commu-nity life. In practical terms, the aim is to set up ways of giving back to the young offenders their identity as citizens during their sentences. It was therefore essential to work on the young people's image of the authorities and vice versa.

This part of the module took place in a police station. It was a police officer who spontaneously offered to organise the first session in the police station. The choice of venue was certainly not neutral. It may have had an upsetting side but, because of that, provided a rare opportunity for the youngsters to go freely and without any form of constraint to a police station. Since then, all the sessions took place in police or *Gendarmerie* stations.

During this part of the module the young people met police officers and gen-darmes outside the context of any form of questioning. Furthermore, it gave police officers an important role in the enforcement of sentences and the pre-vention of reoffending. The workshop was not difficult to set up from an insti-tutional point of view; officers were more than willing to establish a dialogue with the young offenders. A wide range of issues was involved in this encounter: How can civic dialogue be re-established between young people, the judicial authorities and the police and on what bases? How can it be extended? What is the value of all that has been said once the youngsters go home to their friends on the estates?

It emerged from the replies to a questionnaire sent to police officers and gendarmes in spring 2001 that they were not anxious about facing a group but were afraid of the negative image their forces had among young people. Given that, how could civic dialogue be established with young people? How could young people be made to understand that a police or *Gendarmerie* station can be a welcoming place of protection as well as one of repression?

As for the young offenders, they were often nervous about the session in the police station. Those who agreed to take part in the workshop displayed two types of behaviour: some took part in the dialogue, whilst others clammed up, although this could change in the course of the session.

Laurent Sambourg, Chief Inspector of Vernon (Eure), took part in one of the first workshops of this kind. He says that at that time he had little idea what to say and knew only that he had to say it in the police station, where the young people had to go "cold". The aim was to destroy their negative image of the police. "In order to do this I began by explaining what the police are for, starting with the Interior Ministry and going down to the neighbourhood police station. The youngsters seemed to be attentive, although they did not understand all the details. Anyway, one of them told me that what I had said was interesting but that they did not see why young people and police officers went on making each other's lives impossible." As it said in *L'Humanité*,[4] "In order to defuse the hatred of the police prevalent on some estates, meetings between cops and robbers are proliferating, often resulting in stormy but fruitful debate." One afternoon was devoted to the subject of the much discussed police checks that young people resent so much and the police had to justify. The young offenders had the opportunity to say why they resented them so much and the police why they conducted them as they did. At the end of the afternoon, one of the young men said that he understood things better, so the dialogue had not been pointless.

The meeting with the police is the one the youngsters most look forward to and fear most. The police also hold a fascination for them, however. They are fascinated by these men and women who embody force. When they arrive at the police station it is sometimes difficult for the police officers to manage this dual attitude of fear and fascination.

It was decided that one half-day would be spent making the young offenders visit places where citizenship is constructed, symbolically or in practical terms. There are many possibilities in the area and only a few of them were exploited. This aspect of the module is important because it turned out that many of the youngsters were unfamiliar with such places, either remarkable buildings, such as the Congress Chamber in the Chateau of Versailles where parliament met to pass the most important laws of the nation such as the ones that abolished

---

4. 25 December 2000, social affairs pages, "Flics et jeunes: le processus de paix?", in a series entitled "Banlieue 1990-2000: la politique de la ville à l'épreuve des quartiers (I)".

slavery in the nineteenth century, or places close to home like the Town Hall or a sub-prefecture (two sessions were organised with the sub-prefects of Mantes-la-Jolie and Rambouillet). Part of the session was devoted to explaining the role of an elected representative, the speaker being such a representative, for example Ms Onfray, a municipal councillor in Les Mureaux who says:

> "For such young people a mayor is someone they never see or only in certain circumstances. One of the young men in one group knew the mayor professionally. He was amazed to learn that people are not born elected! During the session the youngsters realised that elected representatives spend their time working for a town. They were astonished that anyone should be willing to give their free time to such a task. During the break they asked the elected representatives whether they had children and a family life. They also discovered what the town provides in the way of facilities. These are very important to them and have a price and are largely funded from local taxes. We reminded them that it is their parents who pay those taxes. This aspect of things surprised them and made them aware of community life. In the end, they understood that the things they damaged had to be paid for."

Martine Aymé, sub-prefect of Rambouillet, had a group of young offenders at the sub-prefecture for half a day. She says:

> "It was interesting because they had no idea what the role of a sub-prefect was and thought of a subprefect as someone who lives in a lovely house and has a chauffeur-driven car. When they visited the sub-prefecture, they saw that people were working hard in far from ideal conditions in dilapidated premises. They also realised there were rules. The work of civil servants is also governed by rules. They thought some social groups were exempt from respecting rules. To give one example, they thought that as a sub-prefect I was exempt from prosecution for misdemeanours. It is important to tell them that this is not true. It is essential that the authorities and the law should transmit a consistent message. Regular meetings between authorities are therefore essential in order to determine what rules everyone should respect."

During this visit one young man said that stealing from the state was not theft. I explained that the reality was quite different, taking the example of taxes. Ultimately, theft from the state would penalise his parents and his parents' friends because they paid taxes. Nikola Tietze, a sociologist from CADIS, believes that, for young people, an authority is seen as a "block" which cannot act. Dialogue enables them to understand that the authorities are living organisms.

With various people from the cultural sphere, half-day workshops using dance, theatre and sculpture were organised to work on self-control and controlling one's own violence.

The last half-day was devoted to the issue of victims. For this, a very exciting approach was developed with psychologists specialising in counselling the employees of a public transport network who had been victims of aggression. The exchange was often stormy at the beginning but gradually made the young offenders realise that an attitude, one word, can sometimes be perceived as a serious attack.

In the course of the various sessions a number of flexible operating principles were identified:

- first, the groups should be heterogeneous and come from different towns in the area;
- there should be heterogeneity of offences (violent and otherwise) and history (first offenders and reoffenders);
- there should be mobility: all the sessions should be held in different places in order to acquaint young offenders with new environments.
- there should be assessment and punishment: as we saw above, failure to attend constitutes an incident in the enforcement of community service.

One of the original features of the experiment was the fact that a specific assessment mechanism was put in place from the outset. It was developed by a group of sociologists from CADIS – the Ecole des Hautes Etudes en Sciences Sociales – around three main focal points:

- observation: a sociologist attended as an observer throughout the three days to analyse group dynamics and include the analyses in the successive phases of assessment;
- assessment with the offenders: at the end of each session, an hour was spent with participants and offenders analysing their evaluation of each of the sessions with the judge and probation officers.
- assessment with the speakers: there was a half-day meeting with the speakers in order to obtain their assessment of the session and its limitations and advantages.

These two assessment meetings enabled any problems that might have arisen to be rectified before the next session.

A more quantitative follow-up mechanism is now being developed to measure some of the results, in particular, improved enforcement of community service orders and reoffending.

Development of the experiment in prisons

After holding some ten sessions in the framework of community service orders, that is as an alternative to prison, it was thought that some of the lessons learned might be transposed to prison. A lot of the young people in Yvelines Prison are there for urban violence offences; doubtless more serious than those committed by those sentenced to community service, but nevertheless of the same kind. Two sessions were organised, not without some difficulty. For example, work with remand prisoners, who have yet to be tried, created problems when the subject of responsibility was raised. There was another significant difference, namely that the "civic dialogue" session could last only two days instead of three. The participants' arrival was on each occasion delayed by situations specific to prison life (opening of the doors, gathering together juveniles and adults housed in different buildings, etc.).

Workshops were formed with eight prisoners. The workshops were obviously not held on visiting days. Firefighters, public transport workers and actors took part.

In prison, participation in the session was not subtracted from the sentence. Only one refusal was received. Generally, the young people were very interested: for example, they were pleased to meet the police. Obviously in some cases they are simply happy to get out of their cells for a while. As Marie Françoise Goldberger, a specialist in town policy and the representative of the ombudsperson in Les Mureaux, said: "I believe the 'civic dialogue' experiment brings citizenship into the prison. It is above all very important to stress yet again the need for elected representatives to take part in all these sessions."

It is difficult to draw any conclusions from so little experience. The hard part was the meeting with the police. Everyone stuck to their position. The youngsters found body searches and searches of their cells humiliating. They also thought the prison system was responsible for suicides. Their speech when they met the police was therefore violent. However, the dialogue with the firefighters, for whom the young people expressed great respect, was more positive. Thanks to the combined experience of the speakers and the young people's goodwill, the dialogue was eventually taken up with enthusiasm. Very soon a real civic dialogue began during which the speakers and participants opened up. The life stories which had made an appearance during the afternoon of the first day reappeared in a genuine desire to talk. For the first time in the session, the concept of exchange seemed to have been understood and put into practice uninhibitedly. During the following session the prefect himself came to meet the young prisoners.

This experiment in prison is comparable to a similar initiative involving the opening of a law centre in Fleury-Mérogis through the "jobs for young people" scheme, enabling prisoners to ask people totally unconnected with the prison questions about law, the idea being to set up law centres in prisons; or, again, the work being done to deal with endemic violence in the Fleury-Mérogis centre for young offenders, for example. As Maud Dayet, the director of the centre says, "We need to convey the image of a sympathetic team that knows what goes on in prisoners' lives and is able to do something about it."

Results

Clarisse Buono and Nikola Tietze, sociologists from CADIS – EHESS, made a number of essential recommendations:

- the participants should be treated as adults and citizens and not simply as "young people". Any contribution by a representative of the authorities resembling what happens in schools is rejected or boycotted with the remark, "It is too like school". Real exchange develops, however, when speakers bring in their personal experience, tell the participants about their own lives and beliefs, ask open questions and show that they are prepared to question what they have said. This is indicative, not only of the difficult relationships in schools, but above all of the participants' wish to be treated as adults capable of thinking for themselves. They do not want to be "young people" – a term which identifies them with difficult neighbourhoods, failure and a sort of inferiority;

- the word "conflict" should be given positive connotations: the participants, their sentence and the session should be placed in a social context affected by political issues, the structural oppositions in society and various forms of discrimination so that the session does not have a school or disciplinary atmosphere;

- prefabricated representations of "difficult neighbourhoods", "young people" and "the lives of decent people" should be deconstructed: the speakers should call themselves into question and take part in the dialogue on the same terms as the young offenders.

The context of enforcement of a sentence needs to be clearly understood. There is a sentencing scale in which "civic dialogue" community service is not the first level. Community service was introduced in 1984 and is therefore relatively new. As regards sentencing, the sanction is very often prison or nothing. Community service needs to be a credible alternative. It is a sentence that is new in character since various partners are involved, not only the criminal justice system. In this respect, all the partner bodies are authorised by the judge responsible for the enforcement of sentences. Those authorisations conceal a great deal of explanatory work and training. The sentence under discussion is socially visible. The civic dialogue sessions are a means of optimising community service. It is not particularly effective to rub out tags without understanding why they are a problem in a particular place. Young offenders need to have the rules of community life they have violated explained to them, otherwise they will get up in the morning to go to work but will not have learnt anything.

Extensions

It is also important not to keep bringing dialogue back to the police and the criminal justice system, but rather to show that institutions form a common front. It would be a good thing if the young people were to meet everyone together so that they could realise that there was such a common front. More generally, it is a way of thinking that is being put into place, one based on the development of responsible citizens. This work should begin at school. As Alain Koegler, sub-prefect of Mantes-la-Jolie (Yvelines), said:

"Every class should draw up its regulations and then all the students should sign them. In that way they would know what all the rules were. But all the authorities should be involved in this dialogue, so long as it is not disjointed. Partnership and a common front by the authorities in their dialogue with young people are therefore required. Moreover, the dialogue should not only concern young offenders, since the rejection of the judicial system is not peculiar to them; some young people who are not offenders are equally critical of the authorities."

Sidi El Haimer from Mantes-la-Jolie explained how in his town a disagreement between two drivers or a routine control could end up in stone throwing and spitting at police officers.

"Following this incident we organised a meeting between young people and the police in the Agora. We also took action to foster dialogue between young people and the authorities by holding a football match with the participation of SNCF ticket collectors, bus drivers, etc. The initiative worked well and the young men agreed to take part in the tournament. Other activities have been organised involving police officials coming to meet the associations and inhabitants of neighbourhoods before taking up their duties. This enabled them to find out to whom they could turn in the event of problems. We also observed that firefighters were finding it more and more difficult to work in certain neighbourhoods of the town."

Yazid Kherfi organised a meeting between young people and the police at the youth centre in Chanteloup, rather than at the Town Hall, so that more young people would attend. It was held at night, in order to bring in the most violent young men, with the participation of the Crime Squad because relations between young people and police were very violent. Kherfi asked the young people to face the police officers so that they could tell them exactly what their criticisms of them were. This was certainly a risky strategy but, if one wants to move forward, risks have to be taken. Many (80 to 100) young people, some of them very violent, attended the meeting. Members of the Crime Squad also came, all of them on a voluntary basis. The first hour of the debate was very conflictory. The young people began by talking about their personal problems, while the police officers tried to make them understand that they were human beings. Eventually, at the end of the debate, the young people admitted it was not the Crime Squad they hated, but another police unit.

The problem is that there has been no real follow-up. Young people and police really should converse more naturally. Furthermore, young people realise that the situation in their neighbourhoods would be worse if there were no police (although it has to be admitted that some of them do not do their jobs well). In the final analysis, bad police officers may be preferable to no police at all. Ordinary local people are also important since sometimes the action of a single person is enough to prevent confrontation between young people and the police.

A very similar experiment took place in similar circumstances with children in Mulhouse in the framework of the criminal compensation measure known as the citizenship initiation course. Its substance was very similar to the "civic dialogue" session. The mechanism provides in particular for meetings with adults, police officers and professionals, the focal point being dialogue. All agree that the value added of this system was the opportunity it gave for questioning and discussion, namely its educational value. The sub-prefect of Mulhouse explained that he invited the director of the city's Peugeot factory which employs 4 000 people. The young people told him that, once his factory had dismissed someone, there was no way of ever being re-employed. He replied that it was normal not to be able to work again in a company from which one had been sacked for a serious misdeed. They also said that the temporary employment agencies regarded them as "unemployable", giving a final con-notation to the term and leaving no room for hope. The director of the Peugeot factory then decided to review recruitment procedures to enable persons who had been dismissed for a serious misdeed to be re-employed by Peugeot after some time had elapsed.

It is in legislation that advances have been made, however. The Green Paper on the prison service and the meaning of sentences drafted by Marylise Lebranchu, Minister of Justice in Lionel Jospin's government, contained provisions to introduce a civic training sentence. The act on programming on the justice system, passed by parliament on 3 August 2002, contains a provision – limited to minors, it is true – that gave the experiment its first serious legal recognition.[5]

And, finally, the recent law of 9 March 2004 on "adaptation of criminal justice to the evolutions of crime" provides a new provision in the French Penal Code[6]: when an offence is punishable by a prison sentence, the court may stipulate, instead of that prison sentence, that the offender has to do a *stage de citoyenneté* (civic training sentence), the purposes of which are to remind him or her of the republican values of tolerance and respect for human dignity, which are the bases of society. Thus there is now a legal provision covering this possibility.

As a provisional conclusion, some points can be made on the basis of the experiment that was conducted for a little over two years. Considering young adults as fully responsible citizens – not victims, as they sometimes claim to be, nor pariahs, but citizens who have committed a criminal offence for which the justice system, following debate, has imposed a sanction – may go some way to changing the way people regard each other and put an end to ceaseless con-frontation. The experiment cannot claim to have, on its own, put in place or put back in place the simple elements of a collective ethics based on mutual respect, tolerance, listening to others, etc. The term "dialogue" is used in a

---

5. Requirement to undergo a civic training course of no more than one month with the purpose of reminding the child of his or her duties under the law, the application of which shall be decreed by the Conseil d'Etat.

6. Penal Code, Article 131-3 and 131-5-1.

more generic sense. Respect, listening to others, dialogue and tolerance are necessary if we want to live together. It is an attempt to overcome the old conflict between public order and personal or social development.

In the framework of this sentence, it is to be understood in terms of a collective ethic in which understanding the other goes both ways. It is no more ambitious than that. This may, however, be a great deal, all of it in the framework of an opportunistic network in the positive sense of the term. One of the young women, H, said:

> "You are being negative. It is enough for one of you to say 'I do not like the police' for all the rest of you to follow. You are living in a fantasy world. You are here and they are over there and there is a red line between you. If you go on like this, you will never shake hands with each other."

References

Barra, M.-G., Bruston, P. and Lenoir, E., "Politique de la ville et prévention de la délinquance. Recueil d'actions locales", *Repères,* Editions de la DIV, Saint-Denis, 2004.

Buono, C., Poli, A. and Tietze, N., *La médiation, une comparaison européenne,* Editions de la DIV, Saint-Denis, 1994.

Chauvenet, A., Gorgeon, C., Mouhanna, C. and Orlic, F., *Contraintes et possibles: les pratiques d'exécution des mesures en milieu ouvert,* 1999.

Chauvenet, A., Gorgeon, C., Mouhanna, C. and Orlic, F., *Les peines alternatives et aménagées, une activité discrète,* La Documentation Française, "Regards sur l'actualité, L'univers pénitentiaire", May 2000, pp. 61-70.

Chauvenet, A., Gorgeon, C., Mouhanna, C. and Orlic, F., "Entre social et judiciaire, quelle place pour le travail social du milieu ouvert?", *Archives de Politique Criminelle,* 23, 2001.

Council of Europe, *Improving the implementation of the European rules on community sanctions and measures – Recommendation Rec(2000)22 and report,* Council of Europe Publishing, Strasbourg, 2002.

Faget, J., "La bureaucratisation du travail d'intérêt general", *Actes,* 73, 1990, pp. 23-27.

Faget, J., "Le travail d'intérêt général", *Information Prison Justice,* 60, March 1992, pp. 12-14.

Faget, J., "L'enfance modèle du travail d'intérêt général", in *Le travail d'intérêt général a dix ans: le résultat en vaut la peine,* Etudes et recherches, Ministère de la Justice, 1994, pp. 101-122.

Faget, J., "Travail d'intérêt général et médiation pénale en France", in *Travail d'intérêt général et médiation pénale. Socialisation du pénal ou pénalisation du social?,* Bruylant, Brussels, 1997, pp. 67-82.

Guillonneau, M., "Sanctions et mesures en milieu ouvert", *Cahiers de Démographie Pénitentiaire,* 8, Direction de l'administration pénitentiaire, Paris, 2000.

Khosrokhavar, F., *L'islam dans les prisons,* Editions Balland, Paris, 2004.

Tietze, N. "Die Herausforderung, Konflikte positiv zu bewerten: Stadtgewalt in Straßburg – Neuho", in Karpe, H., Ottersbach, M. and Yildiz, E. (eds.), *Urbane Quartiere zwischen Zerfall und Erneuerung,* Der andere Buchladen, Cologne, 2001, pp. 123-144.

Tournier, P.V., "Les sanctions alternatives à l'emprisonnement en Europe: synopsis", in *Le travail d'intérêt général 1984-1994, études et recherches, actes du Colloque pour le Xe anniversaire du TIG en France,* Ministère de la Justice, Paris, 1994, pp. 11-20.

Tournier, P.V., "Alternatives à la détention en Europe", *Questions Pénales,* XV, 4, 2002.

Chapter 7

The Czech Republic's path from correction to alternatives

Helena Válková and Jana Hulmáková

As part of its pre-accession negotiations concerning future entry into the European Union, the Czech Republic has already adapted its legislation to nearly all requirements under the so-called "first pillar" of the EU, namely those concerned with the economy. Common foreign and security policy, the EU's "second pillar", and criminal policy and justice, covering primarily police co-operation and co-ordination in criminal/legal matters, which, together with home affairs, make up the "third pillar", have not yet exerted such strong pressure to change national criminal legislation and practice.[1] Consequently, changes on a scale comparable to those that have already taken place in the commercial law field have not yet been made in this area. Measures taken against organised crime have been a positive exception, with the Czech Republic amending its Criminal Code and Criminal Procedure Act in order to meet its international obligations.[2] In comparison, mention could be made of the lengthy approval process of the International Criminal Court Statute (the Rome Statute) of 17 July 1998 – signed by the Czech Republic on 13 April 1999 – which has not yet been ratified even though a necessary criminal law amendment has already been adopted. This example shows a failure to appreciate the full significance of this international criminal and political initiative or an unwillingness to respond flexibly to it.

Even important documents adopted by the Council of Europe in the area of criminal policy, namely conventions, resolutions or recommendations, do not always sufficiently influence legislative changes at national level or existing legal practice, although they are discussed in professional journals and are also addressed in the university curriculum. Consequently, it can by no means be said that they are neglected from the legal theory perspective.

---

1. Lukasek, L., "Role spolecne zahranicni a bezpecnostni politiky v tzv evropskem pravnim prostoru" (The role of the common foreign and security policy in the so-called "European legal context"), *Pravni Rozhledy*, "The European law supplement", No. 4, 2002, pp. 1-5.
2. Válková, H., "Die Problematik der organisierten Kriminalität aus der Sicht der Tschechischen Republik", paper given at the international symposium "Strafrechtsentwicklung in Osteuropa: zwischen Bewältigen und neuen Herausforderungen", Schloss Ringberg am Tegernsee, 26 to 29 June 2002.

In the Czech Republic, as in other central European countries, an important and sometimes even decisive factor is whether, in the area of criminal reforms, there are a sufficient number of qualified domestic experts who are able to create an adequate criminal and political climate for the preparation and enforcement of necessary legislative changes and their application in practice. This can be demonstrated by means of an example where the experts, owing to their long-term efforts, have succeeded in making the essential changes in the introduction of alternative criminal procedures and solutions replacing the traditional sentencing mechanisms. To explain how this happened and why these changes were achieved in a relatively short period of time – in one decade – and specifically in the area of sentencing policy, which is usually watched closely even by the general public, can be inspirational particularly for those countries that have not experienced such a positive development although they are culturally and historically very close to the Czech Republic.[3]

Changes in sentencing policy

In an analysis of the statistical data on criminal sanctions imposed in the last fifteen years – a period that includes the end of the 1980s, marking the final stages of socialist criminal policy in Czechoslovakia, the breakthrough period, then the tentative steps of the early 1990s, and later the stabilisation of society and of criminal policy at the end of the 1990s and the beginning of the twenty-first century – one cannot overlook several essential changes that have taken place (see the appendices for a detailed comparison):

- the number of prison sentences imposed has been reduced greatly in both relative and absolute terms. This is most obvious in the adult age-group, namely those aged 18 and over. In 1987 more than one third of adult offenders (and more than one fifth of juvenile offenders) received prison sentences, while in 2002 the courts imposed this sanction on less than one quarter of adults (and only 6.8% of juvenile offenders). The length of prison sentences has also been considerably reduced: short sentences up to one year imposed by courts on adults in 1987 accounted for 44% of all prison sentences, while in 2002 they accounted for as many as 60% (the opposite trend has occurred in the juvenile offenders category: short sentences up to one year accounted for 71% of all prison sentences in 1987, but only 69% in 2002);
- the number of individuals granted an absolute discharge, traditionally the most lenient response to a criminal act, has grown significantly: the courts proceeded in this way in 1987 with only 0.1% of adult offenders and 5.5% of juvenile offenders, while in 2002 the courts discharged as many as 0.5% of adult offenders and 7.8% of juvenile offenders;

---

3. Compare with the situation in Slovakia, for example, where reforms implemented in the area of criminal sanctions since the break-up of Czechoslovakia (31 December 1992) have not been as far-reaching as in the Czech Republic.

- "straight" suspended sentences (that is, without the supervision of a probation officer, a profession newly recognised in the Penal Code in 1997) represented the most frequent sanction in both the 1980s and the 1990s and are also currently experiencing a significant increase: in 1987 approximately one quarter of adult offenders received a suspended sentence (and approximately two thirds of juvenile offenders), while in 2002 the courts imposed this alternative sanction on more than half of adult offenders (use of this sanction in the juvenile offenders category has decreased slightly to 56%);

- the community service order – which has existed since 1995 for criminal acts carrying a prison sentence of up to five years – has only been mentioned in statistics since 1996, but has experienced remarkable growth in the last five years: in 1996 only 1.2% of adults received this sentence (2.1% of juvenile offenders), while in 2002 21% of adults received this sentence (22% of juvenile offenders);

- new instruments of criminal justice – conditional termination of criminal prosecution and mediation – that were introduced into the Criminal Procedure Act by amendments in 1993 and 1995. The data shows evidence of frequent use of conditional termination of criminal prosecution, which was ordered in 1995 in respect of 5 606 defendants in criminal proceedings (that is, nearly 5.2% of the total) and in 2002 in respect of 10 507 defendants in criminal proceedings (that is 11.3% of the total), while mediation was applied less often: in only 105 cases in 1996 and only 387 cases in 2002 (namely, only in respect of 0.4% of all defendants in criminal proceedings).

Considering the increased number of convicted persons (in 1987, 48 347 adults and 4 938 juvenile offenders were convicted, in 2002 as many as 61 151 adults and 3 948 juvenile offenders) and especially the growing number of persons in custody pending trial or sentence, the above-mentioned positive change in sentencing policy, moving from traditional sentences of imprisonment towards increasing use of alternative options, had not, at the end of 2001, had the desired effect in terms of reducing the number of imprisoned people per 100 000 inhabitants. The figure was around 350 in the Czech Republic in the 1980s and fluctuated between 200 and 220 in the 1990s. This means that the figure was still higher than the average for western European countries. It was only after major amendments to the Criminal Procedure Act, which tightened up the conditions for imposing custodial sentences starting on 1 January 2002, that the ratio of prisoners per 100 000 inhabitants dropped from 192 to 162. As of 2 January 2002, 19 194 persons were being held in prisons (including 203 juvenile offenders), one quarter of them (4 478) in custody pending trial or sentence and the remaining three quarters (14 716) sentenced prisoners, while as of 8 January 2003 the figure was only 16 268 (including 179 juvenile offenders), slightly less than one quarter (3 422) of whom were in custody pending trial or sentence, the remainder (12 846) being sentenced prisoners.

Developments in the Czech Republic over the past fourteen years can be viewed as clearly positive in terms of the number and pattern of alternative sentences and measures applied. In a situation where the mass media and the general public were calling for tighter criminal policy measures (such as reintroduction of the death penalty, lowering of the age of criminal liability from 15 to 14 years, increase in criminal sentences for violent and economic crime, criminal prosecution for personal use of drugs, etc.), in response to a sharp increase in the crime rate – which peaked in the second half of the 1990s – the results of the reform efforts in the area of sentencing policy are, without any doubt, encouraging. It would therefore be informative to see why this reform has been successful, what path has been taken by those who enforced it and whether use can be made of this experience in future.

First experiments and consequent legislative changes

If one disregards early experiments in social work with delinquents in socialist Czechoslovakia[4] – which were never able to develop fully and, at best, were focused on work with delinquent youth[5] since, in relation to adult offenders, a prevailing element was control and supervision[6] – one can say that efforts to reform the present, repression-oriented sentencing policy began immediately after 1989. One of the first experiments of this kind was a project called "Out-of-court alternatives for delinquent youth", which was developed at the Institute for State and Law of the Czechoslovak Academy of Sciences.[7] The project was inspired by German (TOA, Cologne)[8] and Austrian (ATA, Vienna)[9]

---

4. Compare, for example, Kunftova, J., *Postpenitenciarni pece* (Postpenitentiary care), Criminology Research Institute of the General Prosecution Office, Prague, 1972; and Suchy, O., *Priciny a prevence recidivy* (Causes and prevention of reoffending), Criminology Research Institute of the General Prosecution Office, Prague, 1983.

5. Válková, H. and Vonkova, J., "Uvahy nad ucinnosti trestniho postihu mladistvych" (Comments on the effectiveness of youth criminal sanctions), *Prokuratura*, No. 2, 1988.

6. Law No. 44/1973 on protective supervision under which social work with offenders followed only recommended co-operation of police bodies (*Verejna bezpecnost*) with state and social bodies. However, the police bodies always exercised supervision in a repressive way, usually over recidivist delinquents. It is not surprising, therefore, that after November 1989 the amendment of Criminal Law No. 175/1990 discontinued it with effect from 1 July 1990. This amendment also replaced capital punishment with life imprisonment. (For a detailed comparison, see for example Válková, H., *Ochranny dohled* (Protective supervision), Criminology Research Institute of the General Prosecution Office, Prague, 1984.)

7. Válková, H. et al., *Mimosoudni alternativa pro delikventni mladez projekt* (Judicial alternative for delinquent youth project), Institute for State and Law of the Czechoslovak Academy of Sciences, Prague, 1991; and Válková, H. and Kopoldova, B., *Prve zkusenosti z prazskeho experimentu mimosoudniho narovnani* (Non-judicial mediation experiment – First experiences from Prague), Nadace Klic, Ceska Lipa,1996.

8. Kawamura, G., "Arbeitschritte bei der praktischen Durchführung des Täter-Opfer-Ausgleichs, in *Arbeitsgruppe TOA-Standards*, 1989, pp. 23-32; and Herz, R., "Dekonstruktivismus im Jugendstrafrecht.Täter-Opfer-Ausgleich", *Mschr. Krim.*, 74, 1991, pp. 80-89.

9. Jesionek, U., "Die Konfliktregelung im neuen österreichischen Jugendrecht", in *Festschrift für Pallin*, Manz Verlag, Vienna, 1989, pp. 161-181.

experiments in so-called "diversions from criminal proceedings", applied first of all to juvenile and young adult delinquents. The same procedure was chosen by the Czech authors, who concentrated initially on juvenile offenders only because, like their foreign colleagues, they assumed a higher degree of acceptance in relation to this age-group from the general public and the media.

Even if the authors' efforts were confined initially to experimental work within the capital city of Prague, the project offered, probably for the first time in Czechoslovakia, a different response to a criminal act committed by a delinquent (youth). Instead of being only the object of a sentence imposed by the state, a juvenile offender plays the active role of someone who can still, through his or her behaviour, rectify, even if only partially, the consequences of his or her act with which he or she is confronted while facing the victim. Also for the first time a witness/injured party becomes a participant whose purely subjective experiences, feelings and needs can be completely or at least partially addressed. The third party – an expert who is not involved in the conflict, later called a mediator – enters into the negotiation process in order to maximise the benefits and minimise risks involved when the offender comes face to face with the victim.

From the start the experiment elicited two opposite approaches. On the one hand, the project was welcomed by the protagonists of new approaches in dealing with juvenile offenders and, on the other, it came up against the barriers of lack of understanding and critical comments from the experts who, at workshops organised to disseminate the project, drew attention to the fact that its implementation constituted an unacceptable violation of the legality according to which the investigative, prosecuting and adjudicating bodies had to unconditionally initiate criminal proceedings of their own motion in all cases where a criminal act had been committed. Since the Czech law of criminal procedure did not recognise, the principle of discretionary prosecution,the rule of law was being violated in the opinion of some experts.[10] The solution, fortunately, came relatively quickly. In 1993 the Criminal Procedure Act was amended and the new instrument of conditional termination of criminal prosecution was introduced.[11] After that, in the second half of the 1990s, other alternatives followed: mediation,[12] community service orders,[13] conditional discharge with supervision,[14] suspended sentences with supervision[15] and, finally in 2001, a special form of effective repentance leading, in the case of a juvenile offenders, to the extinction of liability (criminal responsibility) for an offence.[16]

---

10. Such comments are voiced also by renowned experts such as D. Cisarova from the Law Faculty at Charles University in Prague, who warns against rash implementation of a project that is in her opinion *contra legem*.
11. Articles 307-308, Law No. 292/1993 Coll., effective from 1 January 1994.
12. Articles 309-314, Law No. 152/1995 Coll., effective from 1 September 1995.
13. Articles 45-45a, Law No. 152/1995 Coll., effective from 1 January 1996.
14. Article 26, Law No. 253/1997 Coll., effective from 1 January 1998.
15. Article 60a, Law No. 253/1997 Coll., effective from 1 January 1998.
16. Article 65, paragraph 2, Law No. 265/2001 Coll., effective from 1 January 2002.

This step confers *ex post facto* legitimacy on the reform efforts of the early 1990s when the removal of the danger posed to society by a criminal act was used to justify the termination of criminal proceedings against a young offender. Moreover, in 2001, the new instrument of conditional release with supervision was introduced (similar to the concept of parole), as a result of which a decline in the high number of prisoners, together with other factors, can be observed.[17]

The efforts to change policy on juvenile crime, which played a Trojan horse role in the rigid system of a conservative criminal justice in the early 1990s, can be said to have triggered reforms in the area of new methods of dealing with offenders. Other reasons for this success – at least as regards the alternatives to criminal prosecution and traditional criminal sanctions – have to be sought elsewhere. A lucky coincidence played a key role in this development.

Beginnings and development of the Probation and Mediation Service

As early as 1990, a well-known sociologist and journalist, Jirina Siklova, developed a new curriculum programme called "social work" at the Faculty of Philosophy of Charles University in Prague. Later on she also became a guarantor of the programme as Head of Department. In 1993, a course of lectures entitled "Social work and criminal policy" was launched within this department, focusing on a critical analysis of present (mostly unsuccessful) efforts to bring under control, through sanctions traditionally oriented towards repression, a crime rate that had been escalating since the beginning of the 1990s, and the interpretation of recent trends in this field in other countries. In 1994 the lecturers and students on this course set up an association called "Association for Social Work Development in the Field of Criminal Justice" (hereinafter abbreviated to ASWDCJ), whose title reflected relatively accurately the purpose of this initiative.[18]

The founders' enthusiasm brought the first fruits: projects involving experimental verification of new alternative ways of settling criminal cases: judicial aid, non-judicial negotiation, mediation and probation.

It was necessary to gain the trust and support of the justice system to be able to implement these projects. The first seminars organised by the ASWDCJ with the aim of promoting the projects among criminal judges and state prosecutors took place in summer 1994. Legislation staff at the Ministry of Justice were also targeted. The practitioners who make decisions about criminal acts in practice and the legislative experts responsible for preparing a new codification of criminal law in the Czech Republic began to support "the idea of alternatives". This

---

17. Article 63, paragraph 1, Law No. 265/2001 Coll., effective from 1 January 2002.

18. The association was registered by the Ministry of the Interior on 26 May 1994. The founder members were the students attending the course of lectures on "Social work and criminal policy". The first probation officers were subsequently recruited from among them.

process culminated in the adoption of a governmental resolution[19] requiring the Minister of Justice to explore experimentally the possibility of introducing a new system of probation officers by the end of 1995. These positions have now been created in most district courts and in some regional courts since 1 January 1996, but they are very rarely filled by specialised social workers. This often leads to purely formal execution of probation activities (reduction of work to administrative and technical aspects) and subsequent justified criticism of insufficient qualification of these officers, who are often recruited from the court's own administrative staff. Fortunately, it is obvious that there is a huge difference between the results of "probation work" done by court officials and really qualified probation activity carried out by specialised social workers. The ASWDCJ repeatedly called and submitted proposals for the adoption of a new law that would eliminate the present lack of clarity concerning the responsibilities and functions of probation officers, and would introduce strict qualification requirements for this position and a related training programme.

Negotiations with a view to the preparation of this law began in May 1997 and were conducted in close co-operation with the Ministry of Justice. The government approved its concept (intent) in June 1999 and parliament approved it as Law No. 257/2000 Coll. on the Probation and Mediation Service (hereinafter abbreviated as PMS) on 14 July 2000, effective from 1 January 2001. Thus, the prerequisites for the qualified execution of existing alternative procedures and sanctions in criminal cases were finally introduced and the conditions for the adoption of other new laws were created. A current reform of youth criminal law is a good example of this.

In winter 2001, parliament was discussing a draft law on juvenile justice at first reading. However, given the upcoming political elections (June 2002) and the lack of will to enforce it, its adoption was temporarily postponed.[20] A new government submitted the same draft law within a relatively short time, on 22 January 2003, to a newly elected parliament – with virtually the same wording, since the omission of the young adults category from the competence of a proposed juvenile court represents the only substantial change. The new Juvenile Justice Act No. 218/2003 Coll. was passed by the Czech Parliament on 25 June 2003 and came into force on 1 January 2004. The provisions relating to the wide powers of the PMS in juvenile cases were not changed. These provisions state the cases in which probation officers not only exercise supervision over young people but also participate in the execution of rehabilitation, and protective and criminal policy measures. They also implement supervision and educational measures in respect of delinquent children without criminal liability

---

19. Resolution No. 341 of the Czech Government of 15 June 1994.
20. For a detailed comparison, see Válková, H., "Jugendstrafrechtsreform in Tschechien in Sicht?", *Mschr. Krim.*, 84, 2001, pp. 396-409; and Válková, H., "Tschechische Republik", in Albrecht, H.-J. and Kilchling, M. (eds.), *Jugendstrafrecht in Europa*, Max-Planck-Institut für ausländisches und internationales Strafrecht, Freiburg, pp. 437-453.

(under 15 years) whose illegal acts would be defined as criminal acts if they were adults. The increasing importance of the PMS is also reflected in the basic principles of the new law that clearly assert the key role of judges, state prosecutors, probation officers and defending counsels specialising in juvenile cases. Social workers appear for the first time, in the new law on juvenile justice, on an equal legislative footing with other representatives of the criminal justice system.

This change of perception of the probation officer's role within the system of criminal justice has had an indirect positive influence on his or her professional and social status. In future, probation officers will no longer be perceived solely as the executors of decisions of other judicial bodies, but will become their partners whose specific expertise is respected also by traditional (conservative) legal professions. This may be another factor speeding up the application of alternative sanctions and procedures in the Czech criminal justice system.

The results achieved by the PMS in its first two years of existence

PMS centres recorded a total of 29 291 new cases in the Czech Republic in 2002. This means an increase of more than one third in comparison with 2001 (19 214), as emerges from the report[21] drawn up at the beginning of 2003. Out of the total number of cases recorded in 2002, 8% (2 267) were cases involving juvenile offenders and around 2.6% (765) were drug-related cases. The PMS analysis shows that cases where the probation service intervenes at the time of enforcement of a sanction still account for a high proportion, while cases settled by the probation service during the pre-trial proceedings or during the trial (namely, before the court decision) are not represented so often (around one fifth). The community service order as an instrument of sentence execution accounted for nearly 70% of all alternative sanctions secured by the probation officers. The most frequent PMS activity during the period after the court decision became effective was supervision and monitoring of compliance with obligations and restrictions imposed by criminal courts under the provisions relating to suspended sentence (similar to probation), conditional release (similar to parole), conditional termination of criminal prosecution and conditional discharge (28%). A positive aspect is that in 2002 there was a considerable reduction in the number of cases where the PMS was forced to restrict its involvement to formal queries concerning the behaviour of the accused within the probationary period of his or her suspended sentence, where probationary supervision had not been imposed on the accused. Thus, the necessary capacity was freed up for the execution of more qualified and more time-consuming activities related mainly to the execution of probationary supervision.

---

21. "Comments on the statistical evaluation of the activities of Probation and Mediation Service Centres in the Czech Republic for 2002", Czech Republic PMS Headquarters, Ref. No. PM/168/2003.

In the area of pre-trial proceedings and judicial proceedings, the probation offi-cers spent most of their time gathering and analysing the essential material necessary for the application for conditional termination of criminal prosecution (approximately 55% of their activity at this stage of criminal proceedings). The next most frequent activity was processing the data of the probation reports as a basis for the court's decision on the imposition of an appropriate sanction (approximately 16.5%). The area of the material preparation needed for the court's decision on an alternative to a custodial sentence saw the most signifi-cant growth. The increasing volume of work of the probation officer with his or her client in the context of supervision imposed as an alternative to a custo-dial sentence was closely related to that. The amendment to the Criminal Procedure Act on reducing the use of custodial sentences has played a major role in this and, starting from 1 January 2002, has opened up further possibili-ties for using alternatives to custodial sentences.

The report analysing the probation service's first two years of activity in the Czech Republic shows a clear shift in the evaluation of the relations between the two most important institutions for the PMS – the courts and the state prosecution offices. While in 2001 only the co-operation between the pro-bation service and the courts could basically be described as good, in 2002 co-operation with the state prosecution offices was gradually extended and improved, although significant differences persist from one district to another. The year 2003 is described in the report as a period during which the PMS would focus also on fostering co-operation with police bodies with the objec-tive of intensifying its activities in the early stages of criminal prosecution. This assessment is related to the fact that judges themselves initiated probation activity in pre-trial proceedings and judicial proceedings in 42% of cases in 2002, while the state prosecution offices were more passive (21%). In 2002 the number of applications initiated by the accused themselves increased consider-ably (22%). As for the stage of sentence execution, which is solely within the jurisdiction of the courts, it is logical that 96% of applications for probation in the context of an alternative sentence or conditional release from prison with supervision were initiated by them. As compared with 2001, the number of applications initiated by the accused themselves also increased, especially by persons seeking conditional released from prison in this way.

The above-mentioned analysis indicates that the PMS expects to see a signifi-cant increase in the coming years in the number of cases where it is asked to take over a case not just at the sentence execution stage, but at the early stages of criminal proceedings. This trend should be accompanied by a corresponding strengthening of the PMS, giving it the organisational structure needed to handle the expected increase in its workload with the appropriate degree of professionalism. In connection with the above-mentioned statistical data show-ing a decrease in the number of prisoners, there are currently around 10 000 prison officers and it is necessary to ask whether, in its current situation, the PMS (approximately 250 probation officers) will be able to tackle demanding tasks successfully in future without a transfer of financial resources from the prison system to the area of alternative sentences and an increase in the staffing of probation centres. If this does not happen, it will be necessary to increase the funds allocated to the justice system in order to cover a sufficient number of probation officers.

New codification of criminal law and planned changes in the area of criminal sanctions

Currently, in accordance with the legislative plan, a general part of the criminal law arranged in sections has been prepared and is being discussed within the commission of experts appointed by the Minister of Justice to draft a new criminal law.[22] As opposed to the criminal law of 1961, which is still in force, the draft mainly specifies the content of non-custodial sanctions on the basis of existing experience. Under the draft, where a criminal act has been committed, the courts may impose sentences and protective measures, which, with some exceptions, are no different from the present sanctions (in the list below those sanctions that are not covered by the existing criminal law are shown in italics):

Sentences

(a) imprisonment
(b) *house arrest*
(c) community service order
(d) loss of honorary titles and awards
(e) loss of military rank
(f) prohibition on engaging in professional activities
(g) forfeiture of property
(h) financial punishment
(i) confiscation of belongings
(j) deportation
(k) prohibition of residence

Protective measures

(a) protective in-patient treatment
(b) *institutional detention*
(c) loss of belongings
(d) institutional education for juveniles

Without going into further details concerning individual sanctions, it is obvious from the list that the draft does not contemplate extending the existing system with new sanctions (only house arrest was added to the sentences, and the long-awaited, controversial instrument of institutional detention was added to the protective measures). In our opinion, this fact cannot be seen as a shortcoming of the draft but rather as the consequence of positive experience with the new sanctions introduced in the criminal law, as mentioned above, by means of numerous amendments during the 1990s. Clarification and removal of some partial defects will be sufficient for incorporation of the present modernised system of criminal sanctions into a new codification of criminal law.

---

22. Draft new criminal law, general part (Articles 36-118, criminal sanctions), Ministry of Justice, Prague, 27 January 2003, No. 946/01-L/25.

At the legislative level this can be perceived as one of the indirect outcomes of the Czech Republic's successful move from prison sentences to alternative sanctions.

In conclusion

Assessing the development of the Czech Republic from the time of the "great amnesty" by the President of the Republic at the beginning of 1990, when the prison gates were opened and around 16 000 prisoners (both sentenced and remanded in custody) were, without any previous preparation and with all the related consequences, set free,[23] we can, on the one hand, be satisfied with the surprisingly favourable results in the enforcement of alternative sanctions and procedures replacing the prison sentences that were embedded in the criminal law. On the other hand, we can be disappointed with the rather cumbersome or lethargic approach of some justice institutions, mainly the Ministry of Justice, in terms of securing the practical application of this new criminal policy. If it were not for the enthusiasm of the first pioneers of alternative responses to the rising crime rate (which reached astronomic levels in the Czech Republic as in other post-communist countries during the 1990s, as compared with the period before 1989), it is very hard to imagine that in the course of one decade it would have been possible to change criminal policy in the way in which the reformers finally succeeded.

However, these conclusions have to be viewed with a certain degree of reserve since the assessment covers only a short period of time. The danger of going the "American way", that is "from probation back towards prison", has still not been definitively averted in the Czech Republic, since even here we hear in the media and in parliamentary circles the "strong voices" of those who think that they have discovered an efficient, quick and reliable prescription for a definite solution to the crime problem, by applying strictly repressive measures (longer sentences, criminalisation of acts of negligence in the commercial field, lowering of the age of criminal liability, reduction in the rights of the accused and sentenced, etc.). However, we can say that so far these efforts have always been successfully neutralised and opposite trends have been set in motion. This topic would warrant a sociological study that should, in addition to the statistical data and legal analysis, also be based on public opinion poll results since these point to an interesting development in the attitudes of the Czech public, including opinions on the crime rate and the possible sanctions.[24]

---

23. For details, see Válková, H., Cernikova, V. and Meclova, K., "The Czech Republic", in Zyl Smit, D.V. and Duenkel, F. (eds.), *Imprisonment today and tomorrow,* second edition, Kluwer Law International, The Hague, London, Boston, 2001, pp. 151-174.
24. For details, see Burianek, J., "Bezpecnostni rizika a jejich percepce ceskou verejnosti" (Security risk and its perception in the eyes of the Czech Public), *Sociologicky Casopis,* Vol. 37, No. 1, 2001, pp. 43-64.

Appendix I

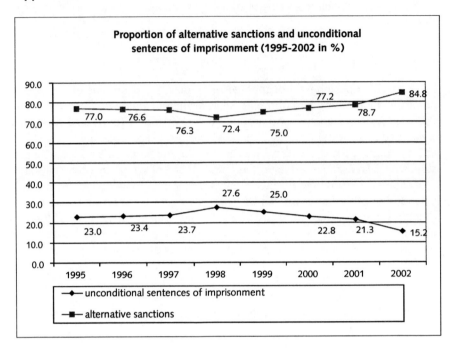

Appendix II

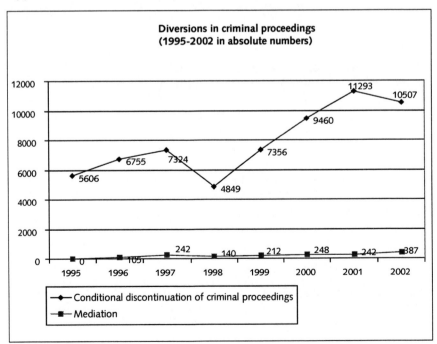

Appendix III

Sanction policy applied by criminal courts between 1995 and 2002

Year	1995	%	1996	%	1997	%	1998	%	1999	%	2000	%	2001	%	2002	%
Type of sanction																
Convicted persons in total	54 957	100	57 974	100	59 777	100	54 083	100	62 594	100	63 211	100	60 182	100	65 099	100
Convicted women	4 588	8.4	5 245	9	5 416	9.1	4 696	8.7	6 226	9.9	6961	11	6 792	11	7 812	12
Principal sanction imposed*	54 583		57 189		58 792		53 045		61 482		61 861		58 853		63 475	
Absolute discharge	8 02	1.5	844	1.5	826	1.4	473	0.9	506	0.8	539	0.9	550	1	589	0.9
Discharge with supervision	0	0	0	0	0	0	18	0.03	82	0.1	92	0.1	118	0.2	131	0.2
Discharge and imposed medical treatment	49	0.1	64	0.1	52	0.1	55	0.1	67	0.1	77	0.1	77	0.1	66	0.1
Discharge and imposed institutional educational treatment	1	0.002	0	0	0	0	2	0.004	7	0.01	13	0.02	10	0	2	0.003
Financial punishment imposed separately	4 978	9.1	4 734	8.3	4 703	8	2 634	5	3 370	5.5	3 571	5.8	3 324	5.6	3500	5.5
Community service order	0	0	722	1.3	1 602	2.7	1 778	3.4	3 218	5.2	7 086	11.5	8 838	15	13424	21.1
Suspended sentence	35 731	65.5	37 021	64.7	37 190	63.3	32 780	61.8	37 597	61.2	34 864	56.4	31 891	54	33 435	52.7
Suspended sentence with supervision	0	0	0	0	0	0	279	0.5	591	1.0	753	1.2	926	1.6	1 505	2.4
Other punishment** imposed separately	470	0.9	429	0.8	486	0.8	370	0.7	704	1.1	752	1.2	586	1	1 165	1.8
Unconditional sentence of imprisonment (in total)	12 552	23	13 375	23.4	13 933	23.7	14 656	27.6	15 340	25.0	14 114	22.8	12 533	21.3	9 658	15.2
Duration:																
Up to 1 year	7 722	61.5	8 290	62.0	8 760	62.9	8 987	61.3	9 926	64.7	9 365	66.4	8 407	67.1	5 826	60.3
Over 1 year and up to 15 years	4 313	34.4	4 502	33.7	4 562	32.7	4 951	33.8	4 728	30.8	4 129	29.3	3 563	28.4	3 291	34.1
Over 5 years and up to 15 years	506	4.0	555	4.1	588	4.2	700	4.8	671	4.4	603	4.3	547	4.4	535	5.5
Over 15 years and up to 25 years	11	0.1	26	0.2	20	0.1	17	0.1	11	0.1	15	0.1	15	0.1	2	0.02
Life sentence	0		4		3		1		4		2	0.0	1		4	0.04

* A sanction is a sentence, absolute discharge or protective measure (medical treatment or institutional educational treatment) imposed on the convicted person.

** Other punishment includes interdiction to undertake professional activities, confiscation of belongings, prohibition of residence, deportation and forfeiture of property.

Source: Statistical data of the Czech Ministry of Justice, Prague, 1995-2002.

Appendix IV

Sanction policy applied by criminal courts between 1995 and 2002 in respect of adults (18 years and older)

Year	1995	%	1996	%	1997	%	1998	%	1999	%	2000	%	2001	%	2002	%
Type of sanction																
Convicted persons in total	48 765	100	51 735	100	53 354	100	49 468	100	57 873	100	58 959	100	56 270	100.0	61 151	100
Convicted women	4 266	8.7	4 847	9.4	5 012	9.4	4 460	9	5915	10.2	6 651	11.3	6 487	11.5	7 552	12.3
Principal sanction imposed*	48 431		51 085		52 544		48 558		56 885		57 758		55 097		59 698	
Absolute discharge	271	0.6	320	0.6	324	0.6	186	0.4	219	0.4	275	0.5	263	0.5	293	0.5
Discharge with supervision	0	0	0	0	0	0	10	0.02	27	0.05	26	0.05	24	0.04	41	0.1
Discharge and imposed medical treatment	44	0.1	54	0.1	43	0.1	49	0.1	61	0.1	67	0.1	60	0.1	55	0.1
Discharge and imposed institutional educational treatment	0	0	0	0	0	0	0	0	0	0	0	0	0	0	0	0
Financial punishment imposed separately	4 847	10	4 635	9.1	4 625	8.8	2 611	5.4	3 351	5.9	3 553	6.2	3 316	6.0	3 495	5.9
Community service order	0	0	596	1.2	1 388	2.6	1 629	3.4	2 970	5.2	6 534	11.3	8 181	14.8	12 598	21.1
Suspended sentence	31 165	64.3	32 475	63.6	32 625	62.1	29 428	60.6	34 220	60.2	32 197	55.7	29 630	53.8	31 323	52.5
Suspended sentence with supervision	0	0	0	0	0	0	250	0.5	521	0.9	699	1.2	848	1.5	1 339	2.2
Other punishment** imposed separately	440	0.9	404	0.8	460	0.9	358	0.7	686	1.2	725	1.3	569	1.0	1 150	1.9
Unconditional sentence of imprisonment (in total)	11 664	24.1	12 601	24.7	13 079	24.9	14 037	28.9	14 830	26.1	13 682	23.7	12 206	22.2	9 404	15.8
Duration:																
Up to 1 year	7 159	61.40	7 787	61.80	8 192	62.60	8 587	61.20	9 585	64.60	9 067	66.3	8 187	67.1	5 651	60.1
Over 1 year and up to 15 years	3 993	34.20	4 239	33.60	4 284	32.80	4 736	33.70	4 566	30.80	3 995	29.2	3 456	28.3	3 213	34.2
Over 5 years and up to 15 years	501	4.30	547	4.30	580	4.40	696	5.00	664	4.50	603	4.4	547	4.5	534	5.7
Over 15 years and up to 25 years	11	0.10	26	0.20	20	0.20	17	0.10	11	0.10	15	0.1	15	0.1	2	0.02
Life sentence	0		2	0.02	3	0.02	1	0.01	4		2	0.01	1	0.01	4	0.04

* A sanction is a sentence, absolute discharge or protective measure (medical treatment or institutional educational treatment) imposed on the convicted person.

** Other punishment includes interdiction to undertake professional activities, confiscation of belongings, prohibition of residence, deportation and forfeiture of property.

Source: Statistical data of the Czech Ministry of Justice, Prague, 1995-2002.

Appendix V

Sanction policy applied by criminal courts between 1995 and 2002 in respect of juveniles (15-17 years old)

Year	1995	%	1996	%	1997	%	1998	%	1999	%	2000	%	2001	%	2002	%
Type of sanction																
Convicted persons in total	6 192	100	6 239	100	6 423	100	4 615	100	4 721	100	4 252	100	3 912	100	3 948	100
Convicted women	322	5.2	398	6.4	404	6.3	236	5.1	311	6.6	310	7.3	305	7.8	260	6.6
Principal sanction imposed*	6 152		6 104		6 248		4 487		4 597		4 103		3 754		3 777	
Absolute discharge	531	8.6	524	8.6	502	8	287	6.4	287	6.2	264	6.4	287	7.6	296	7.8
Discharge with supervision	0	0	0	0	0	0	8	0.2	55	1.2	66	1.6	94	2.5	90	2.4
Discharge and imposed medical treatment	5	0.1	10	0.2	9	0.1	6	0.1	6	0.1	10	0.2	17	0.5	11	0.3
Discharge and imposed institutional educational treatment	1	0.02	0	0	0	0	2	0.04	7	0.2	13	0.3	8	0.2	2	0.1
Financial punishment imposed separately	131	2.1	99	1.6	78	1.2	23	0.5	19	0.4	18	0.4	8	0.2	5	0.1
Community service order	0	0	126	2.1	214	3.4	149	3.3	248	5.4	552	13.5	657	17.5	826	21.9
Suspended sentence	4 566	74.2	4 546	74.5	4 565	73.1	3 352	74.7	3 377	73.5	2 667	65	2 261	60.2	2 112	55.9
Suspended sentence with supervision	0	0	0	0	0	0	29	0.6	70	1.5	54	1.3	78	2.1	166	4.4
Other punishment** imposed separately	30	0.5	25	0.4	26	0.4	12	0.3	18	0.4	27	0.7	17	0.5	15	0.4
Unconditional sentence of imprisonment (in total)	888	14.4	774	12.7	854	13.7	619	13.8	510	11.1	432	10.5	327	8.7	254	6.7
Duration:																
Up to 1 year	563	63.4	503	65	568	66.5	400	64.6	341	66.9	298	69	220	67.3	175	68.9
Over 1 year and up to 15 years	320	36	263	34	278	32.6	215	34.7	162	31.8	134	31	107	32.7	78	30.7
Over 5 years and up to 10 years	5	0.6	8	1	8	0.9	4	0.6	7	1.4	0	0	0	0	1	0.4

* A sanction is a sentence, absolute discharge or protective measure (medical treatment or institutional educational treatment) imposed on the convicted person.

** Other punishment includes interdiction to undertake professional activities, confiscation of belongings, prohibition of residence, deportation and forfeiture of property.

Source: Statistical data of the Czech Ministry of Justice, Prague, 1995-2002.

Chapter 8

Imprisonment for non-payment of fines in Sweden

Hanns von Hofer

This article deals with the practical abolition of imprisonment for non-payment of fines (namely, a prison sentence replacing an unpaid fine) in Sweden and demonstrates that alternative provisions need not necessarily have a negative influence on honest payment of fines. It also attempts to place the *de facto* abolition of imprisonment for non-payment of fines in Sweden in a historical and crime policy context.

As in the other Scandinavian countries, fines in Sweden[1] are of major significance as a penal sanction. In the year 2000, according to official crime statistics, over 70 000 fines were imposed. In addition to these there were approximately 200 000 financial penalties imposed mainly by the police for minor traffic offences. This makes fines the most frequent form of sanction in Sweden, in absolute terms. Fines are also used to a considerable extent for young people between the ages of 15 and 20, with fines being imposed on more than half of all young offenders.

Following the example of Finland, since the 1930s fines have been imposed as day-fines in order to ensure a socially equitable sentencing profile. Under this system, the severity of the crime determines the number of days and the offender's income is used to determine the size of the fine. The number of days can be between 30 and 200, and amounts range from 30 to 1 000 Swedish kronor (namely, between approximately €3 and €100; for further details, see Svensson 1995).

Legal regulation of the collection of fines

The collection of fines and penalties is regulated in the Act on Enforcement of Fines[2] and the Fines Enforcement Ordinance.[3]

---

1.   Since I cannot avail myself of Swedish legal language, I ask the reader to treat all my terminology as colloquial usage rather than *termini technici* with direct equivalents in other legal systems. The status of legislation up to 30 June 2004 is taken into account.
2.   Law of 1979, 189.
3.   Ordinance of 1979, 197.

After final judgment, the defendant receives a payment form from the central police authority which is responsible for the collection process. If the offender pays up promptly, that is the end of the matter. If payment is not forthcoming, the central police authority passes the matter on to the enforcement service to pursue collection. Organisationally, the enforcement service in Sweden is part of the tax administration rather than the judicial system.

The enforcement service initiates collection by sending a demand for payment. An enquiry is then conducted into the economic circumstances of the debtor in order to gain a complete picture of suitable collection measures. According to the provisions of the Act on Collection of Public Debts[4] the enforcement service can grant a respite to pay and produce an instalment schedule. The instalment schedule can be revoked if the debtor does not adhere to its terms.

If further collection measures appear futile or the costs of collection are disproportionate to the sum of money outstanding, collection may be provisionally halted where the public interest does not demand further action.

Collection can be completely halted if it would cause extreme hardship to the debtor or another person dependent upon the debtor, and where this does not contravene the public interest. The limitation period for collection of fines is five years.

A prison sentence for non-payment is only passed if the debtor evades his obligations to pay with intent to deceive. According to the preparatory work for the legislation, this is the case if the debtor deliberately takes steps to evade collection – for instance by signing sham contracts, constantly changing jobs or the like. However, there is also sufficient cause if a general assessment of the debtor's standard of living and other personal circumstances suggest that the debtor is deliberately attempting to evade his obligation to pay. The burden of proof in both cases rests with the state prosecution authorities. Finally, imprisonment for non-payment can also be considered if the public interest demands it in particular cases. According to the preparatory work, this is intended to cover "flagrant" cases of repeat offending, or cases in which the offender's inability to pay would practically equate to an "immunity to sanctioning" (SOU 1995, p. 67).

According to the provisions of the Fines Enforcement Ordinance, it is the role of the enforcement service to initiate proceedings for imprisonment of fine defaulters. This agency must examine whether the conditions for a prison sentence in default of payment are met. If this is found to be the case, the prosecution service is informed, which in turn examines whether the matter should be brought to court. If circumstances require it, the prosecution service can instigate further enquiries by means of a formal preliminary investigation procedure.

---

4. Law of 1993, 891.

The court panel reaches its decision in proceedings to which both the debtor and the prosecutor are called, culminating in a judgment in simplified form. The decision can also be made in the absence of the debtor, however, if the facts of the case have been sufficiently established. The court judgment will consist of either a rejection of the prosecutor's application or a prison sentence of between fourteen days and a maximum of three months. The prison term is not determined in relation to the sum of money owed but is governed by the severity of the default. In practice the usual term is between fourteen days and one month. Appeals against the court's judgment are permissible.

The prison sentence for non-payment is not carried out if the debtor pays the entire fine before commencement of the sentence. If the sentence has already begun, the offender is to be released as soon as full payment has been made. The limitation period for imprisonment of fine defaulters is three years.

Use of imprisonment for non-payment of fines in practice

From the legal description of the procedure, it is apparent that although Sweden retains imprisonment for non-payment of fines as a sanction, its detailed conditions have been made very restrictive. Furthermore, where it is applied, the sentence imposed is on the clement side. What is not clear from the above description, however, is how often prison sentences are actually used for fine defaulters. Up-to-date statistical data are not available, which is associated with the fact that current practice – in harmony with the intentions of the legislature – has reduced the use of imprisonment for fine defaulters to an absolute minimum. The last available data relate to the years 1991 and 1992 (SOU 1995, pp. 68-69). In 1991 there were eight sentences of imprisonment for non-payment of fines, of which one was commuted on appeal to a higher instance; in 1992 there were six such proceedings, in two of which the application of the prosecution service was rejected. Nor do the prison statistics yield any further data indicating sentencing to imprisonment for non-payment of fines. Here the most recent data relate to the year 1983 (RSÅ 1985, p. 113). In that year, nine people were recorded as commencing new prison terms.

For all practical purposes, therefore, imprisonment for non-payment of fines is as good as abolished. This means that Sweden – even in the Scandinavian context – occupies a special status. In all the other Scandinavian countries, imprisonment is used for fine defaulters (Sveri 1998).[5] What made this development possible in Sweden?

---

5. In the year 2001 the average daily occupancy in Denmark was 49 prisoners, in Finland 102 prisoners (31 December) and in Norway 43 prisoners (year 2000). In a recent unpublished paper, Gray (2002) describes the use and enforcement of fines in England and Wales, Scotland, Northern Ireland, Canada, Denmark, Germany, the Netherlands, Sweden, New Zealand, Australia and Israel.

The history of reform

In the year 1969, having just taken up office as Minister of Justice, Lennart Geijer convened a state commission which was appointed to explore the possibilities of complete abolition of imprisonment for non-payment of fines. The late 1960s and early 1970s were eventful years in the modern history of Swedish penal law. At that time – as in other countries – imprisonment and the prison system had come under heavy criticism (see for instance Anttila 1971; Mathiesen 1974). Geijer himself took the view that the Swedish prison population, which numbered approximately 5 500 at that time, could be reduced in the future to 300-700 inmates.

The proposal to abolish imprisonment for non-payment of fines proceeded from a trajectory of development that had already been set in train earlier on in the history of Swedish penal law. Major reforms with regard to imprisonment of fine defaulters had been passed in the 1930s. At the core of these reforms were three important points:

- the possibility of payment in instalments was introduced;
- collection of fines by compulsory enforcement of payment (seizure of assets) became permissible;
- in cases where even seizure of assets would yield nothing, debts could be waived completely.

Whereas prior to 1939 more than 10 000 people per year were placed behind bars in Sweden as a result of unpaid fines, this figure rapidly fell to less than 500 instances of imprisonment per year thereafter.

The state commission of 1969 worked for six years. It put forward the proposal (SOU 1975, No. 55) to abolish imprisonment for non-payment of fines completely since empirical studies – undertaken on behalf of the commission – had shown that in general, honest payment of fines was widespread. Almost 90% of fines imposed were, in fact, paid. They also confirmed the criticism voiced in public debate that those embarking upon prison sentences for fine default, in practice, almost exclusively belonged to marginal groups in society. In accordance with the spirit of that particular era, this circumstance was perceived as "unjust" and implied the need for political action.

Two years later, the government – now a non-socialist coalition – responded with a proposed statute to strike imprisonment for fine defaulters from the statute book without replacement. However, the proposal was rejected by parliament since the majority feared that a small group of debtors would systematically evade any type of payment and thus bring the whole system of fines and their enforcement into disrepute. A new commission was appointed but its proposals were also rejected. Finally, an internal project group within the Ministry of Justice set about the task, and in the year 1983 – now once again under a social democratic government – their suggestions became the law which is still in force today. The problem of "immunity to sanctioning" was solved in that imprisonment for non-payment of fines, as such, was abolished. On the other hand, however, as described above, there was the threat of a prison sentence of between fourteen days and a maximum of three months for those who used deception to evade their obligation to pay or where "in other special cases the public interest demands it".[6]

This wording of the statute laid to rest the fears of the parliamentary majority that a small minority might exploit these liberal provisions. In reality, subsequent practice was to reveal that cases of that kind barely feature, as the extremely low number of sentences proves. Furthermore empirical data allowed the conclusion that even the general level of honest payment did not take a turn for the worse after the reform came into force. As before, some 90% of fines imposed actually found their way into the public coffers (SOU 1995, p. 55). Corresponding data for the present day are unfortunately not available. In the year 2000, incidentally, the sum total of fines collected amounted to around 350 million kronor (approximately €35 million).

Outlook

The abolition, to all intents and purposes, of imprisonment for non-payment of fines is strongly linked with general reform trends in the history of Swedish penal law. The first step in the 1930s came in the era in which the treatment-based approach made its breakthrough. The classical model had stated: "You have been sentenced to a fine. Pay up, otherwise you will be locked up – in proportion to the size of the fine." In contrast, treatment-based approaches opened up the perspective that non-payment of fines was not solely rooted in unwillingness to pay but might also have social causes. In such cases, for example, instalment schedules are a more appropriate alternative to a prison sentence. Another innovation was to make reference to ideas from civil law, as expressed by permitting compulsory collection by means of asset seizure. Finally, it suited the pragmatic vein in Swedish legal thinking to waive fines when collection appeared to be completely futile.

Furthermore, for the successful practical abolition of imprisonment for fine defaulters, it seems significant that the enforcement procedure is located firmly within the remit of the tax administration. By involving the enforcement service, which – as outlined – comes under the Swedish tax administration, the payment of fines has acquired clear fiscal and civil overtones, pushing the idea of penal retribution into the background. The social role of the enforcement service has incidentally developed a great deal further, which is clear from its central position in the process of so-called "debt relief", among other things. This process was introduced in Sweden – following the example set by other countries – in the mid-1990s and means that a private individual who finds himself in payment difficulties and cannot pay high debts within a manageable

---

6. Act on Enforcement of Fines (Law of 1979, 189), paragraph 15.

period of time can make an application for debt relief at the office of the enforcement service.[7]

Finally, another significant circumstance for the successful practical abolition of imprisonment for fine defaulters might have been that reform proposals came at a moment when penal repression was not a guiding light of public policy on crime, and crime policy as such had not yet become a focus for party political posturing. Neither condition remains the case now (Tham 2001). Nor are there vocal demands for current practice to be changed. Whereas other reforms from the 1970s and early 1980s have been wholly or partially reversed in the meantime – the abolition of juvenile imprisonment, for instance, or conditional release after serving half of a prison term – the practical abolition of imprisonment for non-payment of fines has demonstrably endured.

---

7. Law of 1993, 334.

References

Anttila, I., "Conservative and radical criminal policy in the Nordic countries", *Scandinavian Studies in Criminology*, 3, 1971, pp. 9-21.

Gray, C., "Use and enforcement of fines. MBU International note", unpublished paper, October 2002.

Mathiesen, T., "The politics of abolition. Essays in political action theory", Oslo, 1974.

RSÅ, *Rättsstatistisk årsbok 1985* (Legal statistics yearbook 1985), Statistiska Centralbyrån, Stockholm, 1985.

SOU, *No. 55: Bötesverkställighet. Betänkande avgivet av Förvandlingsstraffutredningen* (Enforcement of fines. Report of the committee on imprisonment for non-payment of fines), Stockholm, 1975.

SOU, *No. 91: Ett reformerat straffsystem. Del III. Bilagor. Betänkande av Straffsystemkommittén* (A reformed penal system. Report of the penal system committee. Part III. Appendices), Stockholm, 1995.

Svensson, B., "Criminal justice systems in Sweden", BRÅ report 1995: 1, Stockholm, 1995.

Sveri, K., "Incarceration for non-payment of a fine", in Albrecht, H.-J. et al. (eds.), *Internationale Perspektiven in Kriminologie und Strafrecht. Festschrift für Günther Kaiser* (International perspectives in criminology and penal law. Published in honour of Günther Kaiser), Berlin, 1998, pp. 681-690.

Tham, H., "Law and order as leftist project? The case of Sweden", *Punishment and Society*, 3, 2001, pp. 409-426.

Chapter 9

Reducing the population of fine defaulters in prisons: experiences with community service in Mecklenburg-Western Pomerania (Germany)

Frieder Dünkel

Fines as the predominant sanction in the German criminal justice system

The German penal law for adults provides for only a few sanctioning options. In general there are fines, suspended sentences (probation) and unconditional prison sentences (up to fifteen years or life sentences).

In 1969 the German system of penal sanctions was thoroughly overhauled by the "great reform of criminal law" of that year. This reform intended to strengthen the preventive purposes of punishment as opposed to its purely retributive aspects, and in this way to reduce the significance of imprisonment, in particular, as a form of punishment. Section 47 of the Penal Code (*Strafgesetzbuch* – StGB), which has been in force since then, provides for prison sentences of less than six months, but only if the offender's personality or the special circumstances of the offence require such a sanction in order to influence the offender or protect the legal order. Non-custodial sentences have absolute priority. They range from the dismissal of proceedings combined with the imposition of obligations (for example, compensation or an administrative fine), through pecuniary penalties coupled with a warning that further punishment may be imposed, to fines by the court and the suspension of the sentence on probation. Since 1969, the administration of justice has, to a great extent, put these epoch-making changes to the law into practice. Therefore, in comparison with non-custodial measures, the prison sentence currently plays only a minor role in the system of sanctions. Only about 6% of all sentences are unconditional prison terms, whereas fines (82%) and probation coupled with suspended sentences (12%) predominate. The fact that the prison sentence functions as an *ultima ratio* becomes even clearer if one also considers the informal decisions of the public prosecutors who dismiss, perhaps with the imposition of an administrative fine, almost 50% of all cases (mostly petty offences, but also cases of economic and environmental crimes, see Heinz 2002). All facts considered, one finds that prison sentences account for a mere 3% to 4% of all sanctions. Although the official crime rates have increased considerably during the last thirty years and the average length of prison sentences has also increased *(inter alia,* because of more violent crimes), the incarceration rates have not grown much until recently. Stability has been achieved by extending fines and suspended sentences, especially for property offenders.

Numerically the fine is the most important penal sanction as it is imposed in about 82% of all cases. The Penal Code has created a day-fine system in which one "day-fine" corresponds to one day spent in prison. Section 43 of the Penal Code provides for a maximum of 360 day-fines and for up to 720 day-fines in exceptional cases, such as an accumulation of offences. In practice, 96% of all fines do not exceed ninety day-fines. The amount imposed for a day depends on the financial capacity of the offender. Until the beginning of the 1990s, approximately 6% to 7% of the fines were converted into prison sentences because the fine was not paid (Kaiser 1997, p. 436). Since the early 1980s, "free work" (community service) may be substituted for imprisonment as an alternative to imprisonment for failing to pay a fine. Such a substitution may be made by the judicial administration.[1] Generally, the administration of this alternative is the duty of the social workers who are attached to the courts and who arrange for community service. One day-fine is regarded as the equivalent of six to eight hours of community service (for details see Kerner and Kästner 1986; Jehle, Feuerhelm and Block 1990; Feuerhelm 1997).

The crisis of the 1990s: economic problems of offenders ordered to pay fines and the increase of fine defaulters serving substitute prison sentences

Since the late 1980s the problem of fine defaulters has increased considerably, especially in the new federal states of the former German Democratic Republic (Dünkel and Grosser 1999; Dünkel, Scheel and Grosser 2002). In 1996 about 10% of all adult prisoners served a period of imprisonment in lieu of a fine *(Ersatzfreiheitsstrafe)*: in East Germany 13%, and in West German federal states 7% (Dünkel and Kunkat 1997). The number of admissions to prison in West Germany increased from 25 905 in 1980 to 29 503 in 1990 and not less than 50 586 in 1999, thus almost doubling within 20 years. The East German numbers show an even more dramatic increase from zero to more than 10 000 per year in 2000. The bad economic situation with concomitant high unemployment rates particularly in East Germany (about 20% against 10% in West Germany) is the main reason for this development.

This is the project's starting point, which has been developed under the special situation in Mecklenburg-Western Pomerania where, in 1996, 22% of prisoners in the adult prison system were only incarcerated because of non-payment

---

1. Section 293 of the Introductory Act to the Criminal Code (*Einführungsgesetz zum Strafgesetzbuch* – EGStGB).

of fines. The efforts to reorganise and intensify the social services arranging community service have been a major reform issue of the past five years in many federal states of Germany. A 1999 draft bill provided for the introduction of community service as an independent sanction (that is, not only as a substitute for fines). Another draft paper of the Federal Ministry of Justice wanted to extend community service as a substitute penalty to fines (Kommission zu Reform des Sanktionensystems 2000). In the same way, a draft bill from June 2002 proposed to facilitate community service before substitute imprisonment could take place. The newly elected "red-green" government has declared its readiness to follow this line. One important argument in the debate was the question of whether the social services would be able to organise such projects on a nationwide basis and whether offenders would respond to that offer. The project in Mecklenburg-Western Pomerania was seen as a pilot project that proved the practicability of organising community service and preventing detention for fine defaulters.

Problems of fine defaulters and shortfalls in the organisation of community service as a substitute for fines in German criminal law and practice

Fine defaulters in Germany represent a specific problematic group within the sentenced population. There are, on the one hand, people who are quite well integrated, but simply cannot afford the money requested by the imposed fine. Sometimes this is the result of a peculiarity of the German sentencing system: 70%-80% of all fines are not imposed after an oral hearing at court but after a written request of the Public Prosecutor who estimates income (which is essential in a day-fine system) according to the actual professional situation (this summary procedure is called *Strafbefehlsverfahren*). If the sentenced person is made unemployed or his or her financial situation deteriorates, it could be that the fine is too high and cannot be paid. If the offender is not properly informed about the possibilities of payment by instalments, he or she may go to prison. These relatively well-integrated people can be transferred to community service projects without many problems.

A second group of fine defaulters comprises people who – because of their personal problems and deficiencies – are not able to perform work in regular institutions that provide community work. These people often have alcohol problems, are not used to work because of long periods of unemployment, have problems in their social life, or are sometimes homeless and very unstable (see also Dolde 1999; Wirth 2000). Finally, a third group refuses all offers of community service.

All federal states in Germany dispose of institutions that should provide community service work for fine defaulters. In many cases, however, the only people involved are those attached to the prosecutorial office and those who

129

are not social workers. They offer community service (equivalent to the number of day-fines imposed) by writing a letter to the convicted offender as an alternative to detention. The shortfalls in the system are exposed if the offender does not react. In this case, he or she is taken by the police to prison, often without having been informed of the consequences of not taking up the offer. Only in a few federal states has some form of social work been implemented in order to transfer problematic fine defaulters to community service (see Jehle, Feuerhelm and Block 1990; Feuerhelm 1991 and 1997).

The project that was developed in Mecklenburg-Western Pomerania dealt with the first two groups mentioned above by motivating them, in a systematic way, to do community service instead of serving a substitute detention period. It started in October 1998 and finished its model stage at the end of 2000. Since the beginning of 2001 the project has been administered by the Ministry of Justice of Mecklenburg-Western Pomerania, which guarantees to pay for the costs of social workers attached to the project and for the special intensive proactive social case management.

The organisation of community service in Mecklenburg-Western Pomerania: developing special services for transfer and for treatment arrangements

Community service as a substitute for detention for fine defaulters in Mecklenburg-Western Pomerania was introduced in 1993. Its organisation through the prosecutorial administration has proved rather inefficient due to the problems mentioned above. The new model consists of three innovative "pillars": transfer to community service in two court districts is now organised by probation service social workers and in the two other districts by private organisations in the aftercare system. The second innovative aspect provides intensive care for those problematic fine defaulters who would otherwise not be able to perform community work. They are accompanied to work, sometimes receive special psychological or other treatment, etc. The third element is an administrative regulation of the Ministry of Justice to transfer even those who did not react before being sent to prison. So many fine defaulters after a few days' detention are released from prison by a pardon of the justice administration and transferred to community service.

When the project started in 1998 there were about 500 institutions that offered community work, at the end of the model stage the number of institutions increased to 1 616, 64 of them providing special care and treatment for persons with specific mental or other behavioural problems, for example alcoholics and the long-term unemployed. Institutions for community service are distributed all over the country. No fine defaulter therefore has to travel more than 30 km to get to a place where he or she can perform community service. This is a remarkable result as Mecklenburg-Western Pomerania is the federal state with the lowest population density in Germany (only 1.75 million inhabitants in 23 838 square kilometres). About one third of the institutions for community service are run by the municipalities, almost 50% by lay private organisations and 10% by the churches. The organisational structure of the transfer system for community service in Germany and the peculiarities in Mecklenburg-Western Pomerania can be seen in the following figure.

Figure 1: The execution of fines in Germany and in Mecklenburg-Western Pomerania

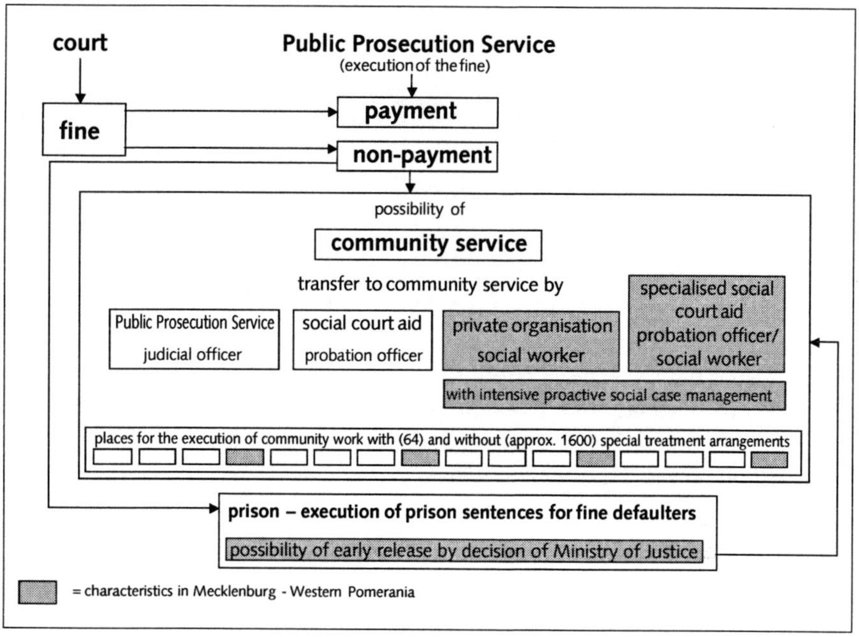

Results of the project: reducing the number of fine defaulters in prison and successful strategies for substitute community service

Since the beginning of the project the average number of fine defaulters in prison per day has been reduced from between 110 and 120 to between 50 and 60 (see Figure 2).

131

Figure 2: Fine defaulters serving prison sentences in Mecklenburg-Western Pomerania (1996-2002)

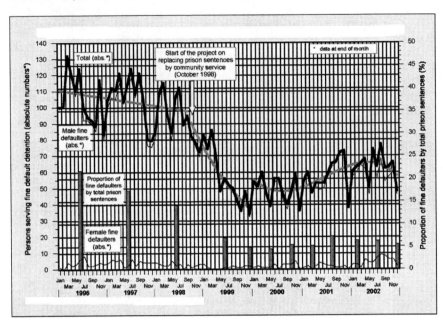

In other words, capacity for fine defaulters has been cut down by half. In 1996, 22% of prison capacity was taken up by fine defaulters, whilst between the beginning of 2000 and 2002 the percentage was reduced to between only 5% and 7% (see also Figure 3).

Figure 3: Proportion of fine defaulters in total prison population in Germany (1996 and 2002)

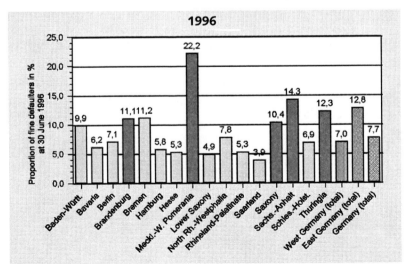

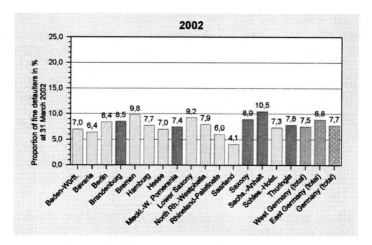

This positive result can also be seen in annual admissions to prison because of non-payment of fines: the number has been reduced by 27%. Only about 5% of fines end in substitute prison sentences, which is one of the lowest percentages in German federal states (see Table 1 below).

Table 1: Admissions to prison for fine defaulters by federal state (1998 and 2000)

Federal state	Admissions for fine defaulters in 1998	Admissions for fine defaulters in 2000	% change with respect to 1998
Baden-Württemberg	4 911	4 664	- 5.0
Bavaria	6 041	5 296	- 12.3
Berlin	4 843	5 317	+ 9.8
Bremen	1 236	1 026	- 17.0
Hamburg	2 994	2 757	- 7.9
Hesse	3 458	3 232	- 6.5
Lower Saxony	6 029	4 446	- 26.3
North Rhine-Westphalia	17 524	15 956	- 8.9
Rhineland-Palatinate	2 412	1 979	- 18.0
Saarland	507	357	- 29.6
Schleswig-Holstein	1 282	1 220	- 4.8
Old federal states total	51 237	46 250	- 9.7
Brandenburg	2 444	2 018	- 17.4
Mecklenburg-Western Pomerania	1 536	1 126	- 26.7
Saxony	3 719	3 655	- 1.7
Saxony-Anhalt	1 691	2 074	+ 22.7
Thuringia	1 590	1 464	- 7.9
New federal states total	10 980	10 337	- 5.9
Germany total	62 217	56 587	- 9.0

Source: Own calculations according to *Statistisches Bundesamt, Rechtspflege,* Fachserie 10, Reihe 4.2, Strafvollzug, 1998 and 2000, Table 1.3.

If we look at the files of those offenders ordered to pay a fine, the great majority – more than 90% – paid in full immediately after the conviction. Only between 1% and 2% of all fines ended in imprisonment, whereas the proportion of orders for community service increased continuously. This is seen in Figure 4, which shows that between 1999 and 2002 the number of transfers to community service doubled or almost tripled. A very interesting result is that in the court district of Stralsund the number is particularly high. This can be explained by the specific proactive case management in this district. Not only did the social workers there offer community work to the offenders, but they systematically visited them at home and tried to motivate them by personal contacts. This form of social casework seems to be the most effective one.

Figure 4: Transfers to community service in different districts of Mecklenburg-Western Pomerania (1996-2002)

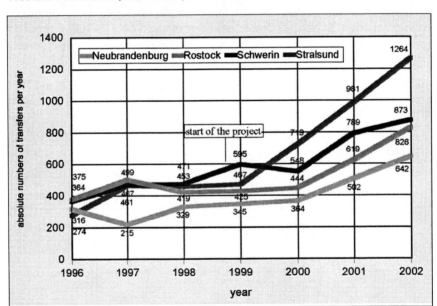

Transfer to an institution with or without special treatment and supervision was successful in most cases. Only 10.6% of those transferred did not appear at community work. Another 8.1% began to work, but then stopped. Interestingly, a relatively large proportion of those who agreed to perform community service later preferred to pay: 2.4% in full immediately after the agreement and another 10.9% in instalments. Some 11.5% started with community service, but later preferred to pay the remainder of the fine instead of working. The majority, however, performed community service in full as a substitute for detention. In total, more than 80% of fine defaulters succeeded in avoiding detention by either completing community service or finally paying at least part of the fine (see Figure 5). The proportion of cases not completing community

134

service or not appearing at all increased with the number of hours to work. With up to 180 hours of work, less than 5% stopped, whereas in the case of more than 540 hours it increased to 17%. Differences concerning fine debtors who never appeared at work followed the same trend. The range was from 6.5% (up to 90 hours) to 17% (more than 540 hours). This lends support to the idea of limiting the duration of community service and changing the number of hours for each day-fine from six to three, as has been proposed in the above-mentioned draft bills.

Figure 5: Payment of fines and execution of community service in Mecklenburg-Western Pomerania 1999-2001 (N=5.547)

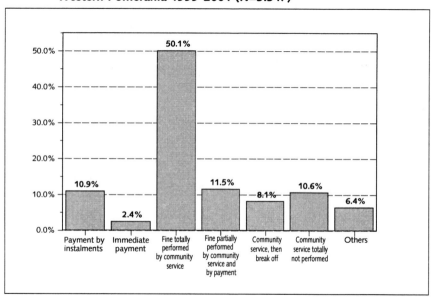

The transfer of very problematic cases (those with alcohol problems, difficulties in performing regular work, etc.) to one of sixty-four institutions providing special care and treatment had almost the same success rate as those not requiring special treatment. This indicates a good selection of problematic fine defaulters in need of special care.

The possibility of being transferred to a community service institution even after being arrested for substitute detention because of non-payment of a fine has also been a success. Some 55% of cases have been successfully completed by community service or payment (by instalments or otherwise). In 45% of the cases released from prison, the judicial pardon had to be revoked, one third of them because of other crimes, another third did not appear at the institution for community work and in the other cases offenders stopped attending. This can be judged as a success, as these cases were extremely difficult involving those with particular personal problems.

Costs and benefits of the project

The costs of the project were covered in the first three years by a private foundation[2] at Munich, and from the beginning of 2001 by the Ministry of Justice in Mecklenburg-Western Pomerania. The annual costs of the community service project consisted of the salaries of the mediators attached to the probation service or private organisations who transferred the offenders to the institutions that executed community service. Furthermore, the institutions providing special care and treatment were paid a certain sum of money for each case (€20 for managing ten hours of community service for each offender). The total costs were €330 000 per year (see in detail Dünkel, Scheel and Grosser 2002, p. 70).

The benefit of the project can be calculated by the money saved by avoiding use of prison capacity. On average at least fifty places were saved per day. The gross cost per day of one prison bed is about €80. However, as there was no cost saving for the prison staff, buildings, etc., the saving represents about €25 per day, which is the cost of food, work remuneration and insurance of prisoners. The total saving is therefore, 50 places for 365 days, namely €456 250.

In addition, one has to consider that the mediators succeeded in making the convicted agree not only to provide community service, but also in a number of cases to pay the fine in full or in part (which would not have been the case if the substitute detention order had been executed). According to the reports of the mediators this strategy represents about €150 000 of savings per year.

So the total benefit of the project in financial terms is about €600 000 per year against an annual cost of only €330 000. These numbers finally convinced the Ministry of Finance and since 2001 the costs have been provided by the budget of the federal state of Mecklenburg-Western Pomerania.

The importance of the project for general reform of German criminal law in extending community service as a criminal sanction

As mentioned before, for several years now German legislators have considered extending community service in the legal framework of penal law. Unlike most other European countries (see Albrecht and Schädler 1986; Cornils 1994; van Kalmthout 2001) it is felt that community service as an independent sanction would be problematic because of constitutional arguments concerning forced labour. Forced labour is prohibited by the constitution.[3] It is, however, allowed by the same article of the constitution in cases of convicted prisoners. The question of whether community service is unconstitutional arises in particular in cases where it does not replace a prison sentence (although the Constitutional

---

2. Internationale Stiftung zur Fôorderung von Kultur und Zivilisation.
3. Basic Law, *Grundgesetz*, Article 12.

Court has accepted community service as an educative measure in the field of juvenile justice).

The latest legislative drafts therefore preferred the model of community service not as an independent sanction, but as a voluntary substitute to fines (and to short-term unconditional prison sentences of up to six months or suspended sentences of up to twelve months, see Kommission zur Reform des Sanktionensystems 2000). In the future, the offender will be offered the choice of community service, so shortening the bureaucratic procedure – in comparison to today where the prosecutor first tries to collect the fine, then imposes substitute detention and only after offers the offender community service so as to prevent detention.

There were, however, federal states which strongly opposed any such reform. It was argued that the organisation of community service in rural areas and the larger federal states would not be possible. The example of Mecklenburg-Western Pomerania, a poor rural state with a large surface area, refutes these arguments. In debates held in the federal legislative chamber the example of Mecklenburg-Western Pomerania therefore played a predominant role. In 2004 a draft bill will probably be passed in the federal parliament which will extend community service in the way it has been implemented on an experimental basis in Mecklenburg-Western Pomerania (with success).

References

Albrecht, H.-J. and Schädler, W. (eds.), *Community service. A new option in punishing offenders in Europe,* Freiburg, 1986.

Cornils, K., "Gemeinnützige Arbeit in den nordischen Ländern", *Monatsschrift für Kriminologie und Strafrechtsreform,* 77, 1994, pp. 322-329.

Dolde, G., "Vollzug von Ersatzfreiheitsstrafen – Ein wesentlicher Anteil im Kurzstrafenvollzug", *Zeitschrift für Strafvollzug und Straffälligenhilfe,* 48, 1999, pp. 330-335.

Dünkel, F. and Grosser, R., "Vermeidung von Ersatzfreiheitsstrafen durch gemeinnützige Arbeit", *Neue Kriminalpolitik,* 11, No. 1, 1999, pp. 28-33.

Dünkel, F. and Kunkat, A., "Zwischen Innovation und Restauration. 20 Jahre Strafvollzugsgesetz - Eine Bestandsaufnahme", *Neue Kriminalpolitik,* 9, No. 2, 1997, pp. 24-33.

Dünkel, F., Scheel, J. and Grosser, R., "Vermeidung von Ersatzfreiheitsstrafen durch gemeinnützige Arbeit", *Bewährungshilfe,* 49, 2002, pp. 56-72.

Feuerhelm, W., "Ergebnisse einer Erhebung bei Staatsanwaltschaften und einer Aktenuntersuchung zu 'Gemeinnütziger Arbeit statt Ersatzfreiheitsstrafe'", in Jehle, J.-M., Feuerhelm, W. and Block, P. (eds.), *Gemeinnützige Arbeit statt Ersatzfreiheitsstrafe,* Kriminologische Zentralstelle, Wiesbaden, 1990, pp. 47-95.

Feuerhelm, W., *Gemeinnützige Arbeit als Alternative in der Geldstrafenvollstreckung,* Kriminologische Zentralstelle, Wiesbaden, 1991.

Feuerhelm, W., *Stellung und Ausgestaltung der gemeinnützigen Arbeit im Strafrecht,* Kriminologische Zentralstelle, Wiesbaden, 1997.

Jehle, J.-M., Feuerhelm, W. and Block, P. (eds.), *Gemeinnützige Arbeit statt Ersatzfreiheitsstrafe,* Kriminologische Zentralstelle, Wiesbaden, 1990.

Kaiser, G., *Kriminologie,* third edition, Heidelberg, 1996.

Kerner, H.-J. and Kästner, O. (eds.), *Gemeinnützige Arbeit in der Strafrechtspflege,* Bonn, 1986.

Kommission zur Reform des strafrechtlichen Sanktionensystems, "Abschlußbericht", Bonn, Internet publication, see www.bmj.bund.de *(Gesetzesvorhaben),* 2000.

van Kalmthout, A., *"Si non solvit in opere ...." Bijdragen over de geschiedenis en ontwikeling van onbetaalde arbeid als strafsanctie,* Wolf Legal Publishers, Nijmwegen, 2001.

Wirth, W., "Ersatzfreiheitsstrafe oder 'Ersatzhausarrest'? Ein empirischer Beitrag zur Diskussion um die Zielgruppen potentieller Sanktionsalternativen", *Zeitschrift für Strafvollzug und Straffälligenhilfe,* 49, 2000, pp. 337-344.

Chapter 10

Reducing the prison population: long-term experiences from Finland

Tapio Lappi-Seppälä

Like in so many other countries, criminal political thinking underwent profound changes during the late 1960s and 1970s in Finland. In the 1960s, the Nordic countries experienced heated social debate on the results and justifications of involuntary treatment in institutions (such as in health care and in the treatment of alcoholics), both penal and otherwise.

In Finland the criticism of the treatment ideology has since merged with that directed against an overly severe Criminal Code and the excessive use of custodial sentences. The resulting criminal political ideology was labelled as "humane neo-classicism". It stressed both legal safeguards against coercive care and the objective of less repressive measures in general.

Between 1970 and 1990 all the main parts of Finnish criminal legislation have been reformed from these starting points. The reform ideology, which guided the law reforms from the early 1970s onwards, represented a pragmatic, non-moralistic approach to crime problems. In this framework, the role of criminal law as a means of crime policy occupies a much less prominent place than before.

This pragmatic-rational approach also had a strong social policy orientation ("good social policy is the best criminal policy"). It entailed, *inter alia,* that measures against social marginalisation and equality work also as measures against crime, and that crime control and criminal policy are part of social justice and not so much an issue of controlling dangerous individuals. This view reflected the values of the Nordic welfare state ideal, and it was widely shared by penological experts as well as leading officials in the Ministry of Justice and the prison administration. Humanisation of the sanction system and the fall of incarceration rates were the tangible effects of this reform work.

This paper discusses some of the results and background factors of that policy, as well as subsequent developments.[1]

---

1. The subject has been dealt with in more detail by the author in Lappi-Seppälä 1998 and 2001, see also Törnudd 1993.

The change

At the beginning of the 1950s, the prisoner rate in Finland was four times higher than in the other Nordic countries. Finland had some 200 prisoners per 100 000 inhabitants, while the figures in Sweden, Denmark and Norway were around 50. Even during the 1970s, Finland's prisoner rate continued to be among the highest in western Europe. However, the steady decrease that started soon after the second world war continued. Even during the 1970s and 1980s, when most European countries experienced rising prison populations, that of Finland kept going down and by the beginning of the 1990s had reached the Nordic level (Figure 1).

Figure 1: Prisoner rates (per 100 000 inhabitants) in four Scandinavian countries (1950-2000)

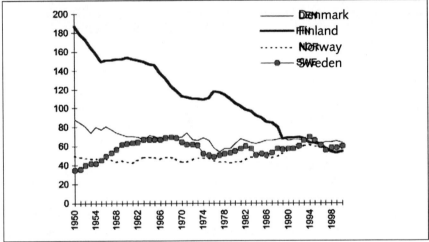

Compiled from Falck, von Hofer and Storgaard 2003.

This long-term change – over almost half a century – cannot be explained with reference to one or two simple factors. The change has been affected both by macro-level structural factors and ideological changes in penal theory, as well as legal reforms and changing practices of sentencing and prison enforcement. The role of these different background reasons obviously varies over time.

Law-reforms and sentencing policies

Since the early 1970s the main parts of Finnish criminal legislation have been reformed from these neo-classical "anti-treatment and anti-repressive" starting points. There has been a purposeful movement towards a more lenient system of sanctions, and especially towards a reduction in the use of custodial sentences. Together with legislative reforms one has to stress also the independent role of the judiciary. In several cases, the courts have taken the initiative of more lenient sentencing levels even before legislators had reached this decision. The major reforms and sentencing changes can be summarised as follows.[2]

General trends in sentencing

The Finnish judge has traditionally had quite a limited number of options when sentencing. The three basic alternatives have been unconditional imprisonment, conditional imprisonment or a fine. The fine was the principal punishment throughout the previous century. However, the most effective alternative to imprisonment has been the conditional sentence. The popularity of this sentencing option has increased steadily. From 1950 to 1990 the number of conditional sentences increased from some 3 000 to 18 000 sentences per year. Growth was especially rapid between 1970 and 1980. A closer look at the sentencing patterns of the courts would reveal two consecutive changes between 1950 and 1990. Both are illustrated in Figure 2.

Figure 2: The average length of prison sentences imposed by the courts and the choice between conditional and unconditional sentences (1950-90)

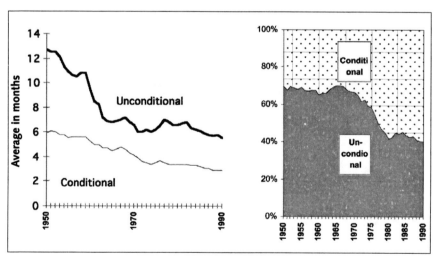

Between 1950 and 1965 the average length of unconditional imprisonment fell from thirteen months to seven months (above left). The graph above right reveals another change. Up to the mid-1960s, two out of three sentences of imprisonment were imposed unconditionally. From the late 1960s onwards the proportion of unconditional sentences fell from 70% (1966) to 42% (1980).

---

2.   The following presentation deals only with major reforms of the sanction system. The first "official recognition" of the high prison rate was given in the form of a general amnesty in 1967. This amnesty shortened prison sentences by one sixth. A list of the legislative reforms that have been carried out in Finland since 1967 can be found in the sources mentioned in the previous footnote.

These two changes can be explained primarily by changes in sentencing for two distinct crime categories: theft and drunken driving.

Penalties for theft offences

Long custodial sentences imposed for traditional property crimes kept the prison population at its peak level during the early 1950s. During the 1950s the courts had started to mitigate the sentences, but high minimum penalties and rigid offence definitions for aggravated forms imposed strict limits to these efforts. However, in 1972 new definitions and new punishment latitudes for larceny were introduced. Again, in 1991 the latitude for the basic form of theft was reduced. As a result, there was a clear change in sentencing practice. In 1971, 38% of offenders sentenced for larceny received a custodial sentence. Twenty years later, in 1991, this proportion had decreased to 11% (for more detail see Lappi-Seppälä 1998; Törnudd 1993). Figure 3 below illustrates the length of prison sentences in between 1950 and 1990 in the case of theft.

Figure 3: The average length of prison sentences for theft (1950-91)

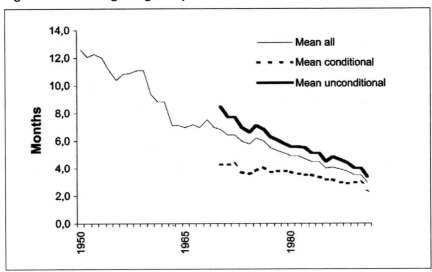

The changes are rather dramatic. For example in 1950 the average length of all sentences of imprisonment imposed for theft was twelve months. In 1971 the sentence was still 7.4 months, but in 1991 it was only 2.6 months of imprisonment.[3] A similar type of change can also be detected in other crime categories (see Figure 4).

---

3. Of course, one has to take into account that in the long run the typical forms of theft have changed. Crimes against individual victims and households have been replaced in part for example by petty shoplifting.

Figure 4: The average length of prison sentence for four different offences (1950-90)

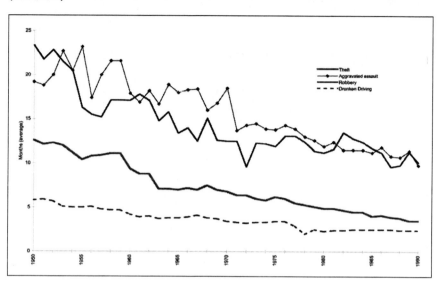

Drink driving

Drink driving plays a special role in Nordic criminal policy. The combination of hard drinking habits and a very restrictive and intolerant attitude towards drinking-and-driving has kept drink driving among the key issues in debates on criminal policy. A substantial part of the Finnish prison problem during the 1960s resulted from fairly long unconditional prison sentences imposed for drink driving. During the 1970s this practice was changed in favour of non-custodial alternatives. The movement was started by the courts themselves, but the development was reinforced by separate legislative acts. The definition of drink driving was modernised by an amendment of the law in 1977. In this connection, legislators took a definite stand in favour of conditional sentence and fines.

On the same occasion, three other bills were passed in order to increase the use of conditional sentences and fines in general (and particularly in the case of drink driving). The reform of the conditional sentence act created the opportunity for combining a fine with a conditional sentence. The reform of the day-fine system raised the amount of day-fines thus encouraging the court to also use fines in more serious cases. The most important 1977 reform from a universal point of view was, however, the enactment of general sentencing rules. These provisions in chapter 6 of the Criminal Code gave the courts general guidance in meting out punishments for all offences. They also provided a framework for further debate concerning the proper sentencing level. The first target of such debate was drink driving. These discussions were, in fact, run by the judges, with only organisational help from the Ministry of Justice (for

143

details, see Lappi-Seppälä 2001). These efforts to change sentencing practice regarding drink driving proved to be a success, as Figure 5 below illustrates.

Figure 5: Sanctions for drink driving (1950-90 in percentages)

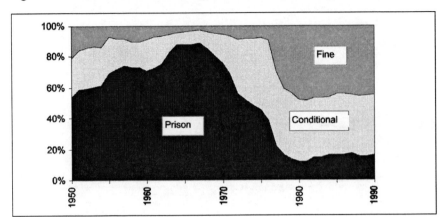

In 1971, 70% of drink drivers received an unconditional sentence. Ten years later, in 1981, this proportion had dropped to 12%. Since the reform in 1977, the normal punishment for aggravated drink driving has been conditional imprisonment together with an unconditional supplementary fine, while "ordinary" drink driving cases (blood alcohol under 0.12%) are dealt with by fines.

The sentencing reforms of the 1970s have turned out to be a criminal policy success. One reason has been that these reforms constituted a coherent and consistent unity with clear aims and systematic strategy. The case of drink driving serves as a good example. Legislators first created the opportunity for combining a fine with a conditional sentence, and then raised the amount of day-fines. After passing a bill on drink driving, new provisions on sentencing were also enacted, and these provided the framework for discussions on the sentencing levels and normal punishment. In a way, all these reforms were part of one well-planned "big package".

New sentencing alternatives: community service

This basic structure of the sentencing system has remained relatively stable during the last decades. The only major amendment in this structure has been the introduction of community service. This took place initially on an experimental basis in 1991. In 1994 the system was extended to cover the entire country and community service became a standard part of the Finnish system of sanctions.

Community service is imposed in lieu of unconditional imprisonment for up to eight months. In order to ensure that community service will really be used instead of unconditional prison sentences, a two-step procedure is adopted. First the court is supposed to make its sentencing decision in accordance with the normal principles and criteria of sentencing, without even considering the possibility of community service. If the result is unconditional imprisonment, then the court may commute the sentence into community service under the following conditions. First, the convicted person must consent to the sanction. Second, the offender must also be capable of carrying out the community service order. Third, recidivism and prior convictions may prevent the use of this sanction. The duration of community service varies between 20 and 200 hours. In commuting imprisonment into community service, one day in prison equals one hour of community service. Thus, two months of custodial sentence should be commuted into roughly sixty hours of community service. If the conditions of the community service order are violated, the court normally imposes a new unconditional prison sentence. Community service does not contain any extra supervision aimed, for example, at controlling the offender's behaviour in general. The supervision is strictly confined to his or her working obligations.

The legislators' idea, thus, was that community service should be used only in cases where the offender would otherwise have received an unconditional prison sentence. As Figure 6 shows, this aim was well achieved.

Figure 6: Imprisonment and community service in Finnish court practice

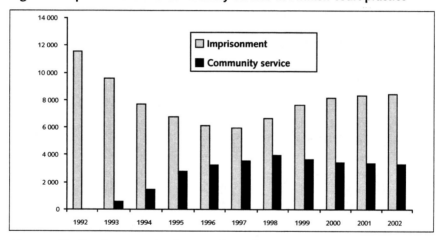

Along with the increase in the number of community service orders, the number of unconditional prison sentences has decreased. In 1998, the average daily number of offenders serving a community service order was about 1 200 and the corresponding prison rate was 2 800. It is therefore reasonable to argue that, within a short period of time, community service has proven to be an important alternative to imprisonment. As the figure shows, the use of community service seems to have reached its peak in 1998-99.

Specific prisoners groups

Over the course of time, different prisoner groups have received different attention. During the 1960s and 1970s the focus was on fine defaulters and recidivists in preventive detention. In the 1970s and 1980s, the use of imprisonment for young offenders was restricted.

Fine defaulters

In the 1950s and 1960s fine defaulters constituted a substantial part of the Finnish prison population (sometimes exceeding 25% of the total population). In the late 1960s the number default prisoners was reduced with two consecutive law reforms: by decriminalising public drunkenness (which led to fewer default sentences since public drunkenness was one of the major offences leading to a default fine) and by raising the amount of day-fines and decreasing the number of day-fines (which led to shorter default sentences).

Figure 7: The number of fine defaulters in prison (1950-2000)

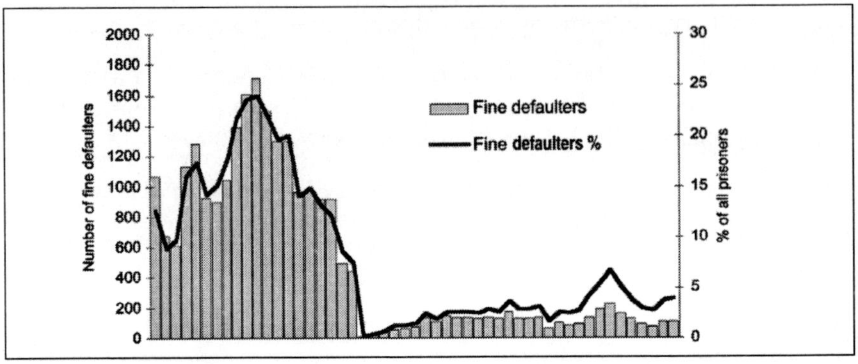

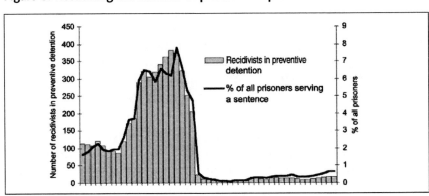

Preventive detention

The Finnish criminal justice system includes a provision for holding chronic recidivists in preventive detention after completion of the sentence, if both the sentencing court and a special court so decide. During the 1960s, the large majority of detainees had been guilty of repeat property crimes. On the basis of an amendment passed in 1971, the option of preventive detention was restricted only to dangerous violent offenders. The number of persons held in detention as recidivists dropped by 90% in one year, from 206 to 24. Since then, the annual average has been between ten and twenty prisoners.

Figure 8: Restricting the number of prisoners in preventive detention

146

Juveniles

There is no special juvenile criminal system in Finland, in the sense that this concept is understood in continental legal systems: there are no juvenile courts and the number of specific penalties only applicable to juveniles has been quite restricted. However, offenders between 15 and 17 receive a mitigated sentence. In addition, the conditions for waiving sanctions (for example, non-prosecution) are much less restrictive for young offenders. Young offenders under 21 who are sentenced to imprisonment are usually released on parole after one third of the sentence has been served, instead of the normal half. Despite the lack of specific measures for juveniles, there has also been a deliberate policy against the use of imprisonment for the youngest age-groups. This has been done mainly by relying on the traditional alternatives. The willingness of the courts to impose custodial sentences on young offenders decreased throughout the 1970s and the 1980s. In addition, the Conditional Sentence Act was amended in 1989 by including a provision which allows the use of unconditional sentences for young offenders only if there are extraordinary reasons calling for this. All of this has had a clear impact on practice (Figure 9). At the moment there are about one hundred prisoners between the ages of 18 and 20 and less than ten in the 15 to 17 age-group, while as recently as the 1960s the numbers were ten times higher.

Figure 9: The number of young prisoners aged between 15 and 17

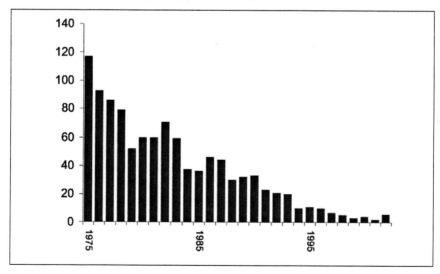

Parole

The system of parole (early release) has also proven to be a very powerful tool in controlling prisoner rates. Any changes in the basic structure of this system will have visible effects on prison figures. In Finland, all prisoners except those few serving their sentence in preventive detention or serving a life sentence will be released on parole. At the moment, the minimum time to be served before a prisoner is eligible for parole is fourteen days. A series of reforms has brought it down to this figure. During the mid-1960s this period was shortened from six to four months, during the mid-1970s from four to three months, and finally in 1989 from three months to fourteen days. Figure 10 illustrates the effects of the 1989 parole reform (and some of the other major changes discussed above).

Figure 10: Prison policy reforms and the number of prisoners (1950-2000)

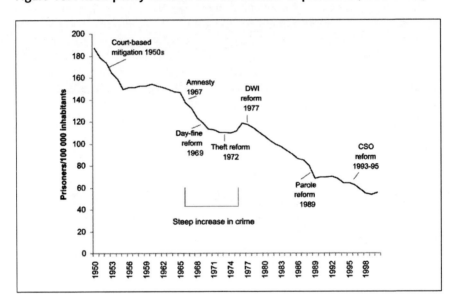

Prison rates and crime rates

A fundamental change in the use of imprisonment naturally leads to the question of its effects on crime rates. Time and time again, research confirms the fact that the use of imprisonment is relatively unrelated to the number of crimes committed or reported. There are, of course, several well-known methodological difficulties in combining crime rates with prison rates (and other changes in sentence severity). However, the possibility of comparing countries which share strong social and structural similarities but have a very different penal history gives an exceptional perspective to the matter. In fact, the Nordic experiences provide an interesting opportunity to test how drastic changes in the penal practices in one country have been reflected in the crime rates, as compared to countries which have kept their penal system more or less stable. Figure 11 provides information on prisoner rates and reported crime in Finland, Sweden, Denmark and Norway from 1950 to 2000.

Figure 11: Prison rates and crime rates (1950-2000)

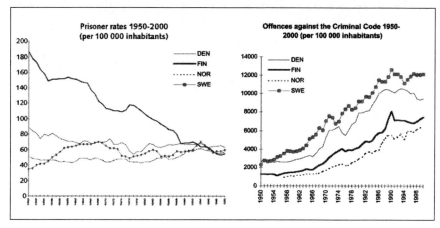

Compiled from: Falck, von Hofer and Storgaard 2003.

A simple comparison between the Nordic countries reveals a striking difference in the use of imprisonment, as well as a striking similarity in the trends in recorded criminality. The fact that Finland has heavily reduced its prisoner rate has not disturbed the symmetry of Nordic crime rates. The figures start to differentiate only during the 1990s, as reported crime in Norway keeps going up, while the Danish figures go down. However, the imprisonment rates in both countries stay at the same level (Norway between 56-60 and Denmark between 63-68).

The figures also confirm, once again, the general criminological conclusion that crime rates rise and fall according to laws and dynamics of their own, and sentencing policies in turn develop and change according to dynamics of their own; these two systems are fairly independent of one another.

Factors behind the change

The decrease in the Finnish prison population has been the result of a conscious, long-term and systematic criminal policy.[4] Legislative reforms in this direction had already started during the mid-1960s. Even before that – during the 1950s – the courts had reduced their sentences. In many cases legislators were strongly supported by the judiciary and especially by the courts of first instance. Quite often the courts had changed their practice even before legislators had changed the law. Still, the critical question remains: What made

---

4.   A short presentation cannot capture all the factors that have influenced this development. For example, one should not forget structural and demographic factors: the ageing of the large birth cohorts born after the war (see Aho 1997) have also contributed to the reduction of the prison population.

149

all this possible, and what made it possible to carry out these law reforms? Describing the techniques used was easy. Explaining why they were adopted and accepted is harder.[5]

Part of the answer could be found in the structure of Finland's political culture. The Finnish criminologist Patrik Törnudd has stressed the importance of the political will and consensus to bring down the prisoner rate. As he summarises, "those experts who were in charge of planning the reforms and research shared an almost unanimous conviction that Finland's internationally high prisoner rate was a disgrace and that it would be possible to significantly reduce the amount and length of prison sentences without serious repercussions on the crime situation" (Törnudd 1993, p. 12). This conviction was shared by the civil servants, the judiciary, the prison authorities and, as was equally important, by the politicians.[6]

Another, and closely related, way to characterise Finnish criminal policy would be to describe it as exceptionally expert-oriented: reforms have been prepared and conducted by a relatively small group of experts whose thinking on criminal policy, at least on basic points, has followed similar lines. The impact of these professionals was, furthermore, reinforced by close personal and professional contacts with senior politicians and with academic research.[7] Consequently, and unlike the situation in many other countries, crime control has never been a central political issue in election campaigns in Finland. At least the "heavyweight" politicians have not relied on populist policies, such as "three strikes" and "truth in sentencing".

This leads to another element in the composition of Finnish criminal policy – the role of the media. In Finland, the media have retained quite a sober and reasonable attitude towards issues of criminal policy. The Finns have largely been saved from low-level populism. But things may be changing. The emergence of a rival in the afternoon paper market about a decade ago, as well as the increase in TV channels and the resulting intensified competition for viewers have brought crime reports onto Finnish TV as well.

"Attitudinal readiness" among the judiciary can also be identified as one relevant factor over the last decades. It would, indeed, be a misinterpretation to conclude that what happened in Finland during the last decades was just a

5. In order to put things into perspective, it should be stressed that instead of a massive move towards decarceration one could also describe the change merely as a "normalisation" of prison rates: a move from a level that was totally absurd to a level that can be considered to be a fair Nordic level – albeit ten times lower than the present US level

6. At least to the extent that they did not oppose the reform proposals prepared by the Ministry of Justice.

7. Several of the Ministers of Justice during the 1970s and 1980s had direct contact with research work; indeed, one of them, Inkeri Anttila, was a Professor of Criminal Law and the Director of the National Research Institute of Legal Policy at the time of her appointment as minister.

skilful manoeuvre of a small group of experts. Collaboration with and assistance from the judiciary was clearly a necessary prerequisite for the change to happen. In many cases, legislators were strongly supported by the judiciary and especially by the courts of first instance. Quite often the courts had changed their practice even before legislators had changed the law. Of course, the fact that criminology and criminal policy are taught in the juridical faculties to lawyers – those who will later implement the laws – is also a part of the larger picture. The majority of Finnish local court judges and prosecutors are relatively young, having completed their university courses during the 1970s and the 1980s in the spirit of liberal criminal policy. In addition, different training courses and seminars arranged for judges (and prosecutors) on a regular basis by judicial authorities – in co-operation with the universities – have also had an impact on sentencing and prosecutorial practices.

Also the crime scene matters. The fact that Finland has been – and still is – a peaceful and safe society with a low level of crime has made it easier to adopt liberal policies in crime control. Even so, it may be argued that this factor has a rather restricted explanatory force. In fact, over a period of approximately twenty years, and especially during the 1960s, Finland experienced severe social and structural changes in its development from a rural/agricultural economy into an industrial urban welfare state. This rapid development had its impact on the crime rate. There was a sharp increase in recorded crime from the mid-1960s to the mid-1970s, and again during the 1980s. However, this did not prevent the prison numbers from falling (and neither is there reason to conclude that this fall had any significant effect on the growth of crime, as discussed above).

Observations on recent trends

Politicisation of criminal policy

All in all, the criminal policy of the past decades in Finland may well be characterised as both rational and humane. But as we are aware, international trends in criminal policy have gone in the opposite direction. Criminal policy has become more and more "a tool of general policy", and with quite unhappy results. The measures adopted are often influenced by motives other than rational criminal policy, to say nothing of a considered analysis of goals, means and values. In the hands of politicians, criminal policy is often just another tool of general politics, a way to transmit "symbolic messages" and a way to "take a stand". Argumentation remains far from the cool and evidence-based criminal political analyses, where criminal law should be treated as *ultima ratio* – to be used only in cases where other means do not apply and only when it produces more good than harm. Instead, criminal justice interventions are often just determined by a political need to "do something". The rule of thumb seems to be that the higher the level of political authority, the more simplistic the approaches advocated. The results can be seen in programmes and slogans that are compressed into two or three words, along the lines of "three strikes", "prison works", "truth in sentencing", "war on drugs" and so on.[8]

This seems, unfortunately, to be the case also when one looks at penal policy at the EU level. This is one reason why a large segment of Nordic scholars in criminal law remain less enthusiastic towards political attempts to harmonise criminal law. The growing international aspect of crime and crime control and the increased pressure on the harmonisation of criminal law within the European Union, as well as the general tendency to politicise criminal policy, all include greater risks of increased repression in Finland too. Signs of this more punitive approach can also be seen in the Finnish debate.

The rise 1999-2002

The number of prison sentences – as well as the number of prisoners – has again started to increase. Between 1999 and 2002 the number of prisoners increased by 25% (Figure 12).

Figure 12: Prisoners by prisoner groups in Finland (1991-2002)

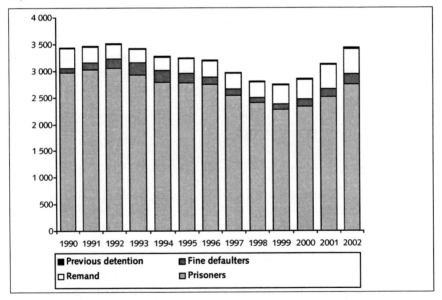

Behind these changes are the increased number of foreign prisoners (mainly from the Russian Federation and Estonia). Between 1999 and 2002 their number has more than doubled. The use of remand has increased by 35% and

---

8. The manifestations of penal populism in five English-speaking countries is well analysed in Roberts et al 2003. An excellent analysis of the social and political forces behind these changes is to be found in Garland 2001.

fine defaulters have almost doubled (Table 1). These three groups account for a little over 50% of the increase. The remainder is mainly the result of changes in the number of convicted persons and sentencing practices (see below).

Table 1: Prisoners in 1999 and 2002 by prisoner groups (annual averages)

	1999	2002	Increase (%)
All	2 743	3 433	+25
– serving a sentence	2 215	2 673	+20
– remand prisoners	354	478	+35
– fine defaulters	102	190	+86
Foreigners	138	293	+112

The change can also be viewed from the point of view of different offence categories (Table 2).

Table 2: Prison population by type of offence (remand and fine defaulters excluded)

	1 May 1999	1 May 2002	1 May 2003	Increase 1999-2003 %
All	2 361	2 762	2 974	+26
– violence	988	1 082	1 254	+38
– drugs	360	498	496	+21
– property	552	684	667	+21
– drunken driving	312	313	355	+14
– other	149	185	202	+35

Drug offences show the most rapid increase (38%). The number of prison sentences for aggravated drug offences has doubled and the sentences have become longer by one third. However, rather than changes in sentencing practice, this increase reflects changes in the nature of the crime (especially in the quantity of the drugs). The good news is that between 2002 and 2003 the situation seems to have been stabilised. The bad news is that violent offences – the largest prisoner group – has shown an increase of 28%, and that this increase has also continued between 2002 and 2003. This is a result of a deliberate overall tightening in the official control of violent offences (in reporting, apprehension and sentencing level). This trend may well continue in the future. During the late 1990s the use of community service also declined (explaining part of the change between 1997 and 2000). However, since the year 2000 the use of community service seems to have stabilised.

Table 3 describes the present situation and the most recent changes (1 January 2003 and 1 January 2004). The total number of prisoners has remained unchanged.

Table 3: The number of prisoners in Finland on 1 January 2003 and 2004

	1 January 2003	1 January 2004
All	3 469	3 463
– serving a sentence	2 819	2 845
– remand	475	450
– fine defaulters	175	168
Foreigners	285	306

Steps backwards, adaptation or signs of new policies?

It is difficult to conclude whether this short-term rise in Finland's prison population is only a "natural step backwards" after a long-term decrease, an adaptation to "new circumstances" and changes in the nature of crime, or a sign of new punitive policies, finally entering Finland too.

The safest guess is that all these three elements have been involved. The increase of drug offenders in prison would have been hard to avoid (for example, mitigating sentences during rapid growth of organised drug-smuggling from the Russian Federation and the Baltic countries was hardly a political option). The short-term decline in the use of community service, in turn, was at least partly an expected move "backwards" after a rapid increase in the use of this new sanction.

But there were also changes in the "criminal political climate". The keywords of the past decades – "humane and rational criminal policy" – have disappeared from political rhetoric and official statements. Policy initiatives by the police for greatly extended investigative powers have been defended with keywords such as "transnational organised crime" which requires a "new kind of criminal policy". However, direct policy initiatives for stiffer penalties have been restricted to only violent and sexual offences. On the other hand, the material costs and practical difficulties following the increase in the prison population have also gained the public's attention and concern. Consequently, plans have been prepared to extend the scope of non-custodial sanctions to a new type of treatment order reserved for those who – due to their alcohol or drug abuse – do not fulfil the conditions of community service. The are also proposals to reduce the use of remand and default imprisonment.

However, in the long run, the shape and content of penal policy is dependent on larger scale social and political conditions. Ultimately, the question whether Finland will also face similar growth in the prison population to that found in so many other countries should be viewed from these premises. Taking into account that very few of the social, political, economic and cultural background conditions which explain the rise of mass imprisonment in the United States and the United Kingdom apply to Finland, there may still be room for some optimism.

Social equality and demographic homogeneity of Finnish society are an essential part of Finland's (possible) guarantees against unfounded repression. There are less racial and class tensions/distinctions, less fear and less frustration to be exploited by marginal political groups and less extreme demands for control and exclusion.

Related to this, the welfare state was never openly discredited in Finland, not even during the deepest recession of the 1990s. The social and economic security granted by the Nordic welfare state model may still function as a social backup system for tolerant criminal policy. But at the same time one has to note that the fear of crime has also grown in Finland, large segments of the population experience deeper insecurity than in the 1970s or 1980s and the general welfare services underwent heavy cutbacks during the 1990s.

Political culture and the reluctance to use tough criminal policy as a general political strategy may still be Finland's salvation. But for how long, the sceptic might ask? Crime is a problem and politicians are responsible for offering solutions to this problem. If nothing else is offered, criminal law and the prison system may become the primary shield against crime in Finland too. Being a realist, the development of convincing crime prevention strategies outside the domain of criminal law also becomes an issue of importance.

The value placed on expert opinions and demands for evidence-based rationality and the strong impact of professional expertise at different levels of the criminal justice system have also contributed to Finland's favourable development. But developments in other countries demonstrate how vulnerable the power of elites may be. Finnish politicians show an increased interest to listen more and more to the voice of the "people" and solid statements of street-credible policemen, than complicated professional analysis from academic ivory towers. However, efforts to inform public opinion, politicians and the media remain increasingly important, as frustrating as they sometimes are.

References

Aho, T., "Land of decreasing prison population", in *Prison population in Europe and North America. Problems and solutions,* Department of Prison Administration, Ministry of Justice, Helsinki, 1997.

Anttila, I., "Conservative and radical criminal policy in the Nordic countries", *Scandinavian Studies in Criminology,* Vol. 3, Universitetsforlaget, Norwich, 1971, pp. 9-21.

Anttila, I. and Törnudd, P., "The dynamics of the Finnish Criminal Code reform", in Lahti, R. and Nuotio, K. (eds.), *Criminal law theory in transition. Finnish and comparative perspectives,* Finnish Lawyers' Publishing Company, Tampere, 1992. Also printed in Törnudd, 1996.

Falck, S., von Hofer, H. and Storgaard, A., *Nordic criminal statistics 1950-2000,* Department of Criminology, Stockholm University, 2003.

Garland, D., *The culture of control. Crime and social order in contemporary society,* University of Chicago Press, 2001.

Lappi-Seppälä, T., *Regulating the prison population. Experiences from a long-term policy in Finland,* National Research Institute of Legal Policy, Research Communications, 38, 1998.

Lappi-Seppälä, T., "Sentencing and punishment in Finland: the decline of the repressive ideal", in Tonry, M. and Frase R. (eds.), *Punishment and penal systems in western countries,* Oxford University Press, New York, 2001.

Roberts, J.V., Stalans, L.J., Indermaur, D. and Hough, M., *Penal populism and public opinion. Lessons from five countries,* Oxford University Press, Oxford, 2003.

Törnudd, P., *Fifteen years of decreasing prisoner rates in Finland,* National Research Institute of Legal Policy, Research Communications, 8, 1993.

Törnudd, P., *Facts, values and visions. Essays in criminology and crime policy,* National Research Institute of Legal Policy, Research Reports, 138, 1996.

PART III
THE PRISON SYSTEM

Chapter 11

Reducing tension and improving rehabilitation by opening prisons: day leave and prison furloughs in Germany

Frieder Dünkel

Reforms of the German prison system in the 1970s

In the late 1960s severe criticism of the German prison system emerged. Prisons were seen as "schools of crime" and many prison riots and disturbances had to be faced by a largely overburdened prison administration. The debate about rehabilitation ("resocialisation") culminated in fundamental changes to the prison system commencing in the late 1960s. After 1967 when, in the course of the general reform of the criminal law, a special commission was charged with drafting new prison legislation, the concept of resocialisation gained acceptance as a guiding principle in the execution of prison sentences. As early as the late 1960s, steps were taken to relax prison regimes and the first experiments with measures such as home leave and work release were launched. In 1976, by which time doubts about the resocialisation model were already being voiced in the United States and Scandinavia, West Germany enacted a Prison Act, which was clearly aimed at specific prevention. Section 2 of the Prison Act (*Strafvollzugsgesetz* – StVollzG) declared that the reintegration of the prisoner into society was the sole objective of the execution of a sentence. There is, however, no clear concept of the means of rehabilitation (resocialisation), and therefore all the different measures mentioned by the act, such as labour, leisure time activities like sport, etc., visits, contacts with the outside world and forms of and periods of prison leave are seen as being "rehabilitative". This paper will discuss the different forms of day leave and other leave of absence and their impact on the "climate" in German prisons as an example of developing "good practices" in this particular field of criminal policy.

After the reunification of Germany in 1990, West German law in its entirety was implemented in the former German Democratic Republic. Thus the same laws apply to offenders and prisoners in all of the *Länder* (federal states) of the Federal Republic of Germany. Another important detail in this context is the "institutional division of labour" (Feest and Weber 1998, p. 234) between the federal and state levels. Legislation in the field of prison law is a matter of federal competence, whereas the prison administration and day-to-day running of prisons is the responsibility of the federal states. The result is a great variation of prison conditions and regional traditions and cultures, which demonstrate different interpretations of the Federal Prison Act (StVollzG).

Opening the prisons

There are different ways of opening prisons and increasing contacts with the outside world. On the one hand, open prisons have been established that have no real impediments to prevent escape.[1] As a rule these prisons are characterised by increased possibilities for contacts with the outside world (for example, visits inside prison and home leave outside prison) and they are seen in the context of the guiding principle of "normalisation" expressed by Section 3.I of the Prison Act, which stipulates that living conditions inside prisons should – as far as possible – be equivalent to those outside prisons.

Sometimes open prisons are used for detainees serving their sentence from the outset, but mainly they are used as a means of preparing prisoners for release, namely for those serving the last few months before their release. When comparing the different *Länder*, the development in Germany shows a widely differing approach to the establishment of open prisons. Figure 1 shows the percentage of prisoners serving their sentence on a given day in an open institution. The range – from about 5% in Bavaria or 10% in Rhineland-Palatinate to around 30% in North Rhine-Westphalia, Berlin or Hamburg, considering only West German states – is astonishing. In the "new" federal states of East Germany the variation of between 2% in Thuringia and 21% in Brandenburg is similarly spectacular. It can be seen clearly that the northern states are more liberal than the southern states and that in western states open prisons are used more frequently than in eastern states. The differences are not due to different prison populations with regard to so-called dangerous or violent prisoners who might not be eligible for this kind of lenient regime. They are simply the result of very different interpretations of the prioritisation of opening prisons and the judgments of the prison administration regarding who would be a risk and who would not. The results concerning abuses of leave through escape or by not returning from day leave or work release programmes do not vary. Therefore, the more liberal regimes have not contributed to increased crime or insecurity. This can also be demonstrated by the long-term effects within some federal states. In the 1980s Baden-Württemberg doubled the proportion of offenders placed in open facilities; the same happened in the 1990s in Mecklenburg-Western Pomerania, both without negative consequences concerning escapes or

---

1. See Sections 141.II and 10 of the Prison Act; Dünkel and Rössner 2001, p. 327 *et seq.*

crimes committed while being detained in an open prison (see, for example, Dünkel 1996 and 1998).

Figure 1: Proportion of sentenced adult prisonners in open facilities on 30 June 2000 in a comparison of the federal states

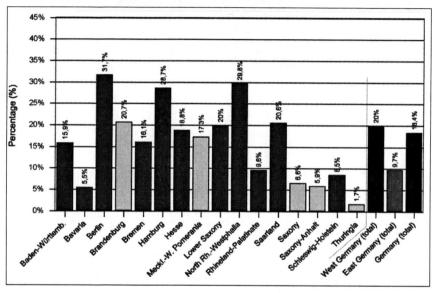

The increased opening up of prisons through home leave (prison furlough, *Hafturlaub*), short prison leave (*Ausgang*) and work release (*Freigang*) represents one of the fundamental novelties of the German prison system. This relaxation of the prison regime was introduced on an experimental basis in 1969 and provisions were incorporated into the Prison Act of 1976. Home leave may be granted regularly for up to twenty-one days per calendar year.[2] Short prison leave means that the prisoner may leave the institution for a few hours per day, in particular to search for work or accommodation or to visit close relatives. Work release means that prisoners work daily outside the institution, without supervision, for an ordinary wage; these prisoners are obliged to pay the institution around €300 per month for board and lodging. All these measures can be granted to prisoners in open as well as closed prisons, although some administrative rules restrict their use in closed prisons, particularly for violent and sexual offenders.

---

2. In addition, special leave of up to seven days may be granted; seven additional days of special leave may also be granted in the three months before release. Prisoners granted work release are permitted six days of special leave per month within the nine months prior to release (Sections 15 and 35 of the Prison Act; see for the legal and administrative regulations Van Zyl Smit 1988).

Short-term day leave and prison furloughs

The quantitative increase in home and short prison leave has been far greater than expected. Figure 2 demonstrates this increase. Between 1977 and 1990 the number of periods of home leave (*furlough*) granted increased from 243 to almost 800 per 100 prisoners of the daily sentenced prison population (30 June of each year). From then until 1994 it decreased. Since the mid-1990s it has remained stable at about 600 (2001: 608). The number of periods of short prison leave (day leave) steadily increased from 219 to 1 184 per 100 prisoners during the period from 1977 to 2001. Even work release increased from 32 to 54 per 100 prisoners at the end of the 1980s. Since then, however, the economy-induced rate of unemployment has also reached the prison system resulting in 38 admissions to work release per 100 prisoners in 2001.

The success of these measures is quite surprising: the proportion of prisoners not returning to the institution on time, or at all, amounts to a mere 1%. Since 1977, failure rates (concerning return to prison) have decreased, although the prison authorities have expanded the system of prison leave considerably (see Figure 3). Even if one considers individual prisoners rather than periods of leave granted, since one prisoner may be granted several periods of leave (Böhm 1986, p. 201 *et seq.*), the success rate is still more than 90% (Dünkel 1992, p. 99 *et seq.*). There is thus no basis for questioning the liberal practice of granting periods of leave (Dünkel 1996 and 1998; Dünkel and Kunkat 1997).

Figure 2: Prison leave and work release in west Germany (1997-2001)

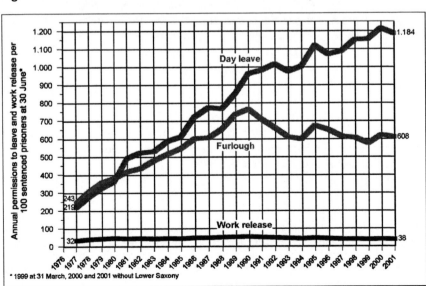

Figure 3: failure to return from leave in West Germany (1997-2001)

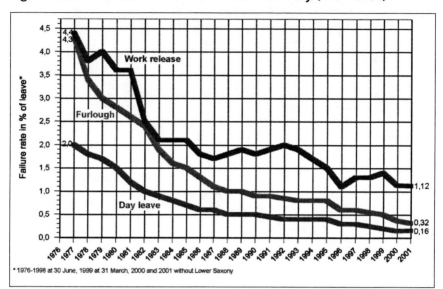

* 1976-1998 at 30 June, 1999 at 31 March, 2000 and 2001 without Lower Saxony

Crimes are committed even less frequently during periods of home leave, although the mass media are fond of sensationalising spectacular individual cases and criticising prison authorities for being too liberal and for no longer guaranteeing the safety of citizens. Under pressure from the public, arising from specific incidents, several federal states have sought to reduce prison leave while others – for example, the city states of Berlin, Bremen and (until recently) Hamburg – have continued to expand their liberal practice. The result is that in Bremen, for example, three to four times as many prisoners are granted home leave as in Baden-Württemberg or Bavaria. These regional practices are set out in Figures 4 and 5. A comparison at regional level reveals the traditional north-south differential with more restrictive prison leave practices being the norm in the southern federal states. However, exceptions do exist in individual institutions and states. Changes in the political climate may also play a decisive role: in Saarland, after the Social Democrats took over government in 1985, the number of periods of home leave granted annually more than doubled and the number of periods of short prison leave almost quadrupled, without the instances of abuse increasing. Special problems can be seen in the new federal states, which are far more restrictive in granting prison furloughs and day leave. Some have not even reached the level of Bavaria, which has the most conservative practice in the old federal states. In the East German states, too, a north-south differential can be seen: Brandenburg and Mecklenburg-Western Pomerania have a slightly more liberal practice than the other new federal states. With regard to prison policy, too much emphasis is placed on security issues, and as a result rehabilitative measures, like the relaxation of prison regimes, develop only slowly (for comments see Dünkel 1995 and 1998).

Figure 4: Day leave in Germany (1997-2001) in a comparison of the federal states

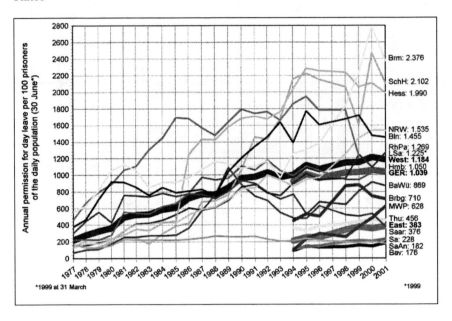

Figure 5: Prison furlough in Germany (1997-2001) in a comparison of the federal states

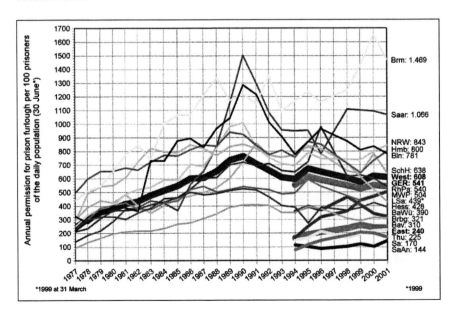

A more extensive granting of leave does not lead to increased failure rates as measured by the number of prisoners failing to return to prison or to the commission of crime whilst prisoners are out on leave (see Figure 6). There is thus no justification for the restrictive trends observed in several federal states.

Figure 6: Prison furlough and failure rates in % in Germany in a comparison of the federal states (2001)

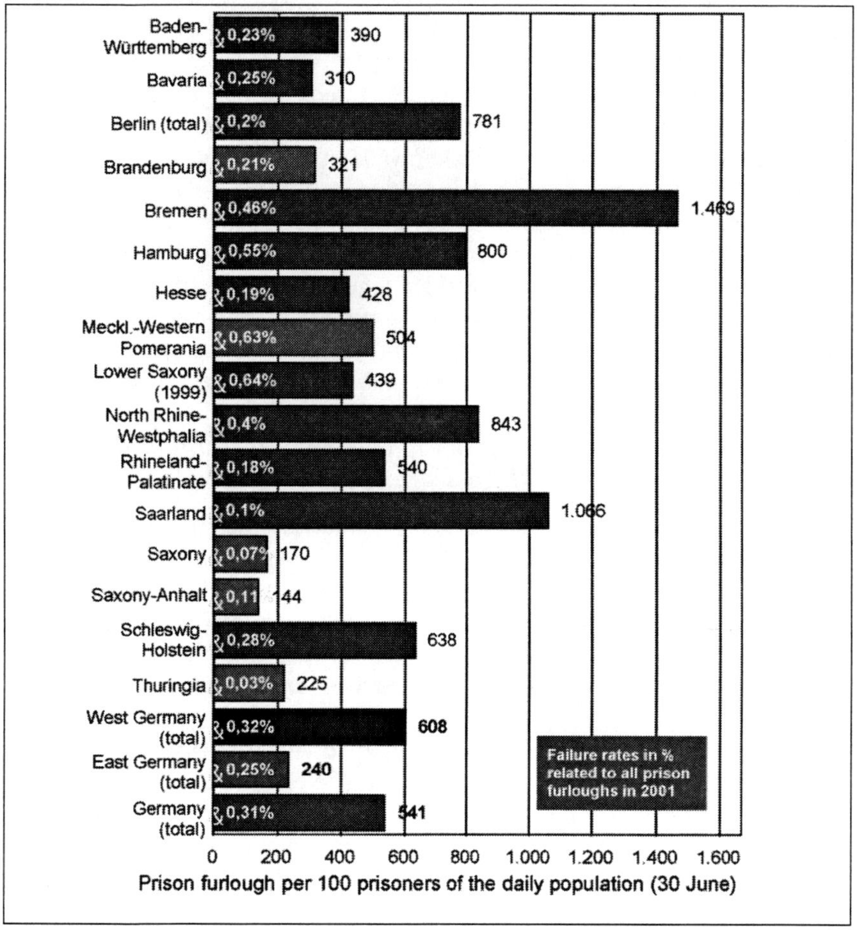

Baden-Württemberg	0,23%	390
Bavaria	0,25%	310
Berlin (total)	0,2%	781
Brandenburg	0,21%	321
Bremen	0,46%	1.469
Hamburg	0,55%	800
Hesse	0,19%	428
Meckl.-Western Pomerania	0,63%	504
Lower Saxony (1999)	0,64%	439
North Rhine-Westphalia	0,4%	843
Rhineland-Palatinate	0,18%	540
Saarland	0,1%	1.066
Saxony	0,07%	170
Saxony-Anhalt	0,11	144
Schleswig-Holstein	0,28%	638
Thuringia	0,03%	225
West Germany (total)	0,32%	608
East Germany (total)	0,25%	240
Germany (total)	0,31%	541

Failure rates in % related to all prison furloughs in 2001

0 200 400 600 800 1.000 1.200 1.400 1.600
Prison furlough per 100 prisoners of the daily population (30 June)

Work release

As far as permission to work outside prison without supervision is concerned (work release, *Freigang*), there are also significant variations between the federal states. Instances of permission per 100 sentenced prisoners on a particular census day (as recorded in 2001) are as follows: Bremen 100, Saarland 54, North Rhine-Westphalia 50, Schleswig-Holstein 22, and in the new federal states in general only 15. Brandenburg and Mecklenburg-Western Pomerania, with 23, are the positive exceptions, whereas in the other new federal states work release is still very much underdeveloped. The failure rate, again, is very low (1% on average), irrespective of a more restrictive or more liberal prison policy (also see Dünkel 1999, p. 88 *et seq.*).

Prison leave, however, should not only be regarded as a liberalisation of a sentence's execution, but also as a disciplinary device, for the prison governor has a wide discretion to decide whether leave should be granted. Occasionally, prisoners criticise this practice for being too arbitrary. Empirical studies have revealed, though, that almost every prisoner (more than 70% of prisoners with sentences longer than six months and nearly 90% in cases of prisoners serving more than one year; Dünkel 1992, p. 99 *et seq.*, p. 235 *et seq.*) is granted prison leave during the release stage. Because of the scope of the prison governor's discretion the special court, known as the *Strafvollstreckungsgericht,* has only limited powers of review at its disposal. Particularly problematic are administrative rules that guide the governor's discretionary decision. Special groups like violent offenders, prisoners sentenced for drug offences or foreigners who will be extradited or expelled are regularly excluded from prison leave or at least the governor has to examine the risk of absconding very thoroughly. In cases of violent offenders, some federal states have set up administrative rules that provide for a special examination by the Ministry of Justice itself.

The principle of resocialisation as a fundamental (constitutional) right of prisoners and its impact on the practice of prison leave

Recently the Federal Constitutional Court emphasised the importance of prison furloughs, such as day leave, in respect of the constitutional principle of resocialisation. This principle requires that the prison authorities give special grounds when refusing prison leave, particularly in the pre-release stage when a decision on early release has to be considered. The courts (*Strafvollstreckungskammer,* see below) must be enabled to realistically assess the risk of further offending. Prison leave is an important means of reintegration and has to be provided as preparation for early release in all regimes, including in closed or high-security prisons.[3] The Federal Constitutional Court furthermore held that the prison authorities could be obliged to transfer prisoners to prisons close to their families in order to make the granting of prison leave easier.[4]

Early release: legal and practical aspects of resocialisation

The Strafvollstreckungskammer of the Regional Court, which also decides prisoners' appeals, may order the remainder of a sentence to be suspended in

---

3. See BVerfG ZfStrVo, 1998, 180; NStZ, 1998, 373; NStZ, 1998, 430; NJW, 1998, 1133; and for more details Heghmanns 1999.
4. BVerfG NJW, 1998, 1133.

terms of Section 57 of the Penal Code. When suspension of a fixed term of imprisonment is being considered, the preconditions, as a rule, are that two thirds of an imposed sentence – with a minimum of two months – must have been served and that the prisoner's legal prognosis must be favourable. The prison authorities must prepare the prisoner for early release with regular prison leave and so forth in order to improve the assessment for a favourable prognosis.

Suspension is even possible after half of the imposed sentence – at least six months – has been served, on condition that, in consideration of the prisoner's offence, personality and institutional conduct, the prognosis is particularly favourable. This "half-time arrangement" applies in general to first-time imprisoned offenders sentenced to periods of less than two years' imprisonment and in exceptional cases also to others.[5] A probation officer may be assigned to the prisoner; the law stipulates that this will normally happen if a prisoner has served at least one year of imprisonment. Moreover, conditions relating to the conduct of the released prisoner may be set. The prisoner must always agree to being released early. The period of parole and of supervision by the probation service[6] lasts between two and five years.

In the case of a life sentence, the remainder of the sentence may be suspended after fifteen years' being served, if the legal prognosis is favourable and if the offence was not so serious that the offender should remain in detention.[7] At present the average period served is approximately eighteen to twenty years (Weber 1990). Critics have pointed out, quite justifiably, that the effect of the provision relating to the seriousness of the offence has been that, in practice, almost no prisoners are released after the minimum period of fifteen years and that the situation that existed before 1981 has not improved (Laubenthal 1987; Weber 1999; Dünkel 2002).[8] The current practice provides support for the repeal of the provision relating to the seriousness of the offence, if not also for the abolition of life imprisonment itself. The Federal Constitutional Court, however, accepted that this legal provision is not unconstitutional if the special seriousness of the homicide is determined by the court at the time of the conviction (and not by the *Strafvollstreckungskammer* fifteen years later).[9]

A prison sentence imposed on a juvenile may already be suspended by the juvenile court judge in his capacity as so-called *Vollstreckungsleiter* after one third of the sentence has been served, with a general minimum requirement

---

5.   See Section 57.II of the Penal Code.
6.   The German Penal Code provides that supervision by a probation officer shall regularly be imposed in cases where the prisoner has served a prison term of at least one year, see Section 57.III of the Penal Code.
7.   Section 57.a of the Penal Code.
8.   Before 1981 a prisoner serving a life sentence could only be released by an act of executive clemency. In 1977 the Federal Constitutional Court decided that this was not sufficient (BVerfGE 45, 187) but that, in other respects, life imprisonment was constitutional.
9.   See BVerfGE 86, 288.

that six months must have elapsed since the beginning of the period of imprisonment.[10] All decisions relating to early release are subject to immediate appeal to the Higher Regional Court.

In the 1980s the practice of suspending the remainder of sentences was expanded considerably. There is, however, a lack of valid statistical data as the prison statistics provided by the Federal Ministry of Justice count all cases of release, including the many fine defaulters who were not eligible for parole. Individual studies have revealed that the proportion of prisoners granted early release amounts to more than 50% if only sentences able to be commuted are taken into consideration (Böhm and Erhard 1984; Dünkel 1992). According to a representative study in Schleswig-Holstein concerning released prisoners in 1989 (see Dünkel 1992), 53% of adult male and 74% of female prisoners received parole; the proportion of prisoners in juvenile correctional institutions was 75%. In the case of prison sentences of more than one year, the percentages of prisoners granted early release went up to 63% (males) and 94% (females). The practice of early release varies considerably according to the regional court involved, the length of the sentence, the type of offence and to other variables such as conduct in prison and periods of home leave without incident (see Dünkel 1992, p. 115 *et seq.*, p. 287). The number of cases assigned to probation officers has increased even more. At present, around 85% of prisoners released early are assigned to a probation officer. Although there are great variations in individual cases, the success rate of prisoners released on parole is slightly more favourable than that of prisoners who serve their full sentence (Dünkel 1981; Böhm and Erhard 1988 and below).

For certain crimes, committed by persons who have served their full term and persons who have been released on parole after a period of preventive detention, supervision of conduct may, in certain circumstances, be ordered after release.[11] The objectives of resocialisation and the protection of society are met simultaneously by such supervision. In practice, probationary assistance is provided mostly for particularly difficult probationers. In this context, increased control sometimes constitutes an obstacle rather than help with reintegration. Moreover, it seems unfair that violations of certain conditions, while a person is subject to supervision of conduct, constitute separate crimes that are punishable with imprisonment of up to one year.[12] This explicitly violates Recommendation No. R (92) 16 of the Committee of Ministers to member states on the European rules on community sanctions and measures (see Morgenstern 2002).

---

10. Section 88 of the Juvenile Justice Act.
11. Provision for this supervision is made in terms of Section 68 *et seq.* of the Penal Code, which substitutes for the police supervision that was abolished in 1975.
12. See Section 145.a of the Penal Code.

Apart from probationary assistance as a form of assistance for released prisoners, it is a characteristic of Germany that various kinds of free (non-judicial) assistance are offered to ex-offenders by public and private associations. The decisive factor is that these associations, which operate on the basis of voluntary participation, can act independently. Most of these associations are advisory bureaux, projects to assist with accommodation, work or recreation, or agencies for debt relief assistance. Fines from criminal proceedings often provide funding for them.

In terms of Section 72 of the Federal Social Assistance Act (*Bundessozialhilfegesetz* – BSHG) released prisoners are entitled to assistance to enable them to overcome special social problems. According to the regulations issued in this regard, such assistance consists mainly of counselling, procuring and maintaining lodging, finding and securing work, as well as vocational training and recreational activities. Although this statutory assistance for released prisoners is defined in great detail, the problematic situation of ex-offenders still means that there is, in practice, a great demand for other forms of post-release assistance.

Empirical data and indicators for the rehabilitative impact of opening the prison system

As mentioned before, the opening of prisons has not resulted in major negative events, such as escape or crime committed during temporary release. The much more difficult question is whether by contributing to better social integration it results in less recidivism. A few German studies have dealt with recidivism after different forms of imprisonment. The major methodological problem is that selection for open prisons makes it difficult, if not impossible, to compare prison population groups in different forms of imprisonment.

However, an extended study in Berlin, mainly aimed at an evaluation of social therapeutic programmes, revealed that prisoners who had been released through a final stage at an open prison after an average risk period of five years had a 10% lower recidivism (in terms of re-incarceration) rate than – with respect to legal and socio-biographic risk factors – comparable ex-prisoners who had served their sentence entirely in closed prisons (see Dünkel 1980, p. 274 *et seq*; see also Rüther and Neufeind 1978).

Dolde ascertained that the recidivism rates in Baden-Württemberg were reduced after the introduction of a special programme where short-term prisoners (up to eighteen months) could serve their sentence at the outset in an open prison (in order to avoid loosing their jobs; see Dolde 1992, p. 28).

Another important question of rehabilitation is the impact of early conditional release on later recidivism. The answer is difficult, as those fully serving their sentence in most cases are prisoners with an unfavourable prognosis and those going on early release are seen as having a good prognosis.[13] Despite variations in practice, it is, none the less, possible to compare cases of similar legal and socio-biographic backgrounds where some such prisoners have been granted early release and others have not. The "production" of a statistically comparable control group to the early released ex-prisoners can be realised by statistical methods of co-variance analysis. This has been done in the research project on the Berlin-Tegel socio-therapeutic treatment unit (see Dünkel 1980 and 1981; Dünkel and Geng 1988). The results concerning reoffending and re-incarceration are encouraging: the early release group from the regular prison had a 13% lower re-incarceration rate than those having served the full sentence (see Dünkel 1980, p. 340 *et seq.*, p. 343; Dünkel 1981, p. 287 *et seq.*, p. 290). In the social therapy group, early release did not make such a big difference (-8%), as those fully serving the sentence had also received rehabilitative forms of relaxations from the prison regime through prison leave, etc. This result is remarkable in so far as two thirds of the social therapy group received early release (usually after two thirds of the sentence) against only one third of the regular prison group. So it can be concluded that the much more extensive practice of early release in the treatment group had rather positive – and in any case no negative – effects. Early release in Germany can be connected to assignment to the probation service. Those prisoners who had been released early with the supervision of a probation officer showed a 16% lower recidivism rate than other early released prisoners from a regular prison who had no such supervision (see Dünkel 1981, p. 291). So there is some indication of a positive impact by the probation service in addition to early release. This is remarkable as German law provides for supervision, in particular, in so-called risk cases that otherwise seem to relapse into crime.[14]

The social therapy group in total had an 18%-20% lower recidivism rate than the "untreated" control group of the regular prison (see also the meta-analyses of Lösel 1993 and 2001). The Tegel prison research showed, furthermore, some differential effects of early release concerning different types of offenders. The differences of recidivism rates in favour of early released prisoners can be shown independently of type of offence, number of pre-convictions and age-group (see Dünkel 1981, p. 289 *et seq.*).

The study in the federal state of Hesse by Böhm and Erhard could not really control the differences of the compared groups (the early released prisoners had a 5%-15% lower recidivism rate), but the authors concluded that early release is at least as favourable as serving a full sentence (see Böhm and Erhard 1988, p. 490 *et seq.*). This can also be demonstrated when looking at the variation of early release rates when comparing the practices of different courts (*Strafvollstreckungskammer*). No negative impact could be seen when the early

---

13. See Section 57 of the Penal Code.
14. See Section 57.III in connection with Section 56.d of the Penal Code.

release rate was 72%, rather than 57% or only 43% in another prison (see Böhm and Erhard 1988, p. 485 *et seq.*, p. 489). One remarkable result was that early released prisoners of foreign nationality showed almost no recidivism (Böhm and Erhard 1988, p. 493).

Another argument for the cost-effectiveness of early release schemes is that early release evidently saves money by avoiding longer imprisonment. Every day of imprisonment in Germany costs on average about €80, so granting release after two thirds of an eighteen-month prison sentence saves about €75 per day (including the costs of the probation service at €5 per day) or €13 500 for the entire period of early release, being six months of the sentence.

The results in Germany correspond with the French research of Kensey and Tournier (1999) and other international studies (see, for example, Sherman et al. 1998 with further references).

These results seem to be plausible when considering the international literature on effective strategies for offender rehabilitation (see Sherman et al. 1998; Lipton 1998; Vennard and Hedderman 1998; Lösel 2001). One of the important means for successful reintegration is the systematic preparation for release through forms of social training aimed at improving social competencies and professional skills. Prison leave and the extension of contacts with the outside world, as they are particularly used in open prisons, are part of such promising strategies. The evaluation literature emphasises the importance of well-structured programmes of social learning and training (see Andrews et al. 1990).

Aside from the "external" rehabilitative success in reducing reoffending, an important question is whether opening the prison system with respect to "internal" criteria, concerning living and working conditions in prison, also indicates some progress. The use of disciplinary and security measures and the coming up of prison disturbances (riots, hunger strikes, etc.) can be seen as indicators of internal conflicts. The hypothesis is that tensions within German prisons have been reduced and the climate in prisons has improved by the opening up of the prison system. First we have to look at the development of registered conflicts indicated by disciplinary and security measures.

The use of disciplinary and security measures as indicators of tension in prisons

Although the 1977 Prison Act reduced the importance of repressive disciplinary measures, it did not wish to dispense with them entirely. Section 102 *et seq.* provide for a number of punishments of disciplinary infringements, ranging from a reprimand, monetary restrictions, restrictions on recreational activities and the suspension from work to solitary confinement for up to four weeks. The question of whether escape and self-mutilation should be met with disciplinary sanctions, as is often the case in practice, is still disputed (Calliess and

Müller-Dietz 2002, Section 102, note 11.f). The majority of scholars refute the need for disciplinary sanctions in cases of non-violent escape.

Even practitioners do not regard the impact of what are to some extent "petty and silly persecutions" (Baumann 1974, p. 114) as very significant. The number of disciplinary sanctions imposed annually in West German penal institutions totals about 35 000 (57 per 100 prisoners in 1996).[15] There was an increase from the mid-1970s onwards (in 1974: 43 per 100 prisoners). Since 1982, however, the number of disciplinary sanctions imposed has remained constant and since 1988 it has decreased slightly. This trend is shown in Figure 7 below. The fact that prisoners are disciplined fairly often is not only proof that a traditional, more repressive concept of treatment and education is widespread, but that regulation of everyday prison life includes a great variety of prohibitions and orders, which lead inevitably to the violation of rules. The widespread freedom of action that flows from the relaxation of prison regimes, such as unlocked cells and communal living, has increased opportunities for violating the rules of the institution.

Figure 7: Disciplinary measures in West German prisons (1970-96)

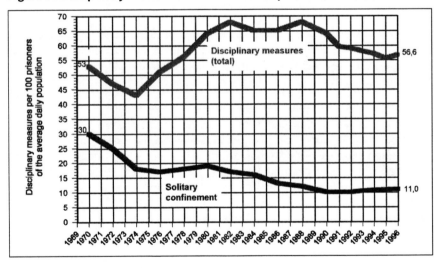

Apart from simple admonitions, possible disciplinary sanctions are: primarily, the withdrawal of the prison allowance (*Hausgeld*) for purchasing tobacco, food and other small items; a ban on participation in communal activities such as recreational groups and sport; and, as the most severe disciplinary measure, detention, that is, solitary confinement in a special cell for a maximum of four weeks (two weeks in juvenile correctional institutions). Since 1970, when the figure was 30 per 100 prisoners, the number of times that detention is imposed

---

15. Since 1996 the federal states (*Länder*) no longer provide statistics on disciplinary measures to the Federal Ministry of Justice and therefore newer statistical data are not available.

has been declining: in 1996 there were 11 per 100 prisoners (see Figure 7). It seems, however, that prisoners consider the withdrawal of the prison allowance and in particular the denial of home leave (prison furlough) or short prison leave as more severe sanctions than detention in solitary confinement. Although the denial of home leave is not officially a disciplinary measure, informally it is often regarded as such.

According to Section 2, paragraph 2, of the Prison Act the treatment approach to the implementation of prison sentences should seek also to protect the general public from further crimes. In addition to general safeguards designed to prevent escape, the law provides for special measures for the incarceration of dangerous prisoners. This is sensible, for if the general safeguards were designed to cope with the most dangerous cases they would burden all prisoners disproportionately. Differentiation of institutions according to varying grades of security is designed to serve this purpose. Therefore formal disciplinary measures are only a part of a system of informal sanctions that are used to guarantee discipline and order in prisons (Walter 1999, p. 447). The withdrawal of privileges or conveniences of daily life, like the possession of certain goods or objects, are not formal disciplinary measures but are sometimes used as such.

It is possible to search both the inmate and his or her cell,[16] to transfer him or her in order to ensure his or her secure incarceration[17] and to record his or her details for purposes of police records.[18]

Section 88 of the Prison Act permits the following measures, which can be defined as security measures in a narrower sense: the withdrawal of certain objects from the control of the prisoner; surveillance at night; isolation from other prisoners; restriction of time spent outdoors; confinement in a specially secure cell ("a calming cell"); and shackling. This provision contains a complete catalogue of the authorised measures and it must be interpreted strictly according to the principle of proportionate means. Confinement in a "calming cell" is particularly problematic. It is a measure resorted to when there is no other way of dealing with a prisoner in an exceptional mental state. It is not a substitute for treatment. To what extent this problem can be dealt with by way of medication – as is the practice in most psychiatric hospitals – is still an open question. The procedure is not regulated by law and hence the problem has not been addressed openly. However, the highly differentiated regional practices are a cause for concern. In 1996, confinements per 100 prisoners ranged from 2 to 6 in Saarland, Mecklenburg-Western Pomerania, Saxony, Saxony-Anhalt and Bavaria (see Figure 8). In contrast, it was imposed 15 to 16 times in Berlin, Brandenburg and Bremen and even 18 times in Schleswig-Holstein. This clearly

---

16. Section 84 of the Prison Act.
17. Section 85 of the Prison Act.
18. Section 86 of the Prison Act.

indicates significant regional differences in practice, rather than different inmate groups that cause security problems. These discrepancies are evident in Figure 8. Secure cells from which all dangerous objects have been removed are to be found in most closed prisons. There were about 300 such cells in the old Federal Republic as a whole (*Bundestags-Drucksache*, 11/4302, p. 9).

Figure 8: Solidarity confinement in German prisons (1996). Disciplinary and security measures in a comparison of the federal states

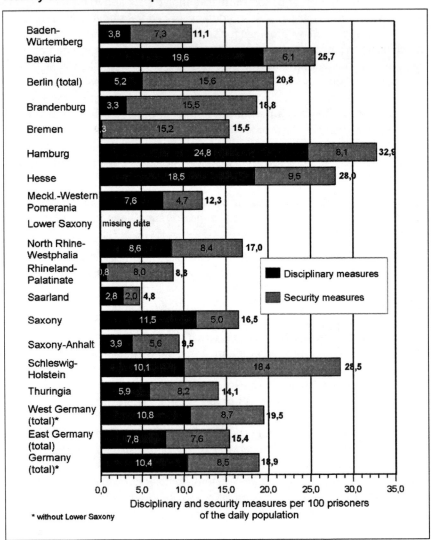

* without Lower Saxony

Reducing tension by opening prisons

There is no clear evidence from longitudinal studies of a correlation between diminished prison disturbances and the opening up of prisons since the early 1970s. However, practitioners clearly state that with the introduction of prison furloughs, etc., everyday prison life has been much easier to manage (or from the prisoners' perspective – everyday life for prisoners has become much more manageable) and that tensions have been reduced considerably (see Preusker 1987; Kaiser and Schöch 2002). The facts can be interpreted ambivalently, as prison leave can also be seen as a measure for disciplining prisoners.

Evidence of reduced tension can also be seen when looking at the number of violent acts by prisoners directed at prison guards.

Interestingly, the relative numbers of violent acts directed at prison guards in the "new" federal states in the early 1990s was twice as high as in the "old" federal states (1994, 1.0 and 0.5 per 100 prisoners respectively, see Dünkel 1996, p. 100), where leave of absence was much more widespread (see Figures 9 and 10). It seems to be a plausible interpretation that the emphasis on secure detention and preventing escapes in the early 1990s in the East German federal states (for criticism, see Dünkel 1995) created tension amongst prisoners that sometimes manifested itself in aggressive behaviour towards prison staff. Since 1994 the East German prison authorities have emphasised, more and more, rehabilitative aspects like the opening up and relaxation of prison regimes. At the same time, physical attacks against prison staff members have declined considerably.

Figure 9: Development of physical attacks against prison staff members in Germany (1993-2000) in comparison of the old and new federal states

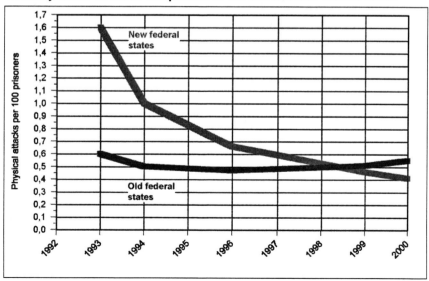

Figure 10: Physical attacks against prison staff members in Germany (1993, 1996 and 2000) in comparison of the federal states

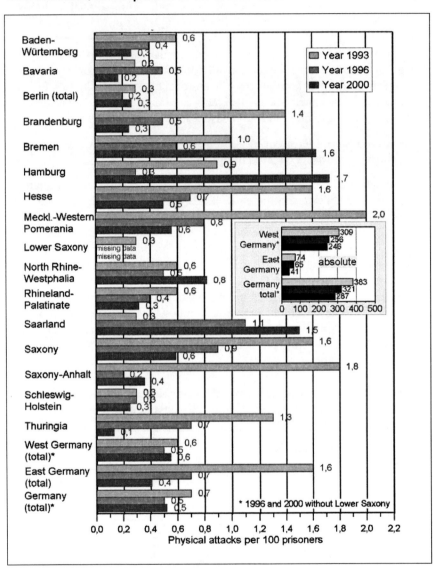

Conclusion

The German prison system has experienced major changes – with liberalised regimes and increased contacts for prisoners with the outside world – since the late 1960s that have contributed considerably to a reduction in prison disturbances and riots, without negative effects for the security of the general public. Furthermore, increases in prison leave have had positive effects in so far as failures to return to prison, as well as serious crimes committed during periods of leave of absence, have been reduced. In the European context, similar developments can be seen in many countries. On the other hand, more repressive prison regimes, particularly for specific groups of offenders, lead to more tensions and, in individual cases, to violence, hostage-taking, etc., by prisoners who cannot hope for prison leave and other forms of relaxations (long-term prisoners and prisoners held in security units). Therefore, the conclusion must be to guarantee relaxation of the prison regime (including leave of absence) and to preserve hope for early release for all groups of prisoners, including those serving life sentences or in preventive detention at the time when they are regarded as no longer being a danger to society. This will contribute to more internal security in the prison and therefore reduce risks of victimisation, both for prison staff as well as for the general public.

References

Andrews, D.A. et al., "Does correctional treatment work? A clinically relevant and psychologically informed meta-analysis", *Criminology*, 28, 1990, pp. 369-404.

Baumann, J. (ed.), *Die Reform des Strafvollzugs*, Goldmann Verlag, Munich, 1974.

Böhm, A., "Vollzugslockerungen und offener Vollzug zwischen Strafzwecken und Vollzugszielen", *Neue Zeitschrift für Strafrecht*, 6, 1986, pp. 201-206.

Böhm, A. and Erhard, C., "Die Praxis der bedingten Strafrestaussetzung. Eine Untersuchung zur Anwendung des § 57 StGB in Hessen", *Monatsschrift für Kriminologie und Strafrechtsreform*, 67, 1984, pp. 365-378.

Böhm, A. and Erhard, C., "Strafrestaussetzung und Legalbewährung. Überblick über Ergebnisse einer Rückfalluntersuchung in zwei hessischen Vollzugs-anstalten mit unterschiedlicher Strafrestaussetzungspraxis", in Kaiser, G. et al. (eds.), *Kriminologische Forschung in den 80er Jahren*, Max-Planck-Institut für ausländisches und internationales Strafrecht, Freiburg, 1988, pp. 481-494.

Calliess, R.-P. and Müller-Dietz, H., *Strafvollzugsgesetz*, ninth edition, C.H. Beck Verlag, Munich, 2002.

Dolde, G., "Zehn Jahre Erfahrung mit dem Vollzug der Freiheitsstrafe ohne soziale Desintegration", *Zeitschrift für Strafvollzug und Straffälligenhilfe*, 40, 1992, pp. 24-30.

Dünkel, F., *Legalbewährung nach sozialtherapeutischer Behandlung*, Duncker und Humblot, Berlin, 1980.

Dünkel, F., "Prognostische Kriterien zur Abschätzung des Erfolgs von Behandlungsmaßnahmen im Strafvollzug sowie für die Entscheidung über die bedingte Entlassung", *Monatsschrift für Kriminologie und Strafrechtsreform*, 64, 1981, pp. 279-295.

Dünkel, F., *Empirische Beiträge und Materialien zum Strafvollzug. Be-stands-saufnahmen des Strafvollzugs in Schleswig-Holstein und des Frauenvollzugs in Berlin*, Max-Planck-Institut für ausländisches und internationales Strafrecht, Freiburg, 1992.

Dünkel, F., "Imprisonment in transition. The situation in the new states of the Federal Republic of Germany", *British Journal of Criminology*, 35, 1995, pp. 95-113.

Dünkel, F., *Empirische Forschung im Strafvollzug. Bestandsaufnahme und Per-spektiven*, Forum Verlag, Bonn, 1996.

Dünkel, F., "Riskante Freiheiten? – Offener Vollzug, Vollzugslockerungen und Hafturlaub zwischen Resozialisierung und Sicherheitsrisiko", in Kawamura, G. and Reindl, R. (eds.), *Wiedereingliederung Straffälliger. Eine Bilanz nach 20 Jahren Strafvollzugsgesetz*, Lambertus Verlag, Freiburg, 1998, pp. 42-78.

Dünkel, F., "Germany", in Van Zyl Smit, D. and Dünkel, F. (eds.), *Prison labour – Salvation or slavery?*, Ashgate, Aldershot, 1999, pp. 77-103.

Dünkel, F., "§§ 38, 39 StGB", in Neumann, U., Puppe, I. and Schild, W. (eds.), *Nomos Kommentar zum Strafgesetzbuch*, Nomos Verlag, Baden-Baden, 2002.

Dünkel, F. and Geng, B., "Aspects of the recidivism of career offenders according to different forms of correction and release from prison", in Kaiser, G. and Geissler, I. (eds.), *Crime and criminal justice. Criminological research in the 2nd decade of the Max Planck Institute in Freiburg*, Max-Planck-Institut für ausländisches und internationales Strafrecht, Freiburg, 1988, pp. 137-185.

Dünkel, F. and Kunkat, A., "Zwischen Innovation und Restauration. 20 Jahre Straf-vollzugsgesetz – eine Bestandsaufnahme", *Neue Kriminalpolitik*, 9, No. 2, 1997, pp. 24-33.

Dünkel, F. and Rössner, D., "Germany", in Van Zyl Smit, D. and Dünkel, F. (eds.), *Imprisonment today and tomorrow. International perspectives on prisoners' rights and prison conditions*, Kluwer, Deventer, Boston, 2001, pp. 288-350.

Feest, J. and Weber, H., "Germany: ups and downs in the resort to imprisonment – Strategic or unplanned outcomes", in Weiss, R.P. and South, N. (eds.), *Comparing prison systems. Towards a comparative and international penology*, Gordon and Breach Publishers, Amsteldijk, 1998, pp. 233-261.

Heghmanns, M., "Die neuere Rechtsprechung des Bundesverfassungsgerichts zur gerichtlichen Überprüfung der Versagung von Vollzugslockerungen – eine Trend-wende?", *Zeitschrift für die gesamten Strafrechtswissenschaften*, 111, 1999, pp. 647-672.

Kaiser, G. and Schöch, H., *Strafvollzug*, fifth edition, C.F. Müller, Heidelberg, 2002.

Kensey, A. and Tournier, P., "Prison population inflation. Overcrowding and recidivism: the situation in France", *European Journal on Criminal Policy and Research*, 7, 1999, pp. 97-119.

Laubenthal, K., *Lebenslange Freiheitsstrafe. Vollzug und Aussetzung des Strafrests zur Bewährung*, Rhömhild, Lübeck, 1987.

Lipton, D.S., "The effectiveness of correctional treatment revisited thirty years later: preliminary meta-analytic findings from the CDATE study", paper presented at the 12th International Congress of Criminology, Seoul, 24 to 29 August 1998.

Lösel, F., "Sprechen Evaluationsergebnisse von Meta-Analysen für einen frischen Wind in der Straftäterbehandlung?", in Egg, R. (ed.), *Sozialtherapie in den 90er Jahren*, Kriminologische Zentralstelle, Wiesbaden, 1993, pp. 21-31.

Lösel, F., "Behandlung oder Verwahrung? Ergebnisse und Perspektiven der Interventionen bei 'psychopathischen' Straftätern", in Rehn, G. et al. (eds.), *Behandlung "gefährlicher Straftäter"*, Centaurus, Herbolzheim, 2001, pp. 36-53.

Morgenstern, C., *Internationale Mindeststandards für ambulante Strafen und Maßnahmen*, Forum Verlag Godesberg, Mönchengladbach, 2002.

Preusker, H., "Erfahrungen der Praxis mit dem Strafvollzugsgesetz", *Zeitschrift für Strafvollzug und Straffälligenhilfe*, 36, 1987, pp. 11-16.

Rüther, W. and Neufeind, W., "Offener Vollzug und Rückfallkriminalität", *Monatsschrift für Kriminologie und Strafrechtsreform*, 61, 1978, pp. 363-376.

Sherman, L.W. et al., *Preventing crime. What works, what doesn't, what's promising*, Office of Justice Programs, National Institute of Justice, US Department of Justice, 1998 (see also: National Institute of Justice, "Research in brief", July 1998; complete documentation: www.preventingcrime.org).

Van Zyl Smit, D., "Leave of absence for West German prisoners: legal principle and administrative practice", *British Journal of Criminology*, 28, 1988, pp. 1-18.

Vennard, J. and Hedderman, C., "Effective interventions with offenders", in Goldblatt, P. and Lewis, C. (eds.), *Reducing offending: an assessment of research evidence on ways of dealing with offending behaviour*, Home Office, London, 1998, pp. 101-119.

Walter, M., *Strafvollzug*, second edition, Boorberg Verlag, Stuttgart, Munich, Hannover, 1999.

Weber, H., "Die Abschaffung der lebenslangen Freiheitstrafe über Tatschuld und positive Generalprävention", *Monatsschrift für Kriminologie und Strafrechtsreform*, 73, 1990, pp. 65-81.

Weber, H., *Die Abschaffung der lebenslangen Freiheitsstrafe*, Nomos Verlag, Baden-Baden, 1999.

Chapter 12

Conditional release and the prevention of reoffending

Annie Kensey

In the framework of examples of good practices with respect to criminal justice and prison, this article deals with conditional release and the work done in France to prevent former prisoners' reoffending.

The article begins by describing the great increase in the prison population in France and the possible means of reducing these alarming figures. The number of prisoners doubled over a twenty-year period and, after falling for five years recently, has now started to rise again.

The research – carried out in the Prison Administration Directorate in association with Pierre V. Tournier – brought out the importance of the relationship between adjusting sentences and the reintegration of released prisoners in society.

Changes in the prison population in France

Between 1975 and 1995, the number of prisoners increased by 100%, from 26 000 to 52 000, while the population at large increased by 10% over the same period. There was then a downward trend for several years, followed by an unprecedented upward trend.

The increase in the prison population since the mid-1970s has been unaffected by three Amnesty Acts and repeated collective pardons decreed every year since 1991, as is shown in Figure 1.

Figure 1: Prison population in France, 1980-2003 (as of the first of each month)

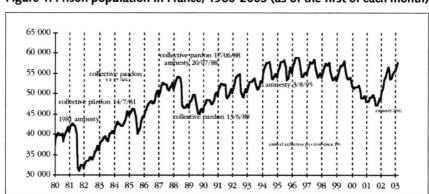

These are the figures for "stock", namely the people in prison on the first of each month. It is important to examine fluctuations in the flow of entries to prison and the length of imprisonment. The main reason behind the upward trend between 1975 and 1995 was that the average period of imprisonment increased from 4.3 months in 1980 to 7.6 months, while the average flow of prison entries stagnated or fell. Between 1996 and 2002, the average length of imprisonment continued to rise but entries to prison fell more sharply.

The fall in entry flows was connected with the work done to find alternatives to prison, especially for less serious offences. It should be emphasised, however, that this is not enough to solve the problem of overcrowding in prisons since ever longer sentences are not affected.

The trend towards longer sentences in France since 1981 is also observable in a number of other European countries. During the 1980s, the number of entries to prison was falling in Belgium, Germany, Italy and Portugal, while the prison population increased as a result of longer sentences everywhere except in Germany.

It is known that the consequences of overcrowding are harmful to prison staff and others working in prisons as well as prisoners. The situation also spells insecurity for everyone living or working in prisons, but is also reflected in the community when the numerical pressure of the prison population works against reintegration programmes and their impact on preventing reoffending.

Why reduce the prison population?

During an international seminar on overpopulation in prisons and the possible solutions[1] the participants showed that social reintegration improved when the enforcement of sentences included individualised early release measures.

The best way of curbing overcrowding in prisons is to reduce the length of imprisonment at the same time as pursuing a policy of reducing entries to prison.

In theory, a number of measures may reduce the length of imprisonment, including cutting the length of pre-trial proceedings, changing the sentencing scale, reforming enforcement of sentences and changing attitudes among judges and juries.

Reducing the sentencing scale may be unpopular, if one believes leniency to be unpopular among the general public. However, such an idea forgets the educational role of government authorities, professionals, associations and researchers who together can inform people rather than follow the barometer of public opinion as it is recorded by public opinion polls.

1. Prison Populations in Europe and North America, Problems and Solutions, Helsinki, March 1997.

The critical situation in prisons may encourage judges to be less severe, but should overcrowding in prisons be taken into account in court decisions? In any case, it is important to inform judges and magistrates of the realities of prison life.

In France, collective pardons have become a tradition on 14 July, the national day, in order to relieve overcrowding in prisons. They exclude some categories of offences, however, and represent only a supplementary reduction in sentences which is applied to prisoners without distinction. This makes collective pardons, of all the measures from which prisoners benefit, the one that places least responsibility upon them. Like reductions in sentences, they are granted almost systematically and therefore are in no way individualised.

Such procedures are purely ways of managing the lack of space and discipline in prisons and have almost nothing in common with conditional release which is a true preventive measure.

Good practice: conditional release and the prevention of reoffending

Research on reoffending conducted by the Prison Administration Directorate of the CNRS[2] has demonstrated the effectiveness of conditional release. Prisoners released in 1982 who had originally been sentenced to at least three years' imprisonment were studied. Their records were examined as of 15 June 1988 for an initial analysis of the return to prison rate. Some 34% of them had returned to prison during a four-year period following release.

One third of those released in 1982 had been released on parole.

The return to prison rate varied enormously according to the type of release: the rate was 23% for those released on parole as against 40% for those who had been released on completing their sentence.

This is a significant difference, though the findings may in part be attributed to the supervision and assistance provided for those released on parole. The widely divergent rates may also be the result of the selection of prisoners granted conditional release.

These two factors, "assistance and supervision" and "selection", have cumulative effects which are obviously difficult to evaluate separately. The nature of the criteria influencing the decision to grant or refuse conditional release can vary considerably and some of those criteria – behaviour in prison, for example – are entirely outside the scope of the present analysis. However, some

---

2. Kensey, A. and Tournier, P.V., *Le retour en prison, analyse diachronique (détenus libérés en 1973 – détenus libérés en 1982, initialement condamnés à trois ans ou plus)*, Direction de l'administration pénitentiaire, CESDIP, "Travaux et documents" No. 40, 1991, and *Libération sans retour? Devenir judiciaire d'un cohorte de sortants de prison condamnés à une peine à temps de trois ans et plus*, Direction de l'administration pénitentiaire, CESDIP, Paris, "Travaux et documents" No. 47, 1994.

structural differences are immediately clear when the proportion of those released on parole is examined. It is double among those who did not have a previous conviction and those who had committed a serious rather than a minor offence, and the proportion increases with age. It is therefore useful to compare the effects of structures on the various return rates between the group leaving at the end of their sentence and those released on parole.

Thus, taking into account the different distributions of the two groups according to criminal record, type of offence and age on release, and with the assistance of a calculation of comparative rates, the rate of return according to type of release is reduced by half, but the difference remains significant: 29% for those released on parole as against 36.5% for the rest.

The findings are set out in the following table:

| | Returns to prison according to type of release | | |
	End of sentence	Conditional release	Difference (percentage points)
Rate observed	39.8%	23%	16.8
Rate with equivalent structure (age, nature of offence, previous conviction)	37.5%	29.4%	8.1

Clearly, this method is rather too rudimentary to be able to claim separation of the "selection" and "assistance and supervision" factors; it simply indicates the possible importance of selection criteria.

The second study looked at the subsequent offending of the same group of prisoners released in 1982. The criminal records of the 1 157 released prisoners in the sample were therefore examined. It was thus possible to observe the rate of new cases which led to further convictions, whether or not a custodial sentence was imposed, and in particular to study the effect of the group's type of release from prison on their subsequent offending.

In almost 50% of the cases studied it was found that a further offence, leading to a conviction, had been committed within four years after release.

The average interval between release and the offence relating to the new case was one year and one month. Slightly fewer than 40% of the released prisoners had committed further offences less than six months after release.

The new offences were on the whole less serious than the initial offences. In the majority of cases, however, they resulted in custodial sentences.

The existence of a criminal record (prior to the first case) had a significant effect on the probability of there being a new case: of those released who had no previous criminal record, 40% committed further offences, as compared with 75.5% of those who had a record of two offences.

The type of release from prison had a significant effect on reoffending: the rate of reoffending by those released at the end of their sentences was 54.5%, while it was 39.6% for those released on parole.

The study went on to look at the group in more detail, according to the initial offence.

This analysis enabled more significant conclusions to be drawn about the effect of conditional release on preventing reoffending. The rates of new cases concern all types of new offences on the criminal record.

Where the initial offence was theft, the category with the highest rate of new cases, the rate was 75% among those who had been released at the end of their sentence and 64.3% for those released on parole.

Where the initial offence was aggravated theft, the rate of new cases was 64.4% of those released at the end of their sentence as against 39.1% for those released on parole.

Where the initial offence was assault and battery, the rate was 60.9% for those released at the end of their sentence and 35.1% for those released on parole. Where the initial offence was rape, the rate was 46.9% for those released at the end of their sentence and 24.9% for those released on parole.

Where the initial offence was murder, the rate of new cases was 41.1% for those released at the end of their sentence and 24.6% for those released on parole.

Where the initial offence was indecent assault (since the entry into force of the new Criminal Code in 1994, indecent assault has been referred to as a sex attack), the rate of new cases was 37% for those released at the end of their sentence and 12.5% for those released on parole, but, since fewer than twenty cases were examined in the target group, this rate is not considered significant.

In order to eliminate the structural effects, as in the analysis of return to prison, typologies were constructed for each offence. It emerged from this that the rate of new cases was reduced in almost all cases by early release on parole, particularly among those convicted for the first time.

Thus the rate of reoffending by prisoners released on parole is considerably lower than among those released at the end of their sentence. The selection of prisoners for conditional release is significant but does not completely explain the lower reoffending rate. The supervision of prisoners after their release is probably more decisive.

Conditional release is in fact the most promising measure since it also concerns long periods of imprisonment and is based on the idea of a prepared and supervised return to the community.

Since the 1970s, however, the number of conditional releases has fallen significantly in France.

If there is a real wish to promote conditional release and see that it can be applied to the great majority of prisoners, it is essential to reduce the risk of reoffending by taking effective measures before release – within the prison – appropriate to the prisoners, but also by developing genuine assistance and supervision measures of varying degrees of severity, as appropriate, following release. Both these conditions are necessary if conditional release is to be made more credible in the eyes of those who sentence and those on behalf of whom sentences are handed down.

The act of 15 June 2000 on the presumption of innocence which strengthens the rights of victims contains a number of provisions on conditional release. Twenty-three measures are proposed: for example, broadening and easing the conditions for granting it, making the procedure more flexible, extending the powers of the judge responsible for applying sentences in this regard, abolishing the power of the Minister of Justice and transferring it to a collegial court, making decisions to grant conditional release judicial decisions and giving the reasons for them, improving supervision and assistance measures, etc.

The drafting of this part of the act was based on the findings of our work much of which was taken up by the commission chaired by Mr Farge set up by the Minister of Justice in 1999 to study ways of reviving conditional release.

In 2003, the new government asked a member of parliament, Mr Jean-Luc Warsmann, to draft a report on the development of alternatives to prison. One of the recommendations is to construct a legal framework enabling the adoption of a general principle of gradual preparation for release by the almost systematic use of a measure other than imprisonment towards the end of sentences.

PART IV
CRIMINAL PROCEDURE

Chapter 13

Treatment of persons co-operating with the judicial authorities and witnesses: the Italian system and good practices

Francesco De Leo, Mariavaleria del Tufo, Gualtiero Michelini and Francesco Patrone

Having been obliged to address organised crime before other European countries, Italy is one of the countries with the most experience in combating this type of crime. Its legislation in this field can serve as a worthwhile example for other systems and may provide some ideas for introducing rules and regulations in this area.

In this report, the authors have set out to highlight a particular aspect of Italy's experience of the treatment of persons who co-operate with the judicial authorities. It has been known for several decades that they are of key importance in combating organised crime.

It became increasingly clear that there was a need to legislate in order to provide an effective level of protection, in order to ensure the security of persons who have to give evidence in court about criminal activities and convince former members of criminal organisations to co-operate with the judicial authorities.

Italy has successfully introduced a number of measures to this end, and this contribution therefore describes the legislation and standards that apply in Italy and the practices used in connection with those who collaborate with the judicial authorities.

The contribution mainly concerns the treatment applicable under criminal and procedural law and during prison custody. Special attention is paid to protection schemes for persons co-operating with the judicial authorities and for witnesses. Ample coverage has been given to the use and organisation of video-conferences, for this technical facility has proved to be of key importance in balancing the need for protection with the rules governing trials and the rights of the defendant.

In this connection, Italy's experience shows that it is necessary to introduce:

- special measures allowing the courts to recognise the existence and extent of mitigating circumstances; these may lead to a significant reduction in the sentence;
- different kinds and levels of protection, depending on the actual risk incurred by the person concerned;
- a variety of appropriate protection methods, ranging from home surveillance to a comprehensive "special protection scheme";
- the possibility of giving evidence from a secret location by means of audiovisual technology, with due regard for constitutional principles and the rules governing a fair trial;
- means of providing compensation for damage, special funds for victims of heinous crimes and arrangements for providing practical assistance and opportunities for a return to a law-abiding life in society for former members of criminal organisations, as part of a comprehensive strategy.

Legislative background

The treatment afforded to those who collaborate with the judicial authorities and to witnesses in Italy has been further refined by Law 45/2001, which improved on the rules and procedures introduced in this field over the last twenty-five years with a view to making it possible to combat organised crime more effectively. The rationale for the new law, which subsequently proved to be correct, was the belief that certain information concerning criminal offences could be acquired only from those directly involved.

One of the earliest instances of the application of the right to preferential or favourable treatment was connected with efforts to combat terrorism. This principle was subsequently extended to persons involved in ordinary organised crime who co-operated with the judicial authorities. It was not until Law No. 45 was passed in 2001 that the matter was properly regulated. In contrast to the previous law on the subject, which was prepared somewhat incoherently, the objectives of the new law are:

- to ensure the authenticity of statements given by those who collaborate with the judicial authorities, so as to avoid the problem of supergrasses who give insincere or false statements (*falsi pentiti*);
- to ensure that protection is given only to those whose statements are found to be relevant to the investigation and, at the same time, reduce the number of people requiring protection, which has increased enormously over time.
- to ensure that all the rights and duties of those who collaborate with the judicial authorities are properly regulated;
- to make a distinction between those who collaborate with the judicial authorities and witnesses.

The Italian legal system does not provide a definition for those who collaborate with the prosecuting authorities. It may, however, be argued that there are two different categories of people. In the narrow sense, the expression may be used to describe anyone who, having been involved in a criminal organisation, is resolved to distance himself or herself from it and collaborate with the judicial authorities by providing them with information about the organisation's structure and offences committed by the organisation or a similar organisation. In the broad sense, the expression may also be used to describe people who, having committed an offence on their own, resolve to distance themselves from it and provide the judicial authorities with information about offences of which they have knowledge – usually offences connected with organised crime. It is clear that the distinction depends on whether or not the person collaborating with the judicial authorities belongs to a criminal organisation. The fact that there are two categories can be explained in the light of the treatment afforded. In the former case, namely when the person was involved in a criminal gang, he or she will be entitled to a reduced sentence and enjoy protection. In the latter case, namely when the person is not part of a criminal gang, no protection will be provided. Moreover, those who collaborate after being involved in a criminal organisation will, if it is a terrorist or Mafia-type organisation, be entitled to protection regardless of the level of collaboration. Finally, those who belong to different types of organisation, for example organisations involved in drug trafficking or kidnapping, will be entitled to protection only if their collaboration is deemed by law to be of great value. The difference in treatment between the two types of criminal organisations has been severely criticised.

The term "witness for the prosecution" is used to describe anyone who has witnessed or been the victim of an offence, whether or not connected with organised crime, but is not involved in it (that is, he or she is not connected or associated with it in any way) and is able to provide the judicial authorities with information about it. This definition is "substantial" in the Italian legal system: from a legal point of view defendants may give factual evidence in criminal proceedings related to the proceedings in which they are involved, where the facts in dispute do not directly concern them. In this case, however, the rules that apply to the defendant are those that govern the protection of persons collaborating with the prosecuting authorities rather than those governing the protection of witnesses for the prosecution, which, as will be seen, are different.

Types of treatment

There are four areas in which the treatment afforded to persons collaborating with the prosecuting authorities differs from ordinary treatment:

- treatment applicable under criminal law (that is, the sentencing system);
- treatment during prison custody;

- treatment applicable under procedural law;

- protection measures.

While preferential treatment is afforded in the first two categories, harsh treatment is meted out to those who obstinately continue to be involved in crime (persistent offenders). This two-tier judicial policy has so far proved to be highly successful in Italy in combating organised crime.

Treatment applicable under criminal law

As far as sentencing is concerned, the law provides for reduced sentences for persons who collaborate with the judicial authorities by providing information in the case of the following offences: abduction or kidnapping for ransom, kidnapping for terrorist purposes, offences committed for terrorist purposes, criminal association for the purposes of drug trafficking, involvement in a Mafia-type criminal organisation, offences committed for Mafia-type criminal purposes, and criminal association for the purposes of smuggling, trafficking and prostitution of minors. These offences have in common the fact that they are all forms of organised crime. It is, however, necessary to add other types of criminal activity, such as drug dealing and smuggling, which are often included in this category, even though they do not necessarily take the form of organised crime. Then there is theft, which is a separate offence and does not come under the heading of organised crime. In the case of each of the above offences, the sentence may be substantially reduced, by up to two thirds.

Further to the restrictions provided for in Law 45/2001 (which applies to protection measures rather than reductions in sentences, which are not covered by the law in question), it has been argued that it would be counter-productive to apply legislative restrictions in such circumstances, given that organised crime is on the increase. On the contrary, it would be appropriate to allow reductions in sentences, especially in the case of co-operation with the judicial authorities, not only in the case of specified forms of criminal association, as is the case today, but in the case of all types of offences committed in association with others.

The possibility of establishing a wide-ranging system of reduced sentences where efforts are made to co-operate with the judicial authorities in the case of all types of offences rather than simply organised crime has been debated on several occasions in Italy. Those who support this approach take the view that the sentence should be reduced by a quarter to a third, the former applying to a more limited range of statutory sentences.

Under the two-tier policy the following situations are dealt with differently:

- sentences that are more severe than the normal statutory sentences (for example, sentences passed on persons committing offences for terrorist purposes or Mafia-type criminal offences); or

- sentences for specific offences that are more serious than ordinary criminal offences (namely, kidnapping for ransom and kidnapping committed for terrorist purposes, as opposed to ordinary kidnapping).

Treatment during prison custody

The two-tier judicial policy operates as follows when it comes to treatment during prison custody: on the one hand, without going into too much detail, severe restrictive measures apply to prison inmates and detainees accused of organised crime, including restrictions on prison benefits, such as good behaviour premiums, opportunities to work outside the prison premises and alternatives to imprisonment. On the other hand, such benefits are available to inmates who are willing to co-operate with the judicial authorities, as an exception to the ordinary rules.

The same two-tier regime applies to persons charged with a criminal offence and remanded in custody during criminal proceedings. On the one hand, those charged with Mafia-type offences must be kept in custody, while on the other those willing to co-operate may be detained elsewhere than in a prison or even be released from custody.

The harsher prison treatment afforded to inmates involved in organised crime can even entail suspension by the Minister of Justice of the ordinary prison rules (for example, the right to outdoor exercise, the right to visits from relatives and the right to receive parcels from outside by post). From a practical point of view, this harsh treatment, which severely affects inmates' lives in prison because they are placed in solitary confinement, has been crucial in preventing regular communication with other criminals. The experience of solitary confinement has often prompted inmates to choose to collaborate.

Investigative interviews can also be an incentive to collaborate with the judicial authorities. The term "investigative interview" speaks for itself, in that such interviews are conducted for Mafia investigation purposes by the State Public Prosecutor and by specialised law enforcement staff in order to obtain information needed for investigations. The State Public Prosecutor is the central public prosecution authority empowered to co-ordinate action against Mafia-type criminal organisations throughout Italy. Investigative interviews can also be useful in encouraging co-operation with investigating experts.

Since there was much criticism of the use and abuse of prison benefits by investigative bodies in the case of those who collaborated with the judicial authorities, Law 45/2001 enshrines three essential features:

- a rigorous procedure for determining whether persons collaborating with the prosecuting authorities deserve benefits (for example, this involves ascertaining whether those who collaborate deserve certain benefits as a result of their behaviour and their conduct in trial proceedings);

- if those who collaborate deserve benefits, those benefits may be granted only once the sentence has been served for a specified length of time;

- detention on remand cannot be automatically revoked simply in return for a contribution from those collaborating; it may, on the other hand, be revoked once it has been ascertained that the persons collaborating have honoured their commitments, and therefore only after a period of time has elapsed.

The prison administration has the discretion to assign prisoners to separate sections or group them together for reasons connected with the dangerousness of certain prisoners or the need to take special precautions for various categories of prisoners. The Prison Administration Department (DAP) has designated special separate sections to which to assign individuals posing personal safety problems because of:

- the traditional antagonistic attitude towards the perpetrators of such heinous crimes as sexual abuse of minors;

- rivalry between criminal organisations;

- co-operation with the judicial authorities.

In the last case, prisoners have to be separated because they are exposed to the risk of revenge attacks.

To qualify for the precautions afforded to those who collaborate with the judicial authorities, it is necessary to meet two specific conditions: there must be a serious and real danger to the safety of the person concerned stemming from his or her co-operation, and his or her statements must concern one of the most serious types of crime.

At the suggestion of the police or the judicial authorities, a special protection scheme can be arranged, the Central Committee provided for by Law 8/1991 being responsible for devising and authorising such a scheme.

The law provides for the adoption of a decree specifying how the Penitentiary Act provisions should be implemented in the case of persons put forward for admittance or admitted to the special protection scheme.

Three types of prison section are currently available in the prison system for persons collaborating with the judicial authorities:

- sections designed for prisoners currently co-operating with the judicial authorities, once it has been suggested that they be admitted to, or put forward for, the special protection scheme;

- sections designed for prisoners who have been given the status of "persons collaborating with the judicial authorities" but who have been neither admitted to, nor put forward for, the special protection scheme;

• sections designed for prisoners who enjoy the status of persons collaborating with the judicial authorities, who have been admitted to, or put forward for, the special protection scheme.

According to the established policy of the central office which handles such matters, before a prisoner is admitted to one of the above-mentioned sections, summary proceedings take place with a view to having the prisoner classified or having the appropriate judicial authority certify that the prisoner has acquired the status of a person collaborating with the judicial authorities.

As soon as the central office has been informed, often from more than one source, that a prisoner has expressed the intention of co-operating with the judicial authorities, or indeed has already started to do so by making initial statements to this end, it notifies the Governor of the prison where the prisoner is being held, issuing instructions concerning custody arrangements (that is, detention in an individual cell) and making provision for special precautions (namely, prohibition of any contact with other prisoners co-operating with the judicial authorities, prohibition of visits from relatives if they are co-operating of their own free will, total separation from other inmates who are co-operating, and separate administration of food and medicine if necessary) needed to ensure the safety of the person who is expected to collaborate and to prevent dangerous outside pressure that might affect his or her statements.

Special precautions are continued for no more than six months, until the person collaborating has finished providing the prosecutor with all the information in his or her possession about the responsibility of other persons and of the criminal organisation.

During this stage, the office responsible gets in touch with the judicial authority, which is requested to report on developments in the prisoners' position as regards trial, on the measures taken to ensure his or her protection (such as the drafting of the proposal for admission to the special protection scheme) and, lastly, on the acquisition of the status of a person collaborating with the judicial authorities.

Should urgent measures have been adopted, or should the prisoner have been formally admitted to the special protection scheme, information on the places of residence of family members is requested and obtained direct by the Central Protection Office.

Once the prisoner has been classified and admitted to the relevant section, the administrative work of the office responsible becomes routine and is limited to normal prison management, with due regard for the special arrangements required by virtue of the specific category into which the prisoner falls.

Lastly, persons collaborating with the judicial authorities may be afforded a number of special prison benefits, which may result in their release (for example, they may be put under house arrest or convicted persons may be assigned to the Probation Service), and may even exceed the benefits provided for by law for other prisoners.

Treatment applicable under procedural law

Where procedural law is concerned, a person collaborating with the judicial authorities is someone who reports events and facts concerning other people and is therefore regarded as a witness for the prosecution. For this reason, such persons are obliged to answer questions and tell the truth. On being questioned for the first time, however, persons collaborating are warned that their statement(s) will disclose information about the liability of other people and that they will therefore no longer be able to refuse to perform their duties as witnesses for the prosecution. There is only one case in which they have the right not to reply when questioned, and that is when they themselves have been charged with the same crime as that for which legal proceedings have been instituted (one example is when they have been accused of acting as driver in a murder case). Although they are regarded as witnesses for the prosecution, their criminal record will be taken into account and it is considered that any statement they give may well have repercussions on their procedural status, as a result of which they have the right to be represented by a defence counsel.

They are, admittedly, regarded as suspect witnesses, and any statements they may make will therefore be subject to stricter rules than in the case of ordinary witnesses. This means that a carefully thought out, prudent assessment by the judicial authorities is required in such circumstances. It is first necessary to establish the credibility of the person collaborating, on the basis of his or her character, past experience and history and his or her relations with the accused person. Secondly, the statements should be proved to be reliable in terms of accuracy and coherency, and in the light of the spontaneity with which the information is provided. Lastly, the content of the statement should be supported from other sources, including statements by other persons collaborating with the judicial authorities. In order, however, to avoid the possibility that a number of persons collaborating will provide statements by mutual agreement (a matter that has elicited great concern during political debate), more restrictive procedures have been adopted and enshrined in the new regulatory framework. They require that persons collaborating with the judicial authorities be placed in a detention centre and be refused contact with the outside world; moreover, they may not be given investigative interviews while in custody.

During the trial hearing, persons collaborating with the judicial authorities are, as has been said, obliged to answer questions. Failure to do so will result in penalties being imposed under criminal law on the grounds of their being hostile witnesses. By the same token, the host of prison benefits described above (such as the possibility of having prison custody revoked) will not apply to them or, if they already apply, will be withdrawn. The same holds for the granting of protection and related benefits enjoyed by persons collaborating with the judicial authorities. Lastly, it should be pointed out that court judgments allowing persons who collaborate to benefit from mitigating circumstances are subject to review.

In connection with procedural law, it can happen that persons collaborating with the judicial authorities fail to answer questions (or avoid being questioned), or provide statements that differ from their previous ones. Their earlier statements may be used only if:

- the statements were given as evidence at the pre-trial stage of criminal proceedings, namely during cross-examination in the presence of the party who stands accused as a result of their statements; the hearing must, of course, have taken place before the judge responsible for the preliminary investigation;
- the parties agree;
- the statements at later stages in the investigation process cannot be relied on (for example, where one of the parties accused has died);
- it is proved that the persons collaborating were subject to violence or coercion, or that they were bribed or otherwise corrupted.

If none of the above circumstances applies, statements given at an earlier stage by the persons collaborating must be challenged and will be taken into account by the competent court only in order to assess the credibility of the persons concerned.

With regard to records of proceedings, a sound recording is always made in the case of trials in which persons collaborate with the judicial authorities. There is express provision to the effect that a sound recording must be made when inmates are questioned. This rule has been extended in practice to investigative interviews.

Protection measures

With regard to protection, it is clear that, as has already been said, one of the reasons for reforming the protection system was to reduce the number of protected people (over 7 000 collaborators, witnesses and relatives). By 31 December 2001 the number had fallen to 5 124 (1 104 collaborators, 74 prosecution witnesses, 3 748 close relatives of collaborators and 198 close relatives of witnesses). At that date, the cost of the special protection scheme exceeded €33 million.

The procedure based on qualitative parameters for deciding which persons collaborating with the judicial authorities require protection was established mainly by tightening the rules governing the protection system. As has already been said, protection is now granted only to persons who are willing to co-operate with the judicial authorities and who were formerly involved in criminal organisations and gangs, whether terrorist or ordinary criminal organisations (defined in the following way: (a) Mafia-type criminal organisations; (b) organisations dealing in illegal drugs or involved in kidnapping or smuggling; and (c) organisations dealing in trafficking of persons or in prostitution of minors; it should not be forgotten, however, that in the last two cases protection may be granted only if the co-operation of the person concerned is considered to be of great relevance for investigation purposes). In the past, by contrast, protection was afforded in the case of a wider range of crimes. In practice, the provision in Law 45/2001 for association offences has been a useful criterion for reducing the scope of protection measures to particular circumstances in which collaboration is deemed to be of value.

It should be added that the criteria referred to above are now more restrictive. To illustrate this point, mention should be made of those cases in which a contribution is made belatedly, namely when it is found to be concurrent with evidence already established. In such cases, protection will not be granted. What is more, persons collaborating with the judicial authorities are called on to provide statements regarding any criminal offences and facts of which they have knowledge, as well as any assets owned by members of criminal organisations. This means that their collaboration must be complete; otherwise the above-mentioned benefits arising from collaboration will be withdrawn. This is not the only obligation incumbent on persons collaborating with the judicial authorities. For example:

- they are obliged to declare all assets, of whatever type, that they own which are of illegal origin (these assets will subsequently be seized);
- they must undertake to be interviewed during the investigation and take part in any other procedures the law requires;
- they must not meet other persons collaborating with the judicial authorities.

Their conduct must therefore be proper, in that they must honour the specific obligations imposed on them by law. Needless to say, failure to honour any of the formal commitments referred to above will result in their benefits being revoked.

To prevent collaboration from being spread over a long period, with the provision of statements at long intervals – which would make them open to exploitation – investigating experts must collect statements within a period of six months (these statements should, at least, provide information about key facts and events). In addition, in order to ensure that statements are made openly and are truthful, a group of persons collaborating who are accusing the same person are forbidden to use the same defence counsel.

Protection measures may be introduced only gradually, according to the degree of danger faced by the person collaborating. The simplest form of protection comprises very general measures (namely, occasional inspections, moving detainees from one cell to another), taken either directly by the police or by the prison administration, the latter being accountable to detainees for their protection.

If these protection measures prove to be inadequate, special protection measures will apply. Such measures are of two types, the decision as to which type to take is left to a Central Committee chaired by the Under-Secretary of State of the Ministry of the Interior and made up of two judges and five officials. It is the responsibility of either the Public Prosecutor or the Head of the Police Department to propose the adoption of such special measures.

Protection measures at the first level are largely decided on by the Prefect and may, for example, include:

- surveillance and protection measures carried out by territorial police forces;
- surveillance security measures, such as remote alarm systems;
- transfer to other municipalities;
- social rehabilitation measures;
- special custody measures.

If the situation is one which poses serious risks to personal security, a second level of special protection will apply. Here the measures can be so complicated as to be described as an alternative "life programme". It is clear that in this case there is scope for additional measures, in the light of the actual situation in question. Examples are:

- moving non-detainees to protected places;
- providing cover documents;
- changing personal details (in other words, providing a new personal identity);
- providing personal assistance (health, legal assistance, assistance with housing, etc.);
- providing financial assistance, possibly in the form of personal maintenance payments.

In particularly urgent and serious circumstances, it is possible for protection measures to be taken on a temporary basis, but they lapse unless they are made final within 180 days. In fact, this is the means whereby protection is normally granted, because the degree of danger to which persons collaborating with the judicial authorities are exposed prompts the latter to deal with the large majority of cases as a matter of urgency. In exceptional cases (which quite often occur), special protection measures are afforded immediately by the police if the Central Committee has not had time to meet.

The calculation of maintenance payments is set out in the law. To ensure transparency in the financial management of persons collaborating with the judicial authorities, despite some criticism in the past, the court can obtain details of expenditure incurred and the amount of any possible maintenance payment supplement. In such cases, the court will issue an order at the request of the defence counsel of those persons being accused by collaborators.

Measures to conceal personal details are provisional, and are specifically designed to enable persons collaborating with the judicial authorities to hide in a protected place. The false personal details cannot under any circumstances be used in drawing up contracts, but they are useful for health care and employment card purposes.

Measures to change people's personal details are very important. These are exceptional protection measures designed for particularly highly valued collaborators. As such changes are final, they must apply when collaboration ends, namely after the proceedings have been completed. Clearly, they must be extended to all members of the family.

When it comes to social rehabilitation measures, employees set particular store by keeping their own job or being moved to a different place of work while retaining the whole range of benefits they have acquired over time, including pay level, benefits under contributory old age pension schemes and the responsibilities and duties pertaining to their job. The self-employed and persons who do not have a job – and this is the situation that arises most often as the criminal past of persons collaborating with the judicial authorities makes it difficult for them to have experience of work – tend to rely on social welfare. In the circumstances, it is clear that any measures designed to wean them off the protection scheme without difficulty will also help them to become gradually reintegrated in society. At the same time, they are provided with the financial advances needed to start a new job. Later on, they will be given a lump sum corresponding to the financial assistance to which they are entitled, so that the protection scheme can be terminated.

As for minors (who account for 45% of the category of protected persons, most of them being close relatives of the persons collaborating), agreements have been entered into with the Ministry of Education to ensure that they may fully exercise their right to education under a false name, which will subsequently be changed into their original name on their educational qualifications. Similar agreements also exist with the regions in connection with training courses and employment start-up programmes.

Mention should be made of international co-operation concerning protection schemes in the strict sense of the term, but also social integration programmes. Such co-operation makes it possible to transfer protected persons to foreign countries. To this end, apart from international conventions and agreements, Italy enters into bilateral agreements with other countries.

As has been stated, the prefects are responsible for implementing special protection measures in the first category. When, however, protection measures take the form of a comprehensive scheme, they are entrusted to a central protection service set up within the criminal investigation department. The service has two divisions, one dealing with persons collaborating with the judicial authorities and the other with witnesses for the prosecution. It also has local units responsible for assistance measures (housing, etc.). Security tasks (house surveillance, escorting people to hearings, etc.) are performed by the local units of the law enforcement agencies. The service also employs officers from various government departments (for example, the Ministry of Labour) to deal with those aspects that require co-ordinated interdisciplinary action. The service also includes a health unit staffed by police doctors and psychologists, who provide protected people with psychological back-up.

Special measures for witnesses

As stated above, a distinction was made under Law 45/2001 between persons collaborating with the judicial authorities and witnesses for the prosecution through the inclusion of practices that have been used by the central protection service over the last few years. The fact that there had been great confusion in this area meant that witnesses for the prosecution were humiliated, and this led to a decrease in the number of such witnesses. Comparative data over the last six months show, instead, that the number of witnesses is increasing.

The main differences between the rules governing the protection of witnesses and those governing the protection of persons collaborating with the judicial authorities are as follows:

- statements made by witnesses can relate to any type of criminal offence and not only offences that entitle persons collaborating with the judicial authorities to protection;

- statements made by witnesses are not subject to such restrictive assessment requirements as statements made by persons collaborating with the prosecuting authorities, namely there is no fundamental requirement that they be significant, complete and made on time; it is sufficient for them to be reliable;

- the maintenance of the protection is entirely dependent on witnesses and their relatives no longer being in danger;

- witnesses are not obliged to declare their assets;

- financial assistance and social rehabilitation measures prove to be more favourable to witnesses.

The following are examples under the latter heading:

- assistance measures must be such as to ensure that the standard of living of individuals and their families is similar to that which they enjoyed before being admitted to the protection scheme;

- witnesses are entitled to compute the current value of the cost of assistance to them if they so wish, in order, for instance, to start up a business;
- if witnesses are employed in the public sector, they are entitled to keep their job on a paid-leave basis until their employer finds them a job in a different government department;
- witnesses are entitled to compensation for loss of salary in the event of the termination of their job or that of any member of their family;
- if witnesses are obliged to leave real property in its place of origin, they are entitled to sell it to the state at the market rate;
- witnesses are entitled to benefit from mortgage facilities so that they can become fully integrated into the financial and social system.

Proceedings held at a distance by means of video-conferences

Law No. 11 of 7 January 1998, which came into force on 21 February 1998, regulates new arrangements for participation in criminal proceedings. The new system of long-distance or virtual participation means that the person concerned does not appear in person in the courtroom where the trial is being held, but takes part from a remote location connected to the courtroom by a video link.

The use of video-conferencing in proceedings was in fact first introduced into Italian law by Decree 306/1992, which later became Law 356/1992, on the long-distance examination of persons turning state's evidence. The success of this technological innovation, which was solely intended for the protection of persons turning state's evidence, persuaded parliament to introduce general rules and regulations on the subject, applicable at virtually any stage in the proceedings.

Law 11/1998 provides for three main types of long-distance participation: participation in a trial, participation in proceedings in chambers and examination of persons turning state's evidence.

The first type applies:

- when a person who is imprisoned for any reason is being prosecuted for one of the offences provided for in Article 51.3.a of the Code of Criminal Procedure (Mafia-type association, crimes committed in order to help Mafia-type associations, kidnapping and association for the purposes of drug trafficking), if there are serious security or public order reasons or the trial is particularly complex and it is necessary to avoid delaying proceedings, not least in the light of concomitant trial commitments on the part of the prisoners themselves;
- when a prisoner is subject to the special regime provided for in Section 41.a of the Penitentiary Act.

Participation in proceedings in chambers may concern hearings before the Tribunale della Libertà (the court responsible for reviewing detention measures), interlocutory evidentiary hearings, preliminary hearings, enforcement proceedings and review hearings.

Persons under protection may be examined at a distance where:

- the trial is for one of the offences provided for in Article 51.3.a of the Code of Criminal Procedure and a person who has been admitted to a protection scheme or been afforded protection measures is to be examined;
- the person to be examined has been afforded a protective measure entailing a change of identity;
- the trial concerns one of the offences provided for in Article 51.3.a of the Code of Criminal Procedure and a person accused of a relevant crime has to be examined and is also on trial, separately, for one of those offences.

Ten prisons have been designated for inmates covered by the special regime provided for in Section 41.a of the Penitentiary Act, while there are units, in two prison clinical and surgical centres, designed for prisoners needing medical treatment.

An official provision is always required for participation in proceedings held at a distance and reasons must be given: the president of the board issues instructions that are forwarded to the parties concerned and to the defence counsels at least ten days before the hearing. During the trial, the judge makes provision to this effect by means of an order.

The law requires that the video link be such as to guarantee concomitant, genuine, mutual visibility of all those present and make it possible to hear what is being said (this point will be dealt with later).

The defence counsel is free to decide whether to participate in the courtroom or from the remote location where his or her client is located. A deputy may be present in the other location instead of the defence counsel. Both the defence counsel and his or her deputy may confer in private with the accused and with each other.

There are four different technical means of establishing a link for a video-conference: point-point, switching, continuous presence (standard) and continuous presence (advanced).

The point-point link entails directly linking a courtroom with a remote site located inside a prison or in another courtroom. It is the simplest system and the one with the fewest technical problems. It had already been tried out from 1992 until 1998, before the law on participation from a distance came into force, as it was used to examine from afar persons turning state's evidence and people under protection. As 90% of persons turning state's evidence are not in prison, they are examined in courtrooms located in the same region as, or a region near, their place of residence, at a secret location unknown to the prison department. The location is chosen by the judicial authority or by the Central Protection Service, which may, on the other hand, decide independently that a person turning state's evidence and residing in Piedmont should appear in a courtroom in Puglia, in order to guarantee his or her safety as well as that of his or her relatives.

The second kind of link is known as the switching or "active speaker" facility. Different rooms are connected – for instance, a courtroom with various small prison rooms or another courtroom – and everyone can see one image, that of the speaker, on his or her monitor. If more than one person is speaking at the same time, the connection is automatically made with the location where the person is speaking most loudly.

The third kind of link is known as continuous presence (standard) (CPS). The monitor is split into a maximum of four quadrants, making it possible to connect five remote locations – as a rule a courtroom and four small prison rooms. When there are three locations to be linked (the courtroom and two prison video rooms), the monitor is merely split into two (dual view).

Another, more recently acquired facility is the so-called continuous presence (advanced) (CPA) link – advanced in that it is the result of a change in the CPS facility necessitated by a practical legal requirement. Since the early months of video-conferencing, it has been necessary to ensure that prisoners are assigned to different small prison rooms during trials in which many accused people (thirty, forty or even fifty) subject to the special regime provided for in Section 41.a of Law 354/1975 are taking part. In such proceedings, the judicial authorities and the DPA has had to choose whether to give preference to the possibility of seeing all the individuals linked by video at the same time, or to the need to place a restricted number of prisoners in each small prison room and to allocate members of the same criminal organisation to different prisons.

Some months after Law 11/1998 came into force, Telecom Italia placed another facility, CPA, at the prison department's disposal. This makes it possible to connect up a large number of remote locations and, at the same time, to block three locations on one's monitor. The fourth quadrant operates in a dynamic fashion, that is the party who is talking in the loudest voice is automatically connected to each monitor. Naturally, this facility makes it possible to overcome the legal and technical problems connected with the effects of Section 41.a but not all the problems related to the need for concomitant, genuine and mutual visibility, as there will be always someone who is unable to see another party at some point.

Nowadays, it is possible to start forty sessions simultaneously, that is to hold, say, thirty trials a day by means of video-conferencing. The same session may be linked to a maximum of fourteen remote locations (small prison rooms or courtrooms).

The CPA facility may be arranged on the same day for fifteen sessions at most (included in the thirty mentioned above), as it necessitates more technical, structural and human resources than the other facilities.

There are new provisions designed to:

- reduce the very high number of transfers of very dangerous prisoners, which are a source of considerable expense and danger in terms of security;

- avoid contact between particularly dangerous prisoners and the criminal organisations to which they belong, thereby making the special regime provided for under Section 41.a of Law 354/1975 more effective; the regime is basically difficult to enforce in prisons (which are located in places where trials for organised crime take place, which generally correspond to the prisoners' place of origin). The prisons in question are not as rigidly organised as the specially designated premises and are more likely to allow contact between prisoners and those with whom they have dealings;

- guarantee the security of people under protection by ensuring that they are not personally present in the courtroom and are more at ease when giving evidence;

- ensure that perpetual transfers of prisoners involved in trials taking place in different courtrooms in separate locations do not undermine the continuity required in each set of proceedings and the need to ensure that proceedings are not over-long.

It can be said that the above goals have now been almost completely attained.

Attention is drawn, in particular, to the following results:

- a reduction in the overall number of transfers of prisoners covered by the special regime provided for in Section 41.a of the Penitentiary Act, as well as persons turning state's evidence, with definite savings in terms of money and staff and a concomitant increase in security;

- the constant presence of prisoners under the special regime in the twelve specially designated prisons, which are far away from regions where there is a criminal influence;

- the examination of persons turning state's evidence takes place only in protected, secret locations far removed from the courtroom;

- efficiency has been achieved, as far as is humanly possible in view of the current state of criminal justice, in trial proceedings, even in such difficult circumstances as occur when prisoners themselves are concurrently committed for trial before more than one judicial authority in the same or different districts (many important cases were dealt with only recently by means of video-conferencing).

With regard to this last point, an analysis of statistical data confirms that the system is technically efficient as well.

From the time the law came into force on 16 January 2003, only 89 out of 29 205 links (an insignificant percentage) were cancelled because of technical problems, while 519 links went ahead even though there were technical hitches.

There are now some 550 persons who have co-operated with the judicial authorities in prison. In 2002, over 3 000 links concerned the examination of persons co-operating with the judicial authorities in a protected location.

The possibility of using video-conferencing to ensure the protection of people who, for various reasons (as witnesses or accused persons in proceedings), have turned state's evidence seems particularly interesting. It has been already said that arrangements concerning proceedings at a distance were made for the first time precisely in the case of persons turning state's evidence, to protect their safety and ensure the genuineness of their statements.

The people under protection appear by video link from secret locations, chosen by the protection body or the judicial authorities (in the case of people not imprisoned) or the Ministry of Justice (in the case of people in prison). In both cases, locations in the areas in which the persons to be examined live (whether they are under protection or in prison) are chosen; in the former case, they are courtrooms that have been reserved, for the day, exclusively for long-distance proceedings and, in the latter case, a room equipped for video-conferences is chosen in the prison in which the person turning state's evidence is being held in custody or in a prison nearby.

Precisely in order to ensure enhanced protection of persons at liberty who are turning state's evidence, people not in prison have sometimes been allowed, at the request of the protection body or the judicial authority, to enter a prison equipped for long-distance proceedings.

Attention has been drawn to the need to amend the provisions currently in force so that the participation of persons turning state's evidence in long-distance proceedings is not confined to particular hearings, but continues throughout the trial.

The possibility of participating in long-distance proceedings in foreign countries is also very interesting. Every year an increasing number of international video links are arranged with people under protection in various foreign countries.

In most cases the international link has been requested for a witness or for the examination of persons turning very important state's evidence, living under protection (either at liberty or in prison) in the United States or Germany. Other links were established to examine, from Italy, witnesses involved in a trial in the

United States. A series of links with Switzerland is also planned so that pre-trial investigations can be carried out by video-conferencing in response to an international letter of request in a trial for Mafia crimes.

The organisation of these links in practice has required lengthy preparations, because it was necessary to link up and use technical audio and video systems which were very different from one another in type and quality.

The elaborate procedures introduced under the protection system in a major foreign country are a particularly interesting example. The country in question authorised a video link with a remote location where a person turning exceptionally significant state's evidence was being held in custody only on condition that there was a long succession of intermediate links designed to extend the technical route and make it more difficult to locate the person in question. Such precautions, though obviously necessary to ensure the safety of people under protection, have adversely affected the technical quality of audiovisual links, which suffers from repeated rerouting.

The new provisions ran into numerous difficulties during the first months of their enforcement, mainly because of:

- numerous objections raised by the prisoners' defence counsels, particularly with regard to the compatibility of the rules and regulations with the constitutional rights of the defence;
- an objective lack of prison facilities (an insufficient number of small prison rooms – 33 rooms in 5 prisons – and an insufficient number of courtrooms equipped for video-conferencing – about 150 – and their unsatisfactory distribution);
- widespread scepticism on the part of certain judicial authorities about the potential of video-conferencing.

These problems have been overcome as a result of a combination of factors:

- recognition of the constitutional legitimacy of long-distance proceedings (Constitutional Court Ruling No. 342 of 14 to 22 July 1999);
- an improvement in the facilities available to the judicial authorities (there are now 123 small prison rooms, spread over 18 prisons; 182 courtrooms have been equipped, especially in areas with the highest density of offenders);
- positive feedback from the judicial authorities that have used video-conferencing as to the huge potential of the system, which, if properly organised, will make it possible to complete many complex trials with a reasonable number of hearings.

On the other hand, it cannot be said that all the problems have been fully overcome. In particular, although transfers of prisoners under the special regime have considerably decreased in number, they still take place, for two reasons.

Firstly, the fact that the number of small prison rooms equipped for video-conferencing is currently limited means it is necessary to transfer prisoners daily from one prison to another in order to make optimum use of the potential of video-conferencing.

Secondly, some judicial authorities continue to report that it is impossible to resort to long-distance proceedings where the law permits such proceedings or even when it makes them compulsory because of the shortage of courtrooms equipped for video-conferencing.

There is a further problem resulting from the fact that it is impossible, because of the law, to meet the need to separate prisoners under the special regime. In practice, they are assigned to different prisons on the basis of rules that also take account of the requirements of trials involving video-conferencing. In particular, Law 11/1998 lays down rules and regulations whereby people participating in long-distance proceedings must be genuinely, concomitantly and mutually visible. For technical and contractual reasons, the service provided to the state by the telecommunications company responsible, Telecom Italia, does not make it possible to split the monitors present in courtrooms into more than four quadrants each. This means that – given that there are numerous precedents in which courts have not accepted other video link facilities, although the case-law is not uniform – the often numerous persons jointly accused in the same criminal proceedings are inevitably assigned to no more than four prisons. This leads to a concentration of prisoners from the same criminal environment in each prison. A technical solution making it possible to increase the number of links visible simultaneously on the same monitor is being considered, but such a solution would imply a serious reduction in the quality of the images. It would be preferable to amend the provision so as to do away with the obligation that there be concomitant, genuine and mutual visibility for all the people present (indeed, this condition is not fulfilled in many courtrooms where accused persons are present), without restricting prisoners' right to participate in the hearing and to uphold any right that they could uphold by being personally present.

Sales agents for publications of the Council of Europe
Agents de vente des publications du Conseil de l'Europe

BELGIUM/BELGIQUE
La Librairie européenne
Rue de l'Orme 1
B-1040 BRUXELLES
Tel.: (32) 2 231 04 35
Fax: (32) 2 735 08 60
E-mail: mail@libeurop.be
http://www.libeurop.be

Jean de Lannoy
202, avenue du Roi
B-1190 BRUXELLES
Tel.: (32) 2 538 4308
Fax: (32) 2 538 0841
E-mail: jean.de.lannoy@euronet.be
http://www.jean-de-lannoy.be

CANADA
Renouf Publishing Company Limited
5369 Chemin Canotek Road
CDN-OTTAWA, Ontario, K1J 9J3
Tel.: (1) 613 745 2665
Fax: (1) 613 745 7660
E-mail: order.dept@renoufbooks.com
http://www.renoufbooks.com

**CZECH REPUBLIC/
RÉPUBLIQUE TCHÈQUE**
Suweco Cz Dovoz Tisku Praha
Ceskomoravska 21
CZ-18021 PRAHA 9
Tel.: (420) 2 660 35 364
Fax: (420) 2 683 30 42
E-mail: import@suweco.cz

DENMARK/DANEMARK
GAD Direct
Fiolstaede 31-33
DK-1171 COPENHAGEN K
Tel.: (45) 33 13 72 33
Fax: (45) 33 12 54 94
E-mail: info@gaddirect.dk

FINLAND/FINLANDE
Akateeminen Kirjakauppa
Keskuskatu 1, PO Box 218
FIN-00381 HELSINKI
Tel.: (358) 9 121 41
Fax: (358) 9 121 4450
E-mail: akatilaus@stockmann.fi
http://www.akatilaus.akateeminen.com

**GERMANY/ALLEMAGNE
AUSTRIA/AUTRICHE**
UNO Verlag
August Bebel Allee 6
D-53175 BONN
Tel.: (49) 2 28 94 90 20
Fax: (49) 2 28 94 90 222
E-mail: bestellung@uno-verlag.de
http://www.uno-verlag.de

GREECE/GRÈCE
Librairie Kauffmann
28, rue Stadiou
GR-ATHINAI 10564
Tel.: (30) 1 32 22 160
Fax: (30) 1 32 30 320
E-mail: ord@otenet.gr

HUNGARY/HONGRIE
Euro Info Service
Hungexpo Europa Kozpont ter 1
H-1101 BUDAPEST
Tel.: (361) 264 8270
Fax: (361) 264 8271
E-mail: euroinfo@euroinfo.hu
http://www.euroinfo.hu

ITALY/ITALIE
Libreria Commissionaria Sansoni
Via Duca di Calabria 1/1, CP 552
I-50125 FIRENZE
Tel.: (39) 556 4831
Fax: (39) 556 41257
E-mail: licosa@licosa.com
http://www.licosa.com

NETHERLANDS/PAYS-BAS
De Lindeboom Internationale Publikaties
PO Box 202, MA de Ruyterstraat 20 A
NL-7480 AE HAAKSBERGEN
Tel.: (31) 53 574 0004
Fax: (31) 53 572 9296
E-mail: books@delindeboom.com
http://www.delindeboom.com

NORWAY/NORVÈGE
Akademika, A/S Universitetsbokhandel
PO Box 84, Blindern
N-0314 OSLO
Tel.: (47) 22 85 30 30
Fax: (47) 23 12 24 20

POLAND/POLOGNE
Głowna Księgarnia Naukowa
im. B. Prusa
Krakowskie Przedmiescie 7
PL-00-068 WARSZAWA
Tel.: (48) 29 22 66
Fax: (48) 22 26 64 49
E-mail: inter@internews.com.pl
http://www.internews.com.pl

PORTUGAL
Livraria Portugal
Rua do Carmo, 70
P-1200 LISBOA
Tel.: (351) 13 47 49 82
Fax: (351) 13 47 02 64
E-mail: liv.portugal@mail.telepac.pt

SPAIN/ESPAGNE
Mundi-Prensa Libros SA
Castelló 37
E-28001 MADRID
Tel.: (34) 914 36 37 00
Fax: (34) 915 75 39 98
E-mail: libreria@mundiprensa.es
http://www.mundiprensa.com

SWITZERLAND/SUISSE
Adeco – Van Diermen
Chemin du Lacuez 41
CH-1807 BLONAY
Tel.: (41) 21 943 26 73
Fax: (41) 21 943 36 05
E-mail: info@adeco.org

UNITED KINGDOM/ROYAUME-UNI
TSO (formerly HMSO)
51 Nine Elms Lane
GB-LONDON SW8 5DR
Tel.: (44) 207 873 8372
Fax: (44) 207 873 8200
E-mail: customer.services@theso.co.uk
http://www.the-stationery-office.co.uk
http://www.itsofficial.net

**UNITED STATES and CANADA/
ÉTATS-UNIS et CANADA**
Manhattan Publishing Company
2036 Albany Post Road
CROTON-ON-HUDSON,
NY 10520, USA
Tel.: (1) 914 271 5194
Fax: (1) 914 271 5856
E-mail: Info@manhattanpublishing.com
http://www.manhattanpublishing.com

_____

FRANCE
La Documentation française
(Diffusion/Vente France entière)
124, rue H. Barbusse
F-93308 AUBERVILLIERS Cedex
Tel.: (33) 01 40 15 70 00
Fax: (33) 01 40 15 68 00
E-mail:
commande@ladocumentationfrancaise.fr
http://www.ladocumentationfrancaise.fr

Librairie Kléber (Vente Strasbourg)
Palais de l'Europe
F-67075 STRASBOURG Cedex
Fax: (33) 03 88 52 91 21
E-mail: librairie.kleber@coe.int

Council of Europe Publishing/Editions du Conseil de l'Europe
F-67075 Strasbourg Cedex
Tel.: (33) 03 88 41 25 81 – Fax: (33) 03 88 41 39 10 – E-mail: publishing@coe.int – Website: http://book.coe.int